MW01137667

Melancholia and Moralism

The MIT Press   Cambridge, Massachusetts   London, England

Melancholia and Moralism

Essays on AIDS and Queer Politics

DOUGLAS CRIMP

First MIT Press paperback edition, 2004

© 2002 Douglas Crimp

All rights reserved. No part of this book may be reproduced in any form by any electronic or mechanical means (including photocopying, recording, or information storage and retrieval) without permission in writing from the publisher.

This book was set in Utopia Headline by Graphic Composition, Inc.

Library of Congress Cataloging-in-Publication Data

Crimp, Douglas.
  Melancholia and moralism : essays on AIDS and
  queer politics / Douglas Crimp.
    p.   cm.
  Includes bibliographical references and index.
  ISBN 978-0-262-03295-7 (hc. : alk. paper) —— **978-0-262-53264-8 (pb. : alk. paper)**
  1. AIDS (Disease)—Political aspects.   2. Gay men.   I. Title.

RA643.8 .C754 2002
362.1'969792—dc21   2001044076

for Damien Jack

CONTENTS

ACKNOWLEDGMENTS

An enterprise covering fourteen years has indebted me to a great many people, and I can only hope to recall most of the crucial ones here. First things first: Over dinner one summer evening, Diana Fuss and Phillip Brian Harper urged me to collect all of my writing on AIDS; without their perfectly simple idea I wouldn't have conceived the book in this way. And I wouldn't have so easily found the time to carry it out if Carole Vance hadn't goaded me into applying for a Rockefeller Fellowship in her Program for the Study of Sexuality, Gender, Health, and Human Rights and then agreed, after I'd been awarded it, to accommodate my scheduling conflicts by deferring it for a semester. I was thus able to spend the calendar year 2000 at the Columbia University School of Public Health working on the manuscript and participating in a series of interdisciplinary seminars attended by an ever-shifting group of committed human rights activists and sex radicals. I enjoyed lively intellectual exchange with the other fellows in residence during my tenure, Jiemin Bao, Marie-Aimée Hélie-Lucas, Gail Pheterson, Oliver Phillips, and Penelope Saunders; I learned much about human rights advocacy from Columbia faculty members Lynn Freedman and Ali Miller of the Law and Policy Project; and I continued to learn new ways to think and talk about sex from Carole Vance—more important, I made a good friend.

My time at Columbia meant a year off from the University of Rochester, and I am grateful to Dean Thomas Leblanc for supporting my leave during a time of transition for my department and graduate program. The Department of Art and Art History and the Program in Visual and Cultural

Studies have provided me with a congenial academic environment since 1992; I particularly want to acknowledge three Rochester faculty friends who've gone on to bigger things: Michael Ann Holly, Trevor Hope, and Janet Wolff. And thanks to my wonderful, wonderful graduate students.

Other friends have talked over my ideas with me, read and commented on my writing, invited me to lecture and thereby pressured me to do the thinking and writing in the first place, and commissioned versions of these essays for previous publication. Here is a partial list of friends and colleagues who have contributed to this project, by which I mean not only these essays but also the larger project of AIDS activism and queer politics: Akira Asada, Thatcher Bailey, David Barr, Nicholas Baume, Gregg Bordowitz, Christopher Bram, Jean Carlomusto, Rosalyn Deutsche, Carolyn Dinshaw, Richard Elovich, David Eng, Jonathan Flatley, the late Teiji Furuhashi, Gregg Gonsalves, John Greyson, Jan Zita Grover, Daniel Hendrickson, Isaac Julien, Ernie Larsen, Catherine Lord, the late Stuart Marshall, Loring McAlpin, Kobena Mercer, Richard Meyer, Sherry Millner, Donald Moffett, Don Moss, Mark Nash, Cindy Patton, Ann Pelligrini, Laura Pinsky, Jane Rosett, Eve Sedgwick, Draper Shreeve, Marc Siegel, Paula Treichler, Keith Vincent, Frank Wagner, Michael Warner, Simon Watney, and Daniel Wolfe.

Eric Clarke and Damien Jack read the entire manuscript and gave me great encouragement and valuable feedback. Sometimes it makes all the difference to have someone who just plain agrees with you about things that matter—whether prima donnas, sexual politics, or what you're writing at the moment: Damien has been a hugely supportive fan of my work from the day (okay, night) I met him; not for that reason alone I dedicate this book to him.

My student and Eastman House film-going pal Matt Reynolds assisted me with all kinds of details in preparing the manuscript for publication. Roger Conover, my editor at MIT Press, has been unwavering in his commitment to my work as it moved from art to AIDS and back again. Judy Feldmann shepherded my essays through production with care and precision. Willa Cobert pushes me to be honest with myself. Adam Budak is a sweetheart—how else can I put it?

1 MELANCHOLIA AND MORALISM: AN INTRODUCTION

Nothing could be more irresponsible than the

immodest self-certainty of one who rests content in

the good sense of a responsibility properly assumed.

—*Thomas Keenan*, Fables of Responsibility

At the opening plenary of the thirteenth International AIDS Conference, held in Durban during July 2000, Edwin Cameron, gay, HIV-positive, and a justice of the High Court of South Africa, gave the first Jonathan Mann Memorial Lecture. His was perhaps the most impassioned and eloquent statement of what became the central theme of the conference: the glaring inequity whereby the lucky few can afford to buy their health while the unlucky many die of AIDS. "I exist as a living embodiment of the iniquity of drug availability and access," Cameron said. "Amid the poverty of Africa, I stand before you because I am able to purchase health and vigor. I am here because I can afford to pay for life itself." He went on to compare this injustice to the worst inhumanities of modern times:

It is often a source of puzzled reflection how ordinary Germans could have tolerated the moral iniquity that was Nazism, or how white South Africans could have countenanced the evils that apartheid inflicted, to their benefit, on the majority of their fellows. . . . [But] those of us who lead affluent lives, well-attended by medical care and treatment, should not ask how Germans or white South Africans could tolerate living in proximity to moral evil. We do so ourselves today, in proximity to the impending illness and death of many millions of people with AIDS. This will happen, unless we change the present. It will happen because available treatments are denied to those who need them for the sake of aggregating corporate wealth for shareholders who by African standards are already unimaginably affluent.[1]

Just three months after Cameron's speech resounded around the world, Andrew Sullivan, gay, HIV-positive, and a contributing writer for the *New York Times Magazine,* wrote a short opinion column for the magazine entitled "Pro Pharma." "Because I have H.I.V.," he said, "I swallow around 800 pills of prescription drugs a month. . . . I asked my pharmacist the other day to tote up the annual bill (which my insurance mercifully pays): $15,600, easily more than I pay separately for housing, food,

1. Edwin Cameron, "The Deafening Silence of AIDS," *Health and Human Rights* 5, no. 1 (2000).

travel, or clothes."[2] After several paragraphs detailing Americans' expanding use of pharmaceutical products and their growing complaints about the price they pay for them, followed by a defense of profit-driven drug development, Sullivan ended with these lines: "The private sector is now responsible for more than 70 percent of all the pharmaceutical research in this country—and that share is growing. Whether we like it or not, these private entities have our lives in their hands. And we can either be grown-ups and acknowledge this or be infantile and scapegoat them. . . . They're entrepreneurs trying to make money by saving lives. By and large, they succeed in both. Every morning I wake up and feel fine, I'm thankful that they do."[3]

Edwin Cameron had presented a stark moral dilemma. How can we tolerate a situation in which our lives and prosperity are purchased at the price of the deaths of many millions of others throughout the world? Andrew Sullivan resolves that dilemma very simply: This is reality, and we can either be grown-ups and accept it or we can be infantile and oppose it. I need hardly say that Sullivan's view is breathtaking in its flippancy both in its disregard of others' lives and in taking for granted his own privilege to "feel fine."[4] But I am also aware that I have produced an easy effect with my juxtaposition of these two statements: absolute certainty about the moral superiority of Cameron's humble, humane attitude as against Sullivan's callous rationalization of his own entitlement. In doing so, I worry that I reproduce Sullivan's own moral certitude and thus engage in the very moralism that I consider the greatest danger of Sullivan's position. Sullivan's self-assurance about the maturity and righteousness of his opinions is no doubt what allows him to adopt such a glib tone in the first place, and it is that tone that most determines that his argument will give offense. But giving offense would also appear to be just what Sullivan is up to. There can be little question but that he knew at the time of writing "Pro Pharma" the political stir Cameron's

2. Andrew Sullivan, "Pro Pharma," *New York Times Magazine*, October 29, 2000, p. 21.

3. Ibid., p. 22.

4. Sullivan so takes his privilege for granted that he adds as a parenthesis only the note about having insurance that "mercifully" pays the exorbitant cost of his medications.

speech had caused. I therefore assume that Sullivan's intention in writing his opinion piece was to play the bad boy, to provoke outrage among all those "politically correct" activists he so loves to castigate for immaturity.[5] "Grow up," Sullivan scolds, again and again.

Sullivan's equation of maturity with his own conservative sexual politics and infantilism with what he calls liberation politics is consistently produced through a narrative about AIDS and gay men.[6] That narrative goes like this: Prior to AIDS, gay men were frivolous pleasure-seekers who shirked the responsibility that comes with normal adulthood— settling down with a mate, raising children, being an upstanding member of society. Gay men only wanted to fuck (and take drugs and stay out

5. Why the *New York Times Magazine* indulges Sullivan's political whims is another question. "Pro Pharma" followed by several months Sullivan's feature-story paean to getting juiced on testosterone ("The He Hormone," *New York Times Magazine,* April 2, 2000). Eventually the *Magazine* did appear to signal some regret about Sullivan's shilling for the pharmaceutical companies in its pages. Two pieces published in early 2001 were highly critical of the industry. See Tina Rosenberg, "Look at Brazil," *New York Times Magazine,* January 28, 2001 (a report on the viability of generic AIDS medications in stemming the epidemic in developing countries, and on the pharmaceutical industry's callous opposition to their manufacture and distribution); and Stephen S. Hall, "Prescription for Profit," *New York Times Magazine,* March 11, 2001 (an investigation into how a virtually useless allergy medication was turned into a blockbuster drug). An op-ed piece by Anthony Lewis taking the Tina Rosenberg article as its point of departure for criticizing the Bush administration ("Bush and AIDS," *New York Times,* February 3, 2001, p. A13) led Sullivan to write yet another column exonerating the pharmaceutical industry in the *New Republic.* Sullivan's "argument" is the now familiar Republican one that free enterprise will solve all of our problems: "The reason we have a treatment for HIV is not the angelic brilliance of anyone per se but the free-market system that rewards serious research with serious money. . . . Drug companies, after all, are not designed to cure diseases or please op-ed columnists. They're designed to satisfy shareholders" (Andrew Sullivan, "Profit of Doom?" *New Republic,* March 26, 2001, p. 6).

6. Sullivan's arguments against "the liberationists" appear in his *Virtually Normal: An Argument about Homosexuality* (New York, Vintage, 1996). Sullivan sometimes calls himself a liberal, and indeed many of his views are among those that make classical liberalism so problematic. He nevertheless boasted in the pages of the *New York Times* of voting in the 2000 presidential election for George W. Bush, hardly a standard-bearer for liberalism. On the right-wing politics of the current crop of mainstream gay journalists, including Sullivan, see Michael Warner, "Media Gays: A New Stone Wall," *Nation,* July 14, 1997, pp. 15–19.

all night and dance), and at that to fuck the way naughty teenage boys want to fuck—with anyone attractive to them, anytime, anywhere, no strings attached. Then came AIDS. AIDS made gay men grow up. They had to find meaning in life beyond the pleasure of the moment. They had to face the fact that fucking has consequences. They had to deal with real life, which means growing old and dying. So they became responsible. And then everyone else accepted gay men. It turns out that the only reason gay men were shunned was that they were frivolous pleasure-seekers who shirked responsibility. Thank God for AIDS. AIDS saved gay men.

For my argument in this book, there is particular significance in the fact that this narrative structures Sullivan's notorious *New York Times Magazine* cover story "When Plagues End: Notes on the Twilight of an Epidemic," published in November 1996.[7] In the opening of that essay, Sullivan claims that even recognizing the end of AIDS is something many gay men can't do, so wedded are we to our infantile rebelliousness, recently embodied in AIDS activism. He gives proof of just how extreme such attachments are by writing about "a longtime AIDS advocate" responding to the promising outlook for people with HIV disease brought about by a new generation of anti-retroviral drugs: "'It must be hard to find out you're positive now,' he had said darkly, 'It's like you really missed the party.'" That "darkly" suggests Sullivan's relish of what he assumes his readers will understand as the perversity that attends such childish liberation politics as AIDS activism.[8]

4
5

---

7. Andrew Sullivan, "When Plagues End: Notes on the Twilight of an Epidemic," *New York Times Magazine,* November 10, 1996, pp. 52–62, 76–77, 84.

8. Ibid., p. 55. It occurs to me that Sullivan's friend might have meant something quite different from the spin Sullivan puts on his remark by inserting "he had said darkly." Learning that you're HIV-positive after the demise of AIDS activism and the general sense of urgency about AIDS, even within the gay community in the United States, could indeed make you feel that you'd missed the party—if by "party" you mean a system of support and a sense of community based on general agreement that the epidemic constitutes a crisis.

Here is a portion of the "AIDS=maturity" story that Sullivan tells in "When Plagues End":

Before AIDS, gay life—rightly or wrongly—was identified with freedom from responsibility, rather than with its opposite. Gay liberation was most commonly understood as liberation from the constraints of traditional norms, almost a dispensation that permitted homosexuals the absence of responsibility in return for an acquiescence in second-class citizenship. This was the Faustian bargain of the pre-AIDS closet: straights gave homosexuals a certain amount of freedom; in return, homosexuals gave away their self-respect. But with AIDS, responsibility became a central, imposing feature of gay life. . . . People who thought they didn't care for one another found that they could. Relationships that had no social support were found to be as strong as any heterosexual marriage. Men who had long since got used to throwing their own lives away were confronted with the possibility that they actually did care about themselves. . . .[9]

Although Sullivan might believe he is telling an uplifting story about gay men's commendable progress, in doing so, he represents gay men before AIDS as the most odious sort of creatures—men who were all too willing to bargain away self-respect and respect for others to gain a form of freedom that was no more than *freedom from* obligation. For those of us whose prime spanned roughly the years between Stonewall and the onset of the epidemic (these were the years of my mid-twenties to mid-thirties; they were also, of course, the years of the greatest growth of the lesbian and gay movement and of the greatest development of lesbian and gay culture in the United States), it is deeply insulting to read of ourselves as having been closeted, accepted second-class citizenship, cared little for ourselves or one another, had no idea we could form strong relationships, thrown our lives away.[10] But this is what it is to be recruited as the foil of someone's moralistic narrative.

9. Ibid., pp. 61–62.
10. In the expanded version of "When Plagues End" published as a chapter of his *Love Undetectable: Notes on Friendship, Sex, and Survival* (New York: Alfred A. Knopf,

I will return to Sullivan's notion of this "Faustian bargain," because I am interested in its reappearance as an explanation of how he became infected with HIV. For the moment, however, I want to look at the second part of his AIDS=maturity narrative, the part about society's newfound acceptance of gay men. "AIDS has dramatically altered the psychological structure of homophobia," Sullivan writes. "What had once been a strong fear of homosexual difference, disguising a mostly silent awareness of homosexual humanity, became the opposite. The humanity slowly trumped the difference. Death, it turned out, was a powerfully universalizing experience."[11] Amazingly, in Sullivan's account, it takes only the recognition that homosexuals die for the homophobe to get in touch with his suppressed feelings for our humanity. More amazing still, homophobia was not really hatred at all, just a pretense of hatred. The fear of difference, in the end, has no psychic reality.[12] It can thus easily be "trumped" by that magical equalizer on which liberalism always stakes its bet: the universal.

6
——
7

Sullivan's reliance on magical thinking to vanquish both homophobia and AIDS is not, however, a species of optimism; on the contrary, it is mere wish-fulfillment. The continuing presence of illness and death from AIDS throughout the world and in our own lives is, for Sullivan, as it is for much of American society, so repressed that every fact attesting to that continued presence is denied either reality or significance. Moreover, anyone who protests that the AIDS crisis is far from over incurs Sullivan's rebuke. We cling to AIDS as melancholiacs unable to mourn our losses and get on with the business of living, and living now in the

1998), we learn that it was in fact Sullivan himself who conformed to his description of pre-AIDS gay men. He was closeted, had little self-respect, had no idea that gay men could form sustaining relationships. Thus his characterization is a classic case of projection of a hated portion of himself onto others.

11. Sullivan, "When Plagues End," p. 56.

12. This might explain why Sullivan is so hostile toward, or at the very least uncomprehending of, queer theory, which has developed such an acute understanding of the intractable psychosexual mechanisms of homophobia. Among queer theory's insights about homophobia is that what appears to be the acceptance of gay men during the AIDS epidemic is in fact the acceptance—not to say the welcoming—of the mass death of gay men; see "The Spectacle of Mourning," this volume.

world of normal grown-up responsibilities and genuine freedom—freedom from homophobic disapproval. But my argument would reverse the charge. It is Sullivan's view that is melancholic, and his moralism is its clearest symptom. Sullivan is incapable of recognizing the intractability of homophobia because his melancholia consists precisely in his identification with the homophobe's repudiation of him.[13] And his moralism reproduces that repudiation by projecting it onto other gay men in whom he disavows seeing himself. But what I am saying here is not meant to diagnose Sullivan. Rather I am attempting to explain a widespread psychosocial response to the ongoing crisis of AIDS.

It would not surprise anyone if I claimed that AIDS gave dangerous new life to moralism in American culture. But that is not exactly my claim. Although much of my writing about AIDS endeavors to combat moralistic responses to the epidemic, especially as those responses have had murderous consequences, my writing also seeks to understand the moralism adopted by the very people initially most devastated by AIDS in the United States: gay men. I am concerned, in other words, with a particular relation between devastation and self-abasement, between melancholia and moralism, between the turn away from AIDS and the turn toward conservative gay politics.

The turn away from AIDS is no simple matter. No one decided one day, enough of AIDS—and then wrote an essay called "When Plagues End." Nor did the turn away from AIDS come about as late as 1996, when Sullivan wrote his essay in the *New York Times* responding to the promise of protease inhibitors.[14] On the one hand, the turn away from AIDS can

13. Freud proposes that melancholia is the result of identification with and incorporation of the love object who has rejected the melancholiac. The repudiation of the self thus becomes a part of one's own ego, resulting in a moralistic self-abasement. See Sigmund Freud, "Mourning and Melancholia," *The Standard Edition of the Complete Psychological Works* (London: The Hogarth Press, 1957), vol. 14, pp. 237–258. See also "Mourning and Militancy," this volume.

14. Whereas many people would locate the origin of the current lack of attention to AIDS in the United States in the widespread changes brought about by the use of second-generation anti-retroviral medication—protease inhibitors and non-nucleoside analogue reverse transcriptase inhibitors—my essays locate that origin in problems

be seen as one response to the epidemic from the moment it was recognized in 1981. Whether as denial that it was really happening, that it was happening *here*, that it was happening to people *like us*, or as denial of its gravity and scope, the fearsomeness of AIDS always induced this tendency to disavowal. On the other hand, those who did confront AIDS as a crisis, often because they had little or no choice to do otherwise, were often eventually overwhelmed by the enormity and persistence of the tragedy, and they too sought the ostensible relief of turning away. But this second turning away is more complicated than the first. The first entails phobic denial—"this isn't happening"; "this can't affect me"; "I have nothing in common with those people." The second involves too much loss—"I can no longer bear this." If, in this latter case, relief seems possible, who wouldn't grasp it? The denial in this case is less of the actuality of AIDS itself than of the overwhelming effects of cumulative loss. This, too, might be characterized as melancholia.

I have claimed that Andrew Sullivan's moralistic repudiation of gay men in the pre-AIDS years is a symptom of melancholia, but I have now admitted that the denial of loss can produce melancholia too. What are its symptoms, if not moralism? How do these forms of melancholia differ?

Andrew Sullivan's proclamation of the end of AIDS was diagnosed as fetishistic by Phillip Brian Harper in a trenchant critique of "When Plagues End." Using the classic psychoanalytic formula for fetishism— "I know very well, but all the same . . ." (thus, an avowal that is simultaneously a disavowal)—Harper translates Sullivan's obliviousness to the millions for whom the development of protease inhibitors clearly can-

already faced by AIDS activists at least five years before these drugs came on the market. See especially "Mourning and Militancy" in this volume. Sullivan had written a preliminary version of "When Plagues End" as an op-ed piece in the *Times* a year earlier ("Fighting the Death Sentence," *New York Times*, November 21, 1995, p. A21). During the ensuing year, the media was full of "good news" about a turnaround in the epidemic, culminating with *Time* magazine's making AIDS researcher David Ho its 1996 person of the year. Ho was at that time theorizing and clinically testing the possibility of eliminating HIV entirely from the bodies of people who began combination therapy immediately following seroconversion. He soon had to admit that his theory was overly optimistic.

not mean the "plague's end" as "I know that not all people who have AIDS are U.S. whites, but in my narrative they are." Harper explains:

If Sullivan can suggest that "most people in the middle of this plague" experience the development of protease inhibitors as a profound occurrence (indeed as the "end" of AIDS) while he simultaneously admits that "the vast majority of H.I.V.-positive people in the world"—manifest in the United States principally as blacks and Latinos—will not have access to the new drugs and, indeed, will likely die, what can this mean but that, in Sullivan's conception, "most people in the middle of this plague" are not non-white or non–U.S. residents? Thus, while it may be strictly true that, as Sullivan puts it, his words are not "meant to deny" the fact of continued AIDS-related death, the form that his declaration assumes does constitute a disavowal—not of death per se but of the significance of the deaths of those not included in his notion of racial-national normativity. Those deaths still occur in the scenario that Sullivan sketches in his article, but they are not assimilable to the narrative about "the end of AIDS" that he wants to promulgate, meaning that, for Sullivan, they effectively do not constitute AIDS-related deaths at all.[15]

Sullivan's fetishism blinds him also to the fact that he takes his own experience of the development of protease inhibitors not as the experience of a privileged subject—white, male, living in the United States, covered by health insurance—but as a universal subject. Thus Sullivan's liberal universalism is not the enlightened political position he thinks it is; rather it is a sociopolitical fetish, constituted through the psychic mechanism of disavowal.

Recognizing Sullivan's misrecognition of his own subjectivity, Harper begins his essay by taking his distance from Sullivan: "For quite a while now, I have strongly suspected that Andrew Sullivan and I inhabit entirely different worlds."[16] Although I know that Harper's phrasing of his

15. Phillip Brain Harper, *Private Affairs: Critical Ventures in the Culture of Social Relations* (New York: New York University Press, 1999), pp. 93–94.

16. Ibid., p. 89.

differences with Sullivan in this way is deliberately arch, I keep getting hung up on it, because, as fully in accord as I am with Harper's critique, I cannot feel that my disagreements with Sullivan are the result of our inhabiting different worlds. Indeed, I sometimes get the claustrophobic feeling that Andrew Sullivan and I inhabit the very same world.

That world is the world of the well-informed but nevertheless recently infected gay men who find it hard to explain, even to ourselves, how we allowed the worst to happen to us. Let me elaborate. What I share with Sullivan is that my HIV infection occurred not before HIV and AIDS were known to me, nor in ignorance of degrees of risk associated with various sexual acts, nor because of a failure to adopt safe sex as a habitual practice. Like Sullivan, I inhabit a gay world that is particularly well informed about every aspect of HIV, from modes of transmission to methods of treatment. Also like Sullivan, my being gay is part of my public as well as my private identity, and dealing with AIDS has formed a large part of my recent professional life. I have devoted countless hours to thinking, writing, and speaking publicly about AIDS. I thus share with Sullivan a certain privilege concerning AIDS, a privilege that, say, a young African American or Latino gay man is unlikely to share. That privilege only increases the shame of having risked infection.

What I do not share with Andrew Sullivan is the explanation of why that risk was taken. Sullivan attributes his HIV infection to his failure to live up to his ethical ideal of a committed monogamous relationship. Here is a portion of what he says about his risky behavior in the version of "When Plagues End" expanded for his book *Love Undetectable:*

I remember in particular the emotional spasm I felt at the blithe comment of an old and good high school friend of mine, when I told him I was infected. He asked who had infected me; and I told him that, without remembering any particular incident of unsafe sex, I didn't really know. The time between my negative test and my positive test was over a year, I explained. It could have been anyone. "Anyone?" he asked, incredulously. "How many people did you sleep with, for God's sake?"

*Too many, God knows. Too many for meaning and dignity to be given to
every one; too many for love to be present in each. . . .*[17]

I find this passage deeply repulsive. First, I want to respond, What kind
of friend, on learning you've become HIV-positive, asks "Who infected
you?" and then chastises you for having too much sex? But more important, I want to ask, How many sex partners are too many? How do you
quantify meaning? dignity? love? One can only assume from what Sullivan writes that these qualities *redeem* sex, but do so only in inverse proportion to the number of sex partners. *This* is ethics?

Well, of course, it is what passes for ethics in Sullivan's religion, which
requires indeed that sex be redeemed—by procreation—and that it
take place only within sanctified marriage. This is nothing new. What *is*
new is that it also provides Sullivan with a ready excuse for his own
"lapse": "With regard to homosexuality, I inherited no moral or religious teaching that could guide me to success or failure. . . . In over
thirty years of weekly churchgoing, I have never heard a homily that attempted to explain how a gay man should live, or how his sexuality
should be expressed."[18] And yet Sullivan clearly did inherit a sexual
morality, for he is capable of the most standard moralizing statements
about sexual promiscuity, which are at the same time, of course, standard versions of homophobia. The following phrases and sentences appear within a few pages of each other in *Love Undetectable:*

. . . the sexual pathologies which plague homosexuals . . .

*. . . it is perhaps not surprising that [homosexuals'] moral and sexual be-
havior becomes wildly dichotic; that it veers from compulsive activity to
shame and withdrawal; or that it becomes anesthetized by drugs or alcohol or fatally distorted by the false, crude ideology of easy prophets.*

17. Sullivan, *Love Undetectable,* p. 41.
18. Ibid., p. 42.

. . . [gay liberationists] constructed and defended and glorified the abattoirs of the epidemic, even when they knew exactly what was going on. Yes, of course, because their ultimate sympathy lay with those trapped in this cycle, they were more morally defensible than condemning or oblivious outsiders. But they didn't help matters by a knee-jerk defense of catastrophic self-destruction, dressed up as cutting-edge theory.

There is little doubt that the ideology that human beings are mere social constructions and that sex is beyond good and evil facilitated a world in which gay men literally killed each other by the thousands.[19]

Sullivan's diatribe against gay men's sexual culture—whose "abattoirs" he nevertheless finds enticing enough to continue visiting regularly— merges in these latter passages with attacks on liberation politics and queer theory. As someone who published "cutting-edge" theoretical defenses of continuing promiscuity in the face of AIDS, I can only assume this venom is meant for me. So for all that I may share Sullivan's world, I clearly share nothing of his worldview.

But I return to what we do share: our recent HIV infections. I characterize Sullivan's explanation of his infection as symptomatic of melancholia because it entails self-abasement, a self-abasement that in Sullivan's case is also a rationalization. Sullivan locates himself within the moralizing narrative about gay men and AIDS that I outlined above. As someone who grew up before AIDS, he considers himself an irrevocably damaged soul, condemned by his church's homophobia to live out his sexual life in the ethical vacuum that was gay life before the epidemic. He can never attain the responsible adulthood that he sees as the great gift of AIDS to gay men because he is too fundamentally deformed by Catholic homophobia ever to attain his ideals. He can only hold up his ideals for the next generation. "Yes," Sullivan writes, "I longed for a relationship that could resolve these conflicts, channel sex into love and commitment and responsibility, but, for whatever reasons, I didn't find

19. Ibid., pp. 50–53.

it. Instead I celebrated and articulated its possibility, and did everything I could to advance the day when such relationships could become the norm."[20] He presented his case even more pathetically to PBS's talk-show host Charlie Rose in 1997: "I sort of feel like it's too late for me. It's too late for my generation. The damage has already been done. We have already struggled for years to overcome the lower standards that we set for ourselves when we were seven and eight and nine." I feel obliged to call attention to Sullivan's sneaky shift in this statement from blaming homophobia for the damage done to his generation of gay men to simply *blaming his generation of gay men.* But my point is actually an opposite one: Sullivan resorts to this notion that it's too late for him in order to absolve himself of the very responsibilities that he demands of others. "Grow up," he insists, "even though I don't have to, because, you know, I'm forever damaged." Sullivan gets to have his seventh and eighth and ninth birthday cake and eat it too.

Grow up! It's really not so easy, at least not when growing up means growing older. Bette Davis was right: "Old age is not for sissies." I don't know if she meant the kind of sissies who adore Bette Davis, but for *this* sissy getting older has been damned hard. So Sullivan's moralizing admonition to gay men to grow up has a peculiar resonance for me. As I said above, I'm of a generation older than Sullivan, the gay-liberation generation he so loves to denigrate. Thus it was just as I approached middle age that the AIDS epidemic became the most determining fact of gay life in the United States. This meant that much of what had been most vital in my life—most adventurous, experimental, and exhilarating; most intimate, sustaining, and gratifying; most self-defining and self-extending—began slowly but surely to disappear. A world, a way of life, faded, then vanished. Friends and lovers died, and so did acquaintances, public figures, and faces in the crowd that I had grown accustomed to. People whose energies and resources had gone toward the invention of gay life either succumbed or turned their attention to dealing with death. Gay cultural and sexual institutions that had for twenty

20. Ibid., p. 56.

years been expanding began to shrink as they came under attack or came to be too much associated with illness and death. And as all this happened—this may seem trivial, but for me it wasn't—my youthful sexual confidence and sense of desirability waned. The midlife crisis that is a banal event in every privileged person's life was overdetermined for me because it occurred in the midst of an epidemic that devastated my world. Facing my own mortality—the real content of this crisis—was profoundly confusing because I was consumed by it at a time when the truth of my situation was that I was healthy and vigorous while tens of thousands like me were dying.

14
—
15

I cannot say precisely what significance this confusion had for my risking HIV infection. Did I seek unconsciously to resolve the paradox of my own good health when I "should" have been sick? Did I try to reclaim the adventure and exhilaration of my younger self? All I know for sure is that feelings of loss pervaded my life. I felt overwhelming loss just walking the streets of New York, the city that since the late 1960s had given me my sense of being really alive.[21] This was certainly melancholia too, but unlike the melancholia that produces moralistic abjection, this was the opposite; my version of melancholia prevented me from acquiescing in and thus mourning the demise of a culture that had shown me the ethical alternative to conventional moralism, a culture that taught me what Thomas Keenan designates in *Fables of Responsibility* "the only responsibility worthy of the name," responsibility that "comes with the removal of grounds, the withdrawal of the rules or the knowledge on which we might rely to make our decisions for us. No grounds means no alibis, no elsewhere to which we might refer the instance of our decision. . . . It is when we do not know exactly what we should do, when the effects and conditions of our actions can no longer be calculated, and

---

21. Further overdetermination: The AIDS crisis also coincided with profound transformations in New York City, where, for example, previously abandoned or peripheral neighborhoods that were home to gay sexual culture were reappropriated and gentrified by the real-estate industry, thus making them inhospitable to the uses we'd invented for them.

when we have nowhere else to turn, not even back onto our 'self,' that we encounter something like responsibility."[22]

Whereas Andrew Sullivan sees gay men as irresponsible because homophobia prevented the arbiters of morality from providing us with rules by which to live, thus creating a moral vacuum, I see this vacuum as the precondition for the truly ethical way of life that gay men struggled to create. AIDS didn't make gay men grow up and become responsible. AIDS showed anyone willing to pay attention how genuinely ethical the invention of gay life had been. This doesn't mean that gay life is not riven with conflict or that being gay grants anyone automatic ethical claims. But the removal of grounds that Keenan sees as the beginning of authentic responsibility has been a condition of being gay in America—simply because the ground rules that are given are ones that disqualify us from the start. I will therefore call this genuine responsibility queer. And I will suggest that it is identical with, or constitutive of, the vitality that I felt from my participation in queer life prior to the epidemic. Obviously this is not the only place one might experience its vertiginous appeal, but it is where I experienced it. This is also to say that genuine responsibility can be experienced in the exhilarating disorientation of sex itself. Thus responsibility is not that which would obligate us to modify or curtail sex, or to justify or redeem it. On the contrary, responsibility may well *follow from* sex. This has obviously made sex terribly paradoxical for gay men during an epidemic of a sexually transmitted deadly disease syndrome. The paradox has meant that we've had to live with an especially heavy burden of conflict, with deep and enduring ambivalence. And we've had to discern and resist the easy answers that moralistic attitudes toward sex would provide to falsely resolve our conflict and ambivalence. And, adding insult to injury, we've had to watch as the U.S. media have given ever more prominent voice to gay spokesmen who unhesitatingly voice the moralism, gay men who go on *Nightline* and *Charlie Rose* and, with immodest self-certainty, assume their proper responsibility.

22. Thomas Keenan, *Fables of Responsibility: Aberrations and Predicaments in Ethics and Politics* (Stanford: Stanford University Press, 1997), pp. 1–2.

○

I tried to capture something of the paradox gay men have faced in the title of one of the first essays I wrote about AIDS, upping the ante of "How to Have Sex in an Epidemic," the first safe-sex pamphlet, to "How to Have Promiscuity in an Epidemic." That essay was, together with "AIDS: Cultural Analysis/Cultural Activism," the first I wrote about AIDS, and it contained what would become the opening salvo in an on-going critique of moralistic responses to the epidemic. Much has changed since then, but then again much has remained the same. I might mention, for example, that twenty years into the AIDS epidemic, Jesse Helms is still the senator from North Carolina, and he is, if anything, more powerful now than in 1987, when he first succeeded in preventing the federal funding of safe-sex information directed at gay men. Sometimes the déjà vu seems more like a nightmare from which we cannot awaken: In February 2001 artist and AIDS activist Donald Moffett felt compelled to reinstall a public art work he'd initially made in 1990, a light box photo-text work that said, "Call the White House . . . Tell Bush we're not all dead yet"—this time in response to George W.'s intention to close the White House AIDS office within weeks of assuming office.[23]

If the argument contained in the trajectory of these essays is right, however, there *has* been a drastic change, but it is a psychic change, a change in the way we think about AIDS, or rather a change that consists in our inability to continue thinking about AIDS. Throughout the early 1990s AIDS became an increasingly unbearable and therefore more deeply repressed topic, AIDS activism became virtually invisible, and gay politics moved steadily Rightward. I had begun to see this configuration of repression, trouble among activists, and moralistic politics at the turn of the decade. "Mourning and Militancy," the title of which that of this book is meant to echo, was my first attempt to theorize this turn;

23. Bush was unable to follow through on his intention because it caused such an outcry among gay people and public health advocates. Instead Bush appointed to head the White House Office of National AIDS Policy a prominent gay Republican, a Catholic who had been active as an antiabortion fundraiser. See Elizabeth Becker, "Gay Republican Will Run White House AIDS Office," *New York Times,* April 9, 2001, p. A13.

Donald Moffett, *Call the White House*, 1990/2001 (photo: George Kimmerling).

it marks a critical juncture in AIDS activism and serves as a theoretical core of the entire collection.[24]

24. Insofar as these essays are intended to contribute to a historical record of debates about AIDS and queer politics, I have decided against making any substantive changes to my essays as originally written and published. The change that I would most wish to make is in the opening paragraph of "Mourning and Militancy," where I criticize Lee Edelman's deconstruction of the AIDS-activist slogan SILENCE=DEATH in "The Plague of Discourse." That essay was my first encounter with Edelman's work, which I have subsequently grown to admire immensely. Moreover, my opening paragraph tends to drive a wedge between academic theory and activist practice

This configuration is also essential to the questions addressed in "Right On, Girlfriend!" and "Don't Tell." "Right On, Girlfriend!" explores the problems posed for ACT UP's coalition politics when notions of fixed, coherent identities came into conflict; it thus takes up forms of moralism that exist within both gay identity politics and traditional Left politics. "Don't Tell" analyzes the rhetoric of the Campaign for Military Service during the gays-in-the-military debates in the early months of the Clinton presidency, seeing in the portrayal of gay and lesbian military personnel as model patriots—politically conservative, healthy, and chaste—the desire to suppress the increasingly unbearable image of the sick person with AIDS and the image of anal sex that is so inevitably linked, at least in fantasy, to that sickness. The final essay of this collection, "Sex and Sensibility, or Sense and Sexuality" confronts the new moralism head-on in the positions of the new crop of mainstream gay journalists, including Sullivan, and in affiliation with the short-lived activist group Sex Panic!'s attempt to defend gay sexual culture and rejuvenate HIV prevention efforts.

If the defense of gay sexual culture and the critique of moralism are central to my essays, so too is a theoretical understanding of cultural representation as an essential site of political struggle, indeed of the struggle for life itself. As against the real-world-versus-culture reductionism of fundamentalisms Right and Left, my position has remained the one I laid out in "AIDS: Cultural Analysis/Cultural Activism": "If we recognize that AIDS exists only in and through its representations, culture, and politics, then the hope is that we can also recognize the imperative to know them, analyze them, and wrest control of them." This "cultural studies" position came to me not in some idle moment of speculation, or from reading what many would dismiss as "trendy academic theory,"

that I hope the essay itself otherwise contests. Edelman's own deconstruction of that split with regard to the rhetoric of AIDS activism can be found in "The Mirror and the Tank: 'AIDS,' Subjectivity, and the Rhetoric of Activism" (in *Homographesis: Essays in Gay Literary and Cultural Theory* [New York: Routledge, 1994], pp. 93–117); the essay is, among other things, Edelman's extremely tactful—and brilliant—rejoinder to my critique, and one that I find use for in my own later piece "Rosa's Indulgence," in this volume.

but as a lesson learned through my participation in ACT UP. In this, Daniel Harris's preposterous contention that postmodern theory exerted deleterious effects on AIDS activism gets things precisely backwards. What makes Harris's position even more preposterous is his disdain for what were in fact productive new relations between cultural theory and activist practice. For example:

For AIDS activists, this deconstructive skepticism [toward an "objective" reality of AIDS] manifests itself in the new interest not so much in circumventing as in manipulating the media, in seizing hold of the actual apparatus by which various moral interpretations of the disease are conveyed to the average consumer. The Media Committee of ACT UP, for example, has taken its cue from the White House and gone so far as to prepare press kits, which it has distributed before several of its demonstrations. Eager reporters and television crews dutifully plagiarized this material and ultimately reported what was "sold" to them in advance.[25]

To which I can only respond: What could be bad? The fact that ACT UP was able thoroughly to inform the media about the complex issues at stake during its demonstrations—against the Food and Drug Administration, for example—and that this resulted in better informed media coverage when the demonstrations occurred is certainly one of ACT UP's signal accomplishments. Can anyone living in contemporary American society honestly believe that media representations are extraneous to "real" politics?[26]

25. Daniel Harris, "AIDS and Theory: Has Academic Theory Turned AIDS into Meta-Death?" *Lingua Franca,* June 1991, p. 18. In attributing the invention of press kits to the White House, Harris reveals the depth of his ignorance of the media.

26. Harris's numerous journalistic writings about gay and AIDS issues generally give away the fact that he is driven by an embittered disaffection with—or perhaps self-imposed exclusion from—much of gay life; thus: "In the heart of San Francisco's Castro district, where I live, the ACT UP logo itself has so much cachet, offers such tangible proof of one's membership in a snugly insular klatch of one's peers, that it has become the Gucci or Calvin Klein designer label of the 1990s, a clubbish insignia that announces cliquishness rather than political conviction" ("A Blizzard of Images" [a review of my book *AIDS Demo Graphics* (Seattle: Bay Press, 1990)], *Nation,* Decem-

This is not to say that I embraced all of ACT UP's cultural interventions uncritically. In "Portraits of People with AIDS," I voice my skepticism toward the activist demand for positive images of people living with AIDS, arguing for a more complicated understanding of representation and its effects. I return to this question in "Accommodating Magic," where the activist demand is finally met by the mainstream media in its reporting about Magic Johnson's HIV illness—with predictably homophobic results.

But AIDS activism does not speak of representation or make representations with a single voice. In "De-Moralizing Representations of AIDS," I compare Gregg Bordowitz's feature-length account of his own history as a maker of AIDS-activist videos in *Fast Trip, Long Drop* (1993) to *Voices from the Front* (1992), a more conventional AIDS-activist documentary covering the history of ACT UP. While Bordowitz attempts to confront his own impending death as a means of reflecting on the toll that death has taken on the AIDS activist movement, *Voices from the Front* fails to acknowledge that toll. Its failure is, I think, a legacy of activism's history of masculinist heroism; in falling prey to this legacy by mythologizing AIDS activism, *Voices from the Front* also misrepresents a strategic shift in activist politics that was another signal contribution of ACT UP, the insertion of self-deprecating humor into activism as a means of deflating the heroics. A good example of ACT UP's style of humor is Matt Ebert and Ryan Landry's *Marta: Portrait of a Teen Activist,* made at an ACT UP demonstration at the Centers for Disease Control in Atlanta in 1990. The video wonderfully captures how—far from heroic—terribly awkward, how terribly queer it can feel to engage in activism. Marta's perpetual confusion—she can't decide which placard to carry, she carries it upside down once she decides, she keeps checking out fellow activists to figure out how to position herself properly for a "die-

ber 31, 1990, p. 852). "Cachet," "snugly insular klatch," "clubbish," "cliquishness"—
the overkill of his language tells a different story than the one Harris seems to think
he's writing. The question here, like the question as to why the *New York Times* indulges the personal *ressentiment* of Andrew Sullivan toward a wider gay culture, is,
Why does the *Nation* publish it?

in"—is hilariously captured by Ryan Landry in school-girl drag as Marta, named after the acronym for Atlanta's mass-transit system.

Harris's view of this innovation is that "While it is true that ACT UP has infused the flagging political momentum of the 1960s with camp and theatricality, there is a sense in which the intellectual underpinnings of the organization have made activism not more radically interventionist but more passively theoretical."[27] Harris's complaint demonstrates that he is oblivious to the fact that ACT UP's queer antics not only provide an image of an antiheroic activism but also deconstruct the homophobic construction whereby "radical activism" is guaranteed by its upright repudiation of "passive theory." Our ability to see such conventional oppositions *as homophobic* has, of course, been a significant contribution of queer theory. The active/passive binary employed by Harris here is the subject of a shrewd analysis of the more humorless varieties of AIDS-activist rhetoric by Lee Edelman, who asks whether "on the one hand, in our defense of an already beleaguered gay identity, we want to emulate the widespread heterosexual contempt for the image of a gay sexuality represented as passive and narcissistic . . . or whether, on the other hand, we want to refuse the 'choice' ideologically imposed by such a binarism—whether we want to deny the incompatibility of passivity and power, and thereby to undertake the construction of a gay subjectivity that need not define itself against its own subset of demonized 'faggots.'"[28]

Nearly all of these essays seek to expose homophobic representations and their disastrous consequences for public health during the epidemic. These include routine representations of "bad gays": Randy Shilts's murderously irresponsible Patient Zero in *And the Band Played On* ("How to Have Promiscuity in an Epidemic" and "Randy Shilts's Miserable Failure"), a figure who returns as the "gay serial killer" Andrew Cunanan, fantasized by the media as taking revenge for an HIV infection that he never even had ("Sex and Sensibility, or Sense

27. Harris, "AIDS and Theory," p. 18.
28. Edelman, *Homographesis,* pp. 109–110.

and Sexuality"); and Jonathan Demme's homosexualized psychopaths Buffalo Bill and Hannibal Lecter in *Silence of the Lambs* ("Right On, Girlfriend!"). And then there are the reverse, the good nongays (good because they're not gay): Magic Johnson's representation of himself to Arsenio Hall as "far from being homosexual" as the basis for his becoming a positive image of someone living with HIV ("Accommodating Magic"); or the not-so-gay good gays: Demme's de-homosexualized positive-image gay man with AIDS in *Philadelphia* ("De-Moralizing Representations of AIDS"). And then there are representations that conceal the sex in the homosexual: Nicholas Nixon's portrayals of people with AIDS as fleshless and ethereal in phobic defense against the possibility that a person with AIDS might still have sex ("Portraits of People with AIDS"); the Names Project quilt's sanitization of gay lives in order that gay deaths can be mourned ("The Spectacle of Mourning"); the chaste gay soldiers in the rhetoric of the Campaign for Military Service ("Don't Tell"); and my own "overlooking" of the homoerotic codes of Edward Weston's photographs of his child Neil ("The Boys in My Bedroom"). Or again the reverse, the picture that refuses to cover up homosexual sex: Rosa von Praunheim's "narcissistic" representations of his sexual pleasures counteracting his own moralistic rhetoric in *Army of Lovers* ("Rosa's Indulgence"); and Robert Mapplethorpe's *Helmut and Brooks* as a picture of what is most feared and hated about gay men ("Painful Pictures"). These last are not homophobic representations; rather they are representations that show how pictured homosexuality solicits homophobia.

Finally, there is the question of artists' representations of AIDS. I first took up the subject of AIDS as an editor of the cultural journal OCTOBER, thinking it would be useful to evaluate the art world's response to the epidemic. As I became more immersed in the crisis, I expanded my project to include a much broader range of thought and action engaged in the struggle against AIDS. What most struck me as I became more deeply involved were the ways in which the institutions of art marginalized the work of direct political engagement. I thus wrote a polemical introduction to the special issue of the journal calling for direct action on the part of the art world. My polemic provoked some indignant reactions. A well-known gay writer called me a Stalinist in the *L.A. Weekly*.[29] A prominent gay English professor told a mutual friend that he would never forgive me for being mean to Liz Taylor (I had accused her of mouthing platitudes about art's universality in a speech she made for an Art against AIDS fundraising gala). And a gay critic complained in *Artforum* that I had made him feel bad for liking David Wojnarowicz's art.[30] Writing a retrospective essay on art and AIDS some ten years later, the same critic, evidently still hung up on my having championed activist art, quoted the writer who'd called me a Stalinist—by now he was just calling me an "art-hating activist"—and went on to *mis*quote one of my most often-cited manifesto-like statements: "We don't need a cultural renaissance, we need cultural practices actively participating in the struggle against AIDS. We don't need to transcend the epidemic; we need to end it."[31] I unapologetically stand by that statement today.

This is not to say that I don't regret that my polemical views came off to some as doctrinaire, uncharitable, and proscriptive. I guess when I first got caught up in the AIDS maelstrom in the 1980s (remember, this was when Ronald Reagan was president and wouldn't even utter the word *AIDS*, much less spend any government money on it), I got pretty damned angry, in part at what seemed to me inadequate or ineffectual responses. I hope, though, that one result of having these essays all to-

29. "AGAINST NATURE, as has often been true of Dennis [Cooper]'s work, was given a chilly reception; Dennis refers to this as the beginning of the Stalinist period of gay art. Douglas Crimp, in a speech called 'Art and Activism' ['Good Ole Bad Boys' in this volume], went out of his way to castigate AGAINST NATURE, and laid out the position that has become the official gay-politico/ACT Upish line, which stridently rejects the personal" (Eric Latzky, "He Cried: Novelist Dennis Cooper Hits Home," *L.A. Weekly*, July 23, 1990, p. 27).

30. David Deitcher, "Ideas and Emotions," *Artforum* 27, 9 (May 1989), pp. 122–127.

31. Deitcher quoted a note by Dennis Cooper and Richard Hawkins on their exhibition *Against Nature* written for *In a Different Light: Visual Culture, Sexual Identity, Queer Practice*, ed. Nayland Blake, Lawrence Rinder, and Amy Scholder (San Francisco: City Lights Books, 1995, p. 57). See David Deitcher, "What Does Silence Equal Now?" in *Art Matters: How the Culture Wars Changed America*, ed. Brian Wallis, Marianne Weems, and Philip Yenawine (New York: New York University Press, 1999); the misquote of my essay appears on page 106.

gether in strict chronological order will show that I took these early criticisms seriously and tried to make my arguments more nuanced. Just a year after making my case in "AIDS: Cultural Analysis/Cultural Activism" for "a critical, theoretical, activist alternative to the personal, elegiac expressions that dominated the art-world response to AIDS," I wrote "Portraits of People with AIDS." While that essay, too, is a polemic against representations I found counterproductive, in this case I posed as the alternative a deeply moving elegy in the form of the independent video *Danny* by Stashu Kybartas. In thus championing a work of mourning I was attempting to say that I had not meant to be either pre- or proscriptive about the form or genre of artwork about AIDS.

Still, I continued—and continue—to be troubled by the fact that the art world's most unwavering conviction is the old saw *Vita brevis, ars longa,* or "Art lives on forever," to use Elizabeth Taylor's words that caused me to be mean. This conviction generally translates into a repudiation of "political art," politics being far too contingent. "Political art" *doesn't* live on forever; it lives most fully in the moment of its intervention. From my perspective, however—one that I had been elaborating for a decade prior to writing about AIDS—this contingency of political investment is the necessary condition of all art, one that traditional idealist notions of art, summed up in a maxim like *Vita brevis, ars longa,* work to conceal. As Rosalyn Deutsche has recently stated, "I, like many artists and critics, avoid the term 'political art': Precisely because it asserts that other art—indeed art per se or so-called real art—is not political, 'political art' is a powerful political weapon, one that is routinely deployed to ghettoize art that avows the political."[32] I take up this problem in "Good Ole Bad Boys," in which I confront the curators of an exhibition conceived as a repudiation of my *OCTOBER* polemic.

There is, though, a twofold danger in arguing for art's avowal of politics, or to argue for activist art practices as I had: First, it can too easily make

32. "'Every Art Form Has a Political Dimension,'" Chantal Mouffe, interviewed by Rosalyn Deutsche, Branden W. Joseph, and Thomas Keenan, *Grey Room* 02 (winter 2001), p. 100.

it appear that there *is* such a thing as art that is beyond politics rather than art that simply disavows its politics; second, and more important, it can make it appear that what is political—or activist—and what is not is self-evident. I write about this problem of essentializing activism in "A Day without Gertrude," in which I argue that the politics of representation is rarely so simple as the direct avowal of a political position.

Having said that, I nevertheless want to end this introduction by stating a few political positions unequivocally:

I am not now and never have been a member of the Communist Party, Stalinist or otherwise (although I did once vote for Angela Davis for President).

I think Elizabeth Taylor is a great movie star; I love her for being such a good friend to the fabulous Hollywood homos Montgomery Clift, James Dean, and Rock Hudson; and I consider her a saint for all she's done in the fight against AIDS.

I have never suggested that anyone shouldn't like David Wojnarowicz's art; I like it myself.

And finally, I don't hate art; I like it. I've spent my entire professional life thinking about it, and I still like it.

2 AIDS: CULTURAL ANALYSIS/ CULTURAL ACTIVISM

First published as the introduction to OCTOBER *43*

(winter 1987), a special issue on AIDS. This is a

slightly adapted version.

"I assert, to begin with, that 'disease' does not exist. It is therefore illusory to think that one can 'develop beliefs' about it to 'respond' to it. What does exist is not disease but practices." Thus begins François Delaporte's investigation of the 1832 cholera epidemic in Paris.[1] It is a statement we may find difficult to swallow, as we witness the ravages of AIDS in the bodies of our friends, our lovers, and ourselves. But it is nevertheless crucial to our understanding of AIDS because it shatters the myth so central to liberal views of the epidemic: that there are, on the one hand, the scientific facts about AIDS, and, on the other hand, ignorance or misrepresentation of those facts standing in the way of a rational response. I will therefore follow Delaporte's assertion: AIDS does not exist apart from the practices that conceptualize it, represent it, and respond to it. We know AIDS only in and through those practices. This assertion does not contest the existence of viruses, antibodies, infections, or transmission routes. Least of all does it contest the reality of illness, suffering, and death. What it *does* contest is the notion that there is an underlying reality of AIDS, on which are constructed the representations, or the culture, or the politics of AIDS. If we recognize that AIDS exists only in and through these constructions, then the hope is that we can also recognize the imperative to know them, analyze them, and wrest control of them.

Within the arts, the scientific explanation and management of AIDS is largely taken for granted, and it is therefore assumed that cultural producers can respond to the epidemic in only two ways: by raising money for scientific research and service organizations or by creating works that express the human suffering and loss. In an article for *Horizon* entitled "AIDS: The Creative Response," David Kaufman outlined examples of both, including benefits such as "Music for Life," "Dancing for Life," and "Art against AIDS," together with descriptions of plays, literature, and paintings that take AIDS as their subject.[2] Regarding these

1. François Delaporte, *Disease and Civilization: The Cholera in Paris, 1832,* trans. Arthur Goldhammer (Cambridge: MIT Press, 1986), p. 6.
2. David Kaufman, "AIDS: The Creative Response," *Horizon* 30, no. 9 (November 1987), pp. 13–20.

latter "creative responses," Kaufman rehearses the clichés about art's "expressing feelings that are not easily articulated," "shar[ing] experiences and values through catharsis and metaphor," "demonstrating the indomitability of the human spirit," "consciousness raising." Art is what survives, endures, transcends; art constitutes our legacy. In this regard, AIDS is even seen to have a positive value: Kaufman quotes Michael Denneny of St. Martin's Press as saying, "We're on the verge of getting a literature out of this that will be a renaissance."[3]

In July 1987, PBS's *McNeil/Lehrer Newshour* devoted a portion of its program to "AIDS in the Arts." The segment opened with the shibboleth about "homosexuals" being "the lifeblood of show business and the arts" and went on to note the AIDS-related deaths of a number of famous artists. Such a pretext for a special report on AIDS is highly problematic, and on a number of counts: First, it reinforces the equation of AIDS and homosexuality, neglecting even to mention the possibility that an artist, like anyone else, might contract HIV heterosexually or by sharing needles when shooting drugs. Second, it suggests that gay people have a *natural* inclination toward the arts, the homophobic flip side of which is that "homosexuals control the arts" (ideas perfectly parallel with anti-Semitic attitudes that see Jews as, on the one hand, "making special contributions to culture," and, on the other, "controlling capital"). But most pernicious of all, it implies that gay people "redeem" themselves by being artists, and therefore that the deaths of other gay people are less tragic.[4] The message is that art, because it is

3. Denneny is the editor of Randy Shilts's *And the Band Played On,* a discussion of which appears in "How to Have Promiscuity in an Epidemic," in this volume.

4. Redemption, of course, necessitates a prior sin—the sin of homosexuality, of promiscuity, of drug use—and thus a program such as "AIDS in the Arts" contributes to the media's distribution of innocence and guilt according to who you are and how you contracted HIV. Promiscuous gay men and IV drug users are unquestionably guilty in this construction, but so are all people from poor minority populations. The special attention paid to artists and other celebrities with AIDS is nevertheless contradictory. While a TV program such as "AIDS in the Arts" virtually beatifies the stricken artist, for personalities such as Rock Hudson and Liberace the scandal of being found guilty of homosexuality tarnishes the halo of their celebrity status.

timeless and universal, transcends individual lives, which are time-bound and contingent.

Entirely absent from the news report—and the *Horizon* article—was any mention of *activist* responses to AIDS by cultural producers. The focus was instead on the dramatic effect of the epidemic on the art world, the coping with illness and death. Extended interviews with choreographers Bill T. Jones and his lover Arnie Zane, who had been diagnosed with AIDS, emphasized the "human face" of the disease in a way that was far more palatable than is usual in broadcast television, simply because it allowed the positive self-representation of both a person with AIDS and a gay relationship. Asked whether he thought "the arts are particularly hit by AIDS," Zane replied, "That's the controversial question of this month, right?" but then went on to say, "Of course I do. I am in the center of this world, the art world. . . . I am losing my colleagues." Colleen Dewhurst, president of Actors Equity, suggested rather that "AIDS-related deaths are not more common among artists, only more visible," and continued, "Artists are supposed to represent the human condition . . ." (a condition that is, of course, assumed to be universal).

"Art lives on forever"—this idealist platitude came from Elizabeth Taylor, National Chairman of the American Foundation for AIDS Research, shown addressing the star-studded crowd at the gala to kick off "Art against AIDS." But strangely it was Richard Goldstein, writer for the *Village Voice* and a committed activist on the subject of AIDS, who contributed the broadcast's most unabashed statement of faith in art's transcendence of life: "In an ironic sense, I think that AIDS is good for art. It think it will produce great works that will outlast and transcend the epidemic."

It would appear from such a statement that what is at stake is not the survival of people with AIDS and those who might now be or eventually become infected with HIV, but rather the survival, even the flourishing, of art. For Goldstein, this is surely less a question of hopelessly confused priorities, however, than a failure to recognize the alternatives to this desire for transcendence—a failure determined by the intractability of the traditional idealist conception of art, which entirely divorces art from engagement in lived social life.

Writing in the catalog of "Art against AIDS," Robert Rosenblum affirms this limited and limiting view of art and the passivity it entails: "By now, in the 1980s, we are all disenchanted enough to know that no work of art, no matter how much it may fortify the spirit or nourish the eye and mind, has the slightest power to save a life. Only science can do that. But we also know that art does not exist in an ivory tower, that it is made and valued by human beings who live and die, and that it can generate a passionate abundance of solidarity, love, intelligence, and most important, money."[5] There could hardly be a clearer declaration of the contradictions inherent in aesthetic idealism that one that blandly accepts art's inability to intervene in the social world and simultaneously praises its commodity value. To recognize this as contradictory is not, however, to object to exploiting that commodity value for the purpose of fundraising for AIDS research and service. Given the failure of government at every level to provide the funding necessary to combat the epidemic, such efforts as "Art against AIDS" have been necessary, even crucial to our survival. I want, nevertheless, to raise three caveats.

1. Scientific research, health care, and education are the responsibility and purpose *of government and not of so-called private initiative, an ideological term that excuses and perpetuates the state's irresponsibility. Therefore, every venture of this nature should make clear that it is necessitated strictly because of criminal negligence on the part of government. What we find, however, is the very opposite: "Confronting a man-made evil like the war in Vietnam, we could assail a government and the people in charge. But how do we confront a diabolically protean virus that has been killing first those pariahs of grass-roots America, homosexuals and drug addicts, and has then gone on to kill, with far less moral discrimination, even women, children, and heterosexual men? We*

5. Robert Rosenblum, "Life Versus Death: The Art World in Crisis," in *Art against AIDS* (New York: American Foundation for AIDS Research, 1987), p. 32.

have recourse only to love and to science, which is what Art against AIDS
is all about." [6]

2. *Blind faith in science, as if it were entirely neutral and uncontami-
nated by politics, is naive and dangerous. It must be the responsibility of
everyone contributing to fundraisers to know enough about AIDS to determine whether the beneficiary will put the money to the best possible
use. How many artists and art dealers contributing to "Art against AIDS,"
for example, know precisely what kinds of scientific research are supported by the American Foundation for AIDS Research? How many know
the alternatives to AmFAR's research agenda, alternatives such as the
Community Research Initiative, an effort at testing AIDS treatments initiated at the community level by people with AIDS themselves? As anyone involved in the struggle against AIDS knows, we cannot afford to
leave anything up to the "experts." We must become our own experts.* [7]

3. *Raising money is the most passive response of cultural practitioners to
social crisis, a response that perpetuates the idea that art itself has no social function (aside from being a commodity), that there is no such thing
as an engaged, activist aesthetic practice. It is this third point that I want
to underscore by insisting, against Rosenblum, that art* does *have the
power to save lives, and it is this very power that must be recognized, fos-*

6. Ibid., p. 28. I hope we can assume that Rosenblum intends his remarks about "pariahs" and "moral discrimination" ironically, although this is hardly what I would call
politically sensitive writing. It could easily be read without irony, since it so faithfully
reproduces what is written in the press virtually every day. And the implication of the
"even women" in the category distinct from "homosexuals" is, once again, that
there's no such thing as a lesbian. But can we expect political sensitivity from someone who cannot see that AIDS is political? That *science* is political? It was science,
after all, that conceptualized AIDS as a gay disease and wasted precious time scru-
tinizing our sex lives, theorizing about killer sperm, and giving megadoses of poppers
to mice at the CDC—all the while taking little notice of the others who were dying of
AIDS, and thus allowing HIV to be injected into the veins of vast numbers of IV drug
users, as well as hemophiliacs and other people requiring blood transfusions.

7. I do not wish to cast suspicion on AmFAR, but rather to suggest that no organization
can be seen as neutral or objective. See in this regard the exchange of letters on Am-
FAR's rejection of the Community Research Initiative's funding applications in the
PWA Coalition Newsline 30 (January 1988), pp. 3–7.

tered, and supported in every way possible. We don't need a cultural re-
naissance; we need cultural practices actively participating in the struggle
against AIDS. We don't need to transcend the epidemic; we need to end it.

What might such a cultural practice be? One example appeared in November 1987 in the window on Broadway of New York's New Museum of
Contemporary Art. Entitled *Let the Record Show* . . . , it is the collective
work of ACT UP (the AIDS Coalition to Unleash Power), which is——I repeat what is stated at the beginning of every Monday night meeting——
"a nonpartisan group of diverse individuals united in anger and committed to direct action to end the AIDS crisis." More precisely, *Let the*
Record Show . . . is the work of an ad hoc committee within ACT UP
that responded to the New Museum's offer to create the window installation. The offer was tendered by curator Bill Olander, himself a participant in ACT UP. Olander wrote:

I first became aware of ACT UP, like many other New Yorkers, when I saw
a poster appear on lower Broadway with the equation: SILENCE=DEATH.
Accompanying these words, sited on a black background, was a pink tri-
angle—the symbol of homosexual persecution during the Nazi period
and, since the 1960s, the emblem of gay liberation. For anyone conver-
sant with this iconography, there was no question that this was a poster
designed to provoke and heighten awareness of the AIDS crisis. To me, it
was more than that: it was among the most significant works of art that
had yet been done which was inspired and produced within the arms of
the crisis.[8]

That symbol, made of neon, occupied the curved portion of the New
Museum's arched window. Below it, in the background and bathed in
soft, even light, was a photomural of the Nuremberg Trials (in addition
to prosecuting Nazi war criminals, those trials established our present-

8. Bill Olander, "The Window on Broadway by ACT UP," in *On View* (New York: New Museum of Contemporary Art, 1987), p. 1. The logo that Olander describes is not the work
of ACT UP, but of a design collective called the SILENCE=DEATH Project, which lent
the logo to ACT UP.

ACT UP (Gran Fury), *Let the Record Show . . .*, 1987, installation view, New Museum
Window on Broadway (collection the New Museum, New York).

day code of medical ethics, involving such things as informed consent to experimental medical procedures). In front of this giant photo were six life-size silhouetted photographs of "AIDS criminals" in separate, boxed-in spaces, and below each one the words by which he or she may be judged by history, cast—literally—in concrete. As the light went on in each of these separate boxed spaces, we could see the face and read the words:

The logical outcome of testing is a quarantine of those infected.
—Jesse Helms, U.S. Senator

It is patriotic to have the AIDS test and be negative.
—Cory Servaas, Presidential AIDS Commission

We used to hate faggots on an emotional basis. Now we have a good reason.
—anonymous surgeon

AIDS is God's judgment of a society that does not live by His rules.
—Jerry Falwell, televangelist

Everyone detected with AIDS should be tattooed in the upper forearm, to protect common needle users, and on the buttocks to prevent the victimization of other homosexuals.
—William F. Buckley, columnist

And finally, there was a blank slab of concrete, above which was the silhouetted photograph of President Reagan. We looked up from this blank slab and saw, once again, the neon sign: SILENCE=DEATH.

But there was more. Suspended above this rogues' gallery was an electronic information display programmed with a running text, portions of which read as follows:

Let the record show . . . William F. Buckley deflects criticism of the government's slow response to the epidemic through calculations: "At most three years were lost . . . Those three years have killed approximately

15,000 people; if we are talking 50 million dead, then the cost of delay is not heavy. . . ."

Let the record show . . . The Pentagon spends in one day more than the government spent in the last five years for AIDS research and education. . . .

Let the record show . . . In June 1986, $47 million was allocated for new drug trials to include 10,000 people with AIDS. One year later only 1,000 people are currently enrolled. In that time, over 9,000 Americans have died of AIDS.

Let the record show . . . In 1986, Dr. Cory Servaas, editor of the Saturday Evening Post, *announced that after working closely with the National Institutes of Health, she had found a cure for AIDS. At the time, the National Institutes of Health officials said that they had never heard of Dr. Cory Servaas. In 1987, President Reagan appointed Dr. Cory Servaas to the Presidential AIDS Commission.*

Let the record show . . . In October of 1986, $80 million was allocated for public education about AIDS. 13 months later there is still no national education program. In that time, over 15,000 new cases have been reported.

Let the record show . . . 54% of the people with AIDS in New York City are black and Hispanic. The incidence of heterosexually transmitted AIDS is 17 times higher among blacks than whites, 15 times higher among Hispanics than whites. 88% of babies with AIDS are black and Hispanic. 6% of the US AIDS education budget has been targeted for the minority community.

And finally:

By Thanksgiving 1981, 244 known dead . . . AIDS . . . no word from the President.

By Thanksgiving 1982, 1,123 known dead . . . AIDS . . . no word from the President.

The text continues like this, always with no word from the President, until finally:

By Thanksgiving 1987, 25,644 known dead . . . AIDS . . . President Reagan: "I have asked the Department of Health and Human Services to determine as soon as possible the extent to which the AIDS virus has penetrated our society."

After each of these bits of information, the sign flashed, "Act Up, Fight Back, Fight AIDS," a standard slogan at ACT UP demonstrations. Documentary footage from some of these demonstrations could be seen in the videotape *Testing the Limits,* programmed at the New Museum simultaneously with the window display. The video about AIDS activism in New York City is the work of a collective (also called Testing the Limits) "formed to document emerging forms of activism arising out of people's response to government inaction in the global AIDS epidemic."

The SILENCE=DEATH Project, the group from ACT UP who made *Let the Record Show . . . ,* and Testing the Limits share important premises that can teach us much about engaged art practices. First, they are *collective* endeavors. Second, these practices are employed by their collectives' members as an essential part of their AIDS activism. This is not to say that the individuals involved are not artists in the more conventional sense of the word; many of these people work within the precincts of the traditional art world and its institutions. But involvement in the AIDS crisis has not left their relation to that world unaltered. After making *Let the Record Show . . .* for the New Museum, for example, the group from ACT UP reconvened and decided to continue their work (soon adopting the name Gran Fury). Among the general principles discussed at their first meeting, one was unanimously voiced: "We have to get out of Soho, get out of the art world."

The New Museum has been more hospitable than most art institutions to socially and politically committed art practices, and it was very courageous of the museum to offer space to an activist organization rather than to an artist. It is also very useful that the museum has a window on lower Broadway that is passed by many people who would never set foot in an art museum. But if we think about art in relation to the AIDS epidemic—in relation, that is, to the communities most drastically affected by AIDS, especially poor and minority communities where AIDS is spreading much faster than elsewhere—we will realize that no work made within the confines of the art world as it is currently constituted will reach these people. Activist art therefore involves questions not only of the nature of cultural production but also of the location, or the means of distribution, of that production. *Let the Record Show . . .* was made for an art-world location, and it appears to have been made largely for an art-world audience. By providing information about government inaction and repressive intentions in the context of shocking statistics, its purpose is to inform—and thereby to mobilize—its presumably sophisticated audience (an audience presumed, for example, to be able to recognize a photograph of the Nuremberg Trials).[9] Such information and mobilization *can* (contra Rosenblum) save lives; indeed, until a cure for AIDS is developed, *only* information and mobilization can save lives.

In New York City, virtually every official campaign of highly visible public information about AIDS—whether AIDS education for schools, public service announcements on TV, or posters in the subways—must meet with the approval of, among others, the immensely powerful and reactionary Cardinal John J. O'Connor. This has resulted in a murderous regime of silence and disinformation that virtually guarantees the mounting deaths of sexually active young people—gay and straight—and of IV drug users, their sex partners, and their children, most of them from poor, minority populations. Recognizing this, small coalitions of cultural workers, including a group calling itself the Metropolitan Health Association and Gran Fury, have taken to the streets and subways to mount education campaigns of their own. Employing sophisticated

9. Whether or not the audience was also presumed to be able to see a connection between *Let the Record Show . . .* and the procedures and devices of artists such as Hans Haacke, Jenny Holzer, and Barbara Kruger is an open question.

graphics and explicit information, printed in English and Spanish, these artists and activists are attempting to get the unambiguous word out about how safe sex and clean works can protect people from contracting HIV. Even apart from the possibility of arrest, the difficulties faced by these people are daunting. Their work demands a total reevaluation of the nature and purpose of cultural practices in conjunction with an understanding of the political goals of AIDS activism. It requires, in addition, a comprehensive knowledge of routes of HIV transmission and means of prevention, as well as sensitivity to cultural specificity—to, say, the street language of Puerto Ricans as opposed to that of Spanish-speaking immigrants from Central or South America.

Even having adopted new priorities and accumulated new forms of knowledge, the task of cultural producers working within the struggle against AIDS will be difficult. The ignorance and confusion enforced by government and the dominant media; the disenfranchisement and immiseration of many of the people thus far hardest hit by AIDS; and the psychic resistance to confronting sex, disease, and death in a society where those subjects are largely taboo—all of these conditions must be faced by anyone doing work on AIDS. Cultural activism is only now beginning; also just beginning is the recognition and support of this work by art-world institutions.

To date, a majority of cultural producers working in the struggle against AIDS have used the video medium. There are a number of reasons for this. Much of the dominant discourse on AIDS has been conveyed through television, and this discourse has generated a critical counterpractice in the same medium; video can sustain a fairly complex array of information; and cable access and the widespread use of VCRs provide the potential for a large audience for this work.[10] In October 1987, the American Film Institute Video Festival included a series entitled "Only Human: Sex, Gender, and Other Misrepresentations," organized

10. For a good overview of both commercial television and independent video productions about AIDS, see Timothy Landers, "Bodies and Anti-Bodies: A Crisis in Representation," *Independent* 11, no. 1 (January–February 1988), pp. 18–24.

by Bill Horrigan and B. Ruby Rich. Of eight programs in the series, three were devoted to videotapes about AIDS. Among the more than twenty videos shown, a full range of independent work was represented, including tapes made for broadcast TV (*AIDS in the Arts*), AIDS education tapes (*Sex, Drugs, and AIDS*, made for the New York City School system), "art" tapes (*News from Home* by Tom Kalin and Stathis Lagoudakis), music videos (*The ADS Epidemic* by John Greyson), documentaries (*Testing the Limits*), and critiques of the media (*A Plague on You* by the Lesbian and Gay Media Group). The intention of the program was not to select work on the basis of aesthetic merit but to show something of the range of representations and counterrepresentations of AIDS. As B. Ruby Rich stated in the program:

> *To speak of sexuality and the body, and not speak of AIDS, would be, well, obscene. At the same time, the peculiarly key role being played by the media in this scenario makes it urgent that counterimages and counterrhetoric be created and articulated. To this end, we have grouped the AIDS tapes together in three special programs to allow the dynamic of their interaction to produce its own discourse—and to allow the inveterate viewer to begin making the aesthetic diagnosis that is quickly becoming every bit as urgent as (particularly in the absence of) the medical one.*[11]

My preparation of a special issue of *October* on AIDS stemmed initially from encounters with several works of or about media: Simon Watney's book *Policing Desire: AIDS, Pornography, and the Media* (Minnesota University Press, 1987); Stuart Marshall's video *Bright Eyes,* made for Britain's Channel 4 television; and the documentary about AIDS activism in New York City *Testing the Limits.* My intention was to show, through discussion of these works, that there was a critical, theoretical, activist alternative to the personal, elegiac expressions that appeared to dominate the art-world response to AIDS. What seemed to me essential was a vastly expanded view of culture in relation to crisis. But the full extent to which this view would have to be expanded became clear only

11. B. Ruby Rich, "Only Human: Sex, Gender, and Other Misrepresentations," in *1987 American Film Institute Video Festival,* Los Angeles, p. 42.

Cultural Analysis/Cultural Activism

through further engagement with the issues. AIDS intersects with and requires a critical rethinking of all of culture: of language and representation, science and medicine, health and illness, sex and death, the public and private realms. AIDS is a central issue for gay men, of course, but also for lesbians. AIDS is an issue for women generally, but especially for poor and minority women, child-bearing women, and women working in the health care system. AIDS is an issue for drug users, for prisoners, and for sex workers. At some point, even "ordinary" heterosexual men will have to learn that AIDS is an issue for them, and not simply because they might be susceptible to "contagion."

3 HOW TO HAVE PROMISCUITY IN AN EPIDEMIC

First published in OCTOBER *43 (winter 1987),*

a special issue on AIDS.

—AIDS: Questions and Answers

—AIDS: Get the Facts

—AIDS: Don't Die of Ignorance

The sloganeering of AIDS education campaigns suggests that knowledge about AIDS is readily available, easily acquired, and undisputed. Anyone who has sought to learn the "facts," however, knows just how hard it is to get them. Since the beginning of the epidemic, one of the very few sources of up-to-date information on all aspects of AIDS has been the gay press, but this is a fact that no education campaign (except those emanating from gay organizations) will tell you. As Simon Watney has noted, the British government ban on gay materials coming from the United States until late in 1986 meant, in effect, that people in the U.K. were legally prohibited from learning about AIDS during a crucial period. The ban also meant that the British Department of Health had to sneak American gay publications into the country in diplomatic pouches in order to prepare the Thatcher government's bullying "Don't Die of Ignorance" campaign.[1]

Among information sources, perhaps the most acclaimed is the *New York Native,* which has published news about AIDS virtually every week since 1982. But, although during the early years a number of leading medical reporters wrote for the newspaper and provided essential information, the *Native's* overall record on AIDS is not so admirable. Like other tabloids, the *Native* exploits the conflation of sex, fear, disease, and death in order to sell newspapers. Banner headlines with grim predictions, new theories of "cause" and "cure," and scandals of scientific infighting combine with soft-core shots of hot male bodies to ensure that we will rush to plunk down our two dollars for this extremely thin publication. One curious aspect of these headlines over the past few years is that they nearly always refer not to a major news or feature story,

1. Simon Watney, *Policing Desire: Pornography, AIDS, and the Media* (Minneapolis: University of Minnesota Press, 1987), p. 13.

but to a short editorial column by the newspaper's publisher Charles Ortleb. These weekly diatribes against the likes of Robert Gallo of the National Cancer Institute and Anthony Fauci of the National Institute for Allergy and Infectious Diseases might appear to be manifestations of a healthy skepticism toward establishment science, but Ortleb's distrust takes an odd form. Rather than performing a political analysis of the ideology of science, Ortleb merely touts the crackpot theory of the week, championing whoever is the latest outcast from the world of academic and government research. Never wanting to concede that establishment science could be right about the "cause" of AIDS, which is now generally (if indeed skeptically) assumed to be the retrovirus designated HIV, Ortleb latches onto any alternative theory: African Swine Fever Virus, Epstein Barr Virus, reactivated syphilis.[2] The genuine concern by informed people that a full acceptance of HIV as *the* cause of AIDS limits research options, especially regarding possible cofactors, is magnified and distorted by Ortleb into ad hominem vilification of anyone who assumes for the moment that HIV is the likely primary causal agent of AIDS. Among the *Native's* maverick heroes in this controversy about origins is the Berkeley biochemist Peter Duesberg, who is so confident that HIV is harmless that he has claimed to be unafraid of injecting it into his veins. When asked by *Village Voice* reporter Ann Giudici Fettner what he *does* think is causing the epidemic, Duesberg replied, "We don't have a new disease. It's a collection of [old] diseases caused by a lifestyle that was criminal 20 years ago. Combined with bathhouses, all these infections go with lifestyles which enhance them."[3] As Fettner notes, this is "a stunning regression to 1982," when AIDS was presumed to be a consequence of "the gay lifestyle."

A scientist pushing "the gay lifestyle" as the cause of AIDS in 1987 might seem a strange sort of hero for a gay newspaper to be celebrating, but

2. For an overview of theories of the cause of AIDS, see Robert Lederer, "Origin and Spread of AIDS: Is the West Responsible?" *Covert Action* 28 (summer 1987), pp. 43–54; and 29 (winter 1988), pp. 52–65.

3. Quoted in Ann Giudici Fettner, "Bad Science Makes Strange Bedfellows," *Village Voice,* February 2, 1988, p. 25.

then anyone who has read the *Native* regularly will have noted that, for Ortleb too, sex has been the real culprit all along. And, in this, Ortleb is not alone among powerful gay journalists. He is joined in this belief not only by right-wing politicians and ideologues, but by Randy Shilts, AIDS reporter for the *San Francisco Chronicle* and author of *And the Band Played On,* the best-selling book on AIDS.[4] That this book is pernicious has already been noted by many people working in the struggle against AIDS. For anyone suspicious of "mainstream" American culture, it might seem enough simply to note that the book *is* a bestseller, that it has been highly praised throughout the dominant media, or, even more damning, that the book has been optioned for a TV miniseries by Esther Shapiro, writer and producer of *Dynasty.* For some, the fact that Larry Kramer is said to be vying for the job of scriptwriter of the series will add to these suspicions (whoever reads the book will note that, in any case, the adaptation will be an easy task, since it is already written, effectively, *as* a miniseries). The fact that Shilts places blame for the spread of AIDS equally on the Reagan administration, various government agencies, the scientific and medical establishments, *and the gay community,* is reason enough for many of us to condemn the book.

And the Band Played On is predicated on a series of oppositions; it is, first and foremost, a story of heroes and villains, of common sense against prejudice, of rationality against irrationality; it is also an account of scientific advance versus political maneuvering, public health versus civil rights, a safe blood supply versus blood-banking industry profits, homosexuals versus heterosexuals, hard cold facts versus what Shilts calls AIDSpeak.

We might assume we know what is meant by this neologism: AIDSpeak would be, for example, "the AIDS test," "AIDS victims," "promiscuity." But no, Shilts employs these imprecise, callous, or moralizing terms just

4. Randy Shilts, *And the Band Played On: Politics, People, and the AIDS Epidemic* (New York: St. Martin's Press, 1987). Page numbers for all citations from the book appear in parentheses in the text.

as do all his fellow mainstream journalists, without quotation marks, without apology. For Shilts, AIDSpeak is, instead, a language invented to cover up the truth. An early indication of what Shilts thinks this language is appears in his account of the June 5, 1981, article in the *Morbidity and Mortality Weekly Report* about cases of *Pneumocystis* pneumonia in gay men. Shilts writes:

The report appeared . . . not on page one of the MMWR *but in a more inconspicuous slot on page two. Any reference to homosexuality was dropped from the title, and the headline simply read:* Pneumocystis *pneumonia Los Angeles.*

Don't offend the gays and don't inflame the homophobes. These were the twin horns on which the handling of this epidemic would be torn from the first day of the epidemic. Inspired by the best intentions, such arguments paved the road toward the destination good intentions inevitably lead. (pp. 68–69)

It was a great shock to read this in 1987, after six years of headlines about "the gay plague" and the railing of moralists about God's punishment for sodomy, or, more recently, statements such as "AIDS is no longer just a gay disease." Language destined to offend gays and inflame homophobia has been, from the very beginning—in science, in the media, and in politics—the main language of AIDS discussion, although the language has been altered at times in order that it would, for example, offend Haitians and inflame racism, or offend women and inflame sexism. But to Shilts AIDSpeak is not this language guaranteed to offend and inflame. On the contrary, it is

a new language forged by public health officials, anxious gay politicians, and the burgeoning ranks of "AIDS activists." The linguistic roots of AIDSpeak sprouted not so much from the truth as from what was politically facile and psychologically reassuring. Semantics was the major denominator of AIDSpeak jargon, because the language went to great lengths never to offend.

A new lexicon was evolving. Under the rules of AIDSpeak, for example, AIDS victims could not be called victims. Instead, they were to be called People With AIDS, or PWAs, as if contracting this uniquely brutal disease was not a victimizing experience. "Promiscuous" became "sexually active," because gay politicians declared "promiscuous" to be "judgmental," a major cuss word in AIDSpeak. . . .

. . . The new syntax allowed gay political leaders to address and largely determine public health policy in the coming years, because public health officials quickly mastered AIDSpeak, and it was a fundamentally political tongue. (p. 315)

Shilts's contempt for gay political leaders, AIDS activists, and people with AIDS, and his delusions about their power to influence public health policy are deeply revealing of his own politics. But to Shilts, politics is something alien, something others have, and political speech is AIDSpeak. Shilts has no politics, only common sense; he speaks only the "truth," even if the truth is "brutal," like being "victimized" by AIDS.

As an immediate response to this view, I will state my own political position: Anything said or done about AIDS that does not give precedence to the knowledge, the needs, and the demands of people living with AIDS must be condemned. The passage from *And the Band Played On* quoted above—and indeed the entire book—is written in flagrant disregard of these people. Their first principle, that they not be called victims, is flaunted by Shilts. I will concede that people living with AIDS are victims in one sense: they have been and continue to be victimized by all those who will not listen to them, including Randy Shilts. But we cannot stop at condemnation. Shilts's book is too full of useful information, amassed in part with the help of the Freedom of Information Act, simply to dismiss it. But while it may be extremely useful, it is also extremely dangerous—and thus has to be read very critically.

In piecing together his tale of heroes and villains—which intersperses vignettes about scientists from the Centers for Disease Control in Atlanta, the National Institutes of Health in Bethesda, and the Pasteur Institute in Paris; doctors with AIDS patients in New York, San Francisco, and Los Angeles; blood-banking industry executives; various people with AIDS (always white, usually gay men living in San Francisco); officials in the Department of Health and Human Services and the Food and Drug Administration; gay activists and AIDS service organization volunteers—Shilts always returns to a single complaint. With all the people getting sick and dying, and with all the scandals of inaction, stonewalling, and infighting that are arguably the primary cause of those people's illness and death, journalists never bothered to investigate. They always bought the government's lies, never looked behind those lies to get the "truth." There was, of course, one exception, the lonely journalist for the *San Francisco Chronicle* assigned full-time to the AIDS beat. He is never named, but we know his name is Randy Shilts, the book's one unqualified hero, who appears discreetly in several of its episodes. Of course, that journalist knows the reason for the lack of investigative zeal on the part of his fellows: the people who were dying were gay men, and mainstream American journalists don't care what happens to gay men. Those journalists would rather print hysteria-producing, blame-the-victim stories than uncover the "truth."

So Shilts would print that truth in *And the Band Played On,* "Investigative journalism at its best," as the flyleaf states. The book is an extremely detailed, virtually day-by-day account of the epidemic up to the revelation that Rock Hudson was dying of AIDS, the moment, in 1985, when the American media finally took notice.[5] But taking notice of Rock Hudson was, in itself, a scandal, because by the time the Rock Hudson story captured the attention of the media, Shilts notes, "the number of AIDS cases in the United States had surpassed 12,000 . . . of whom 6,079 had died" (p. 580). Moreover, what constituted a story for the media was only scandal itself: a famous movie star simultaneously revealed to be gay and to be dying of AIDS.

---

5. The fact that Shilts chose this moment as the end point of his narrative suggests that the book's central purpose is indeed to prove the irresponsibility of all journalists but Shilts himself, making him the book's true hero.

How surprised, then, could Shilts have been that, when his own book was published, the media once again avoided mention of the six years of political scandal that contributed so significantly to the scope of the AIDS epidemic? that they were instead intrigued by an altogether different story, the one they had been printing all along—the dirty little story of gay male promiscuity and irresponsibility?

In the press release issued by Shilts's publisher, St. Martin's, the media's attention was directed to the story that would ensure the book's success:

PATIENT ZERO: The Man Who Brought AIDS to North America *What remains a mystery for most people is where AIDS came from and how it spread so rapidly through America. In the most bizarre story of the epidemic, Shilts also found the man whom the CDC dubbed the "Patient Zero" of the epidemic. Patient Zero, a French-Canadian airline steward, was one of the first North Americans diagnosed with AIDS. Because he traveled through the gay communities of major urban areas, he spread the AIDS virus throughout the continent. Indeed, studies later revealed 40 of the first 200 AIDS cases in America were documented either to have had sex with Patient Zero or have had sex with someone who did.*

The story of Gaetan Dugas, or "Patient Zero," is woven throughout the book in over twenty separate episodes, beginning on page 11 and ending only on page 439, where the young man's death is recounted. "At one time," Shilts writes in a typically portentous tone, "Gaetan had been what every man wanted from gay life; by the time he died, he had become what every man feared." It is interesting indeed that Shilts, a gay man who appears *not* to have wanted from gay life what Gaetan Dugas may or may not have been, should nevertheless assume that what all gay men want is identical.

The publisher's ploy worked, for which they appear to be proud. Included in the press kit sent to me were Xeroxes of the following news stories and reviews:

—New York Times: *Canadian Said to Have Had
Key Role in Spread of AIDS*

—New York Post: *The Man Who Gave Us AIDS*

—NY Daily News: *The Man Who Flew Too Much*

—Time: *The Appalling Saga of Patient Zero*

—McClean's: *"Patient Zero" and the AIDS Virus*

People magazine made "Patient Zero" one of its "25 most intriguing
people of '87," together with Ronald Reagan, Mikhail Gorbachev, Oliver
North, Fawn Hall, Princess Diana, Vincent van Gogh, and Baby Jessica.
Shilts's success in giving the media the scandalous story that would
overshadow his book's other "revelations"—and that would ensure that
the blame for AIDS would remain focused on gay men—can be seen
even in the way the story appeared in Germany's leading liberal weekly
Der Spiegel. Underneath a photograph of cruising gay men at the end of
Christopher Street in New York City, the story's sensational title reads
"Ich werde sterben, und du auch" ("I'm going to die, and so are you"), a
line the Canadian airline steward is supposed to have uttered to his
bathhouse sex partners as he turned up the lights after an encounter
and pointed to his Kaposi's sarcoma lesions.

Shilts's painstaking efforts at telling the "true" story of the epidemic's
early years thus resulted in two media stories: the story of the man who
brought us AIDS, and the story of the man who brought us the story of
the man who brought us AIDS. Gaetan Dugas and Randy Shilts became
overnight media stars. Being fully of the media establishment, Shilts's
criticism of that establishment is limited to pitting good journalists
against bad. He is apparently oblivious to the economic and ideological
mechanisms that largely determine how AIDS will be constructed in the
media, and he thus contributes to that construction rather than to its
critique.

The criticism most often leveled against Shilts's book by its gay critics is that it is a product of internalized homophobia. In this view, Shilts is seen to identify with the heterosexist society that loathes him for his homosexuality and through that identification to project his loathing onto the gay community. Thus, "Patient Zero," the very figure of the homosexual as imagined by heterosexuals—sexually voracious, murderously irresponsible—is Shilts's homophobic nightmare of himself, a nightmare that he must constantly deny by making it true only of others. Shilts therefore offers up the scapegoat for his heterosexual colleagues in order to prove that he, like them, is horrified by such creatures.

It is true that Shilts's book reproduces virtually every cliché of homophobia. Like Queen Victoria's proverbial inability to fathom what lesbians do in bed, Shilts's disdain for the sexual habits of gay men extends even to finding certain of those habits "unimaginable." In one of his many fulminations against gay bathhouses, Shilts writes, "Just about every type of unsafe sex imaginable, and many variations that were unimaginable, were being practiced with carefree abandonment [*sic*] at the facilities" (p. 481).

Shilts's failure of imagination is in this case merely a trope, a way of saying that certain sexual acts are beyond the pale for most people. But in resorting to such a trope, Shilts unconsciously identifies with all those who would rather see gay men die than allow homosexuality to invade their consciousness.

And the Band Played On is written not only as a chronology of events, but also as a cleverly plotted series of episodes. Hundreds of narrative threads are woven around individual characters described in conventional novelistic fashion. Often Shilts uses people's regional accents and physiques metonymically to stand for their characters: "Everyone cheered enthusiastically when Paul Popham [president of the Gay Men's Health Crisis] addressed the crowd in his broad, plainspoken Oregon accent" (p. 139). A hundred pages earlier, Popham is introduced with the sentence, "At the Y, Larry [Kramer] had told Paul that he had such a naturally well-defined body that he didn't need to work out, and Paul responded with a shy aw-shucks ingenuousness that reminded Larry of Gary Cooper or Jimmy Stewart" (p. 26). Shilts's choice of novelistic form allows him these tricks of omniscient narration. Not only does he tell us what Paul said and Larry thought, he also reveals his characters' dreams and nightmares, and even, in a few cases, what people with AIDS were thinking and feeling at the moment of death. These aspects of bourgeois writing would seem to represent a strange choice indeed for the separation of fact from fiction,[6] but I want to argue that it is precisely this choice that determines Shilts's homophobia. For it is my contention not simply that Shilts has internalized homophobia, but that he has sought to escape the effects of homophobia by employing a particular cultural form, one that is thoroughly outmoded but still very much with us in its vulgarized variants. In *Writing Degree Zero*, Roland Barthes writes, "Until [the 1850s], it was bourgeois ideology itself which gave the measure of the universal by fulfilling it unchallenged. The bourgeois writer, sole judge of other people's woes and without anyone else to gaze on him, was not torn between his social condition and his intellectual vocation."[7]

52
—
53

"Sole judge of other people's woes and without anyone else to gaze on him," Shilts adopted a no-longer-possible universal point of view—which is, among other things, the heterosexual point of view—and thus erased his own social condition, that of being a gay man in a homophobic society. Shilts wrote the story of Gaetan Dugas not because it needed telling—because, in the journalist's mind, it was true and factual—but because it was required by the bourgeois novelistic form that Shilts used as his shield. The book's arch-villain has a special function, that of securing the identity of his polar opposite, the book's true hero.

6. Shilts writes in his "Notes on Sources": "This book is a work of journalism. There has been no fictionalization. For purposes of narrative flow, I reconstruct scenes, recount conversations and occasionally attribute observations to people with such phrases as 'he thought' or 'she felt.' Such references are drawn from either the research interviews I conducted for the book or from research conducted during my years covering the AIDS epidemic for the *San Francisco Chronicle*" (p. 607).

7. Roland Barthes, *Writing Degree Zero,* trans. Annette Lavers and Colin Smith (Boston: Beacon Press, 1967), p. 60.

Shilts created the character of "Patient Zero" to embody everything that the book purports to expose: irresponsibility, delay, denial, ultimately murder.[8] "Patient Zero" stands for all the evil that is "really" the cause of the epidemic, and Shilts's portrait of "Patient Zero" stands for Shilts's own heroic act of "exposing" that evil.

If I have dwelt for so long on *And the Band Played On,* it is not only because its enthusiastic reception demands a response. It is also because the book demonstrates so clearly that cultural conventions rigidly dictate what can and will be said about AIDS. And these cultural conventions exist everywhere the epidemic is constructed: in newspaper stories and magazine articles, in television documentaries and fiction films, in political debate and health-care policy, in scientific research, in art, in activism, and in sexuality. The way AIDS is understood is in large measure predetermined by the forms these discourses take. Randy Shilts provided the viciously homophobic portrait of "Patient Zero" because his thriller narrative demanded it, and the news media reported that story and none of the rest because what is news and what is not is dictated by the form the news takes in our society. In a recent op-ed piece about his recognition that AIDS is now newsworthy, A. M. Rosenthal, executive editor of the *New York Times* during the entire five-year period when the epidemic was a *non*story for the *Times,* offered the following reflection on the news-story form: "Journalists call events,

8. I say *created* because, though Gaetan Dugas was a real person, his character—in both senses of the word—was invented by Shilts. Moreover, contrary to the St. Martin's press release, Shilts did not "discover" "Patient Zero." The story about how various early AIDS researchers were able to link a number of early cases of the syndrome—which was done not to locate the "source" of the epidemic and place blame but simply to verify the transmissibility of a causal agent—was told earlier by Ann Giudici Fettner and William A. Check. Dugas is called "Eric" in their account, and his character is described significantly differently: "'He felt terrible about having made other people sick,' says [Dr. William] Darrow [a CDC sociologist]. 'He had come down with Kaposi's but no one ever told him it might be infectious. Even at CDC we didn't know then that it was contagious. It is a general dogma that cancer is not transmissible. Of course, we now know that the underlying immune-system deficiency that allows the cancer to grow is most likely transmissible'" (*The Truth about AIDS* [New York: Henry Holt, revised edition, 1985], p. 86). Thanks to Paula Treichler for calling this passage to my attention.

trivial or historic, 'stories' because we really are tellers of tales and to us there is no point in knowing or learning if we can't run out and tell somebody. That's just the way we are; go ask a psychiatrist why."[9]

"Patient Zero" is a news story while the criminal inaction of the Reagan administration is not—"go ask a psychiatrist why." Rock Hudson is a story, but the thousands of other people with AIDS are not—"go ask a psychiatrist why." Heterosexuals with AIDS is a story; homosexuals with AIDS is not—"go ask a psychiatrist why." Shilts laments this situation. His book contributes nothing to understanding and changing it.

Among the heroes of *And the Band Played On* is Larry Kramer, who shares Shilts's negative view of gay politics and sexuality. Here is how Shilts describes the reception of Kramer's play about AIDS, *The Normal Heart:*

April 21 [1985]

PUBLIC THEATER
New York City
A thunderous ovation echoed through the theater. The people rose to their feet, applauding the cast returning to the stage to take their bows. Larry Kramer looked to his eighty-five-year-old mother. She had always wanted him to write for the stage, and Kramer had done that now. True, The Normal Heart *was not your respectable Neil Simon fare, but a virtually unanimous chorus of reviewers had already proclaimed the play to be a masterpiece of political drama. Even before the previews were over, critics from every major news organization in New York City had scoured their thesauruses for superlatives to describe the play. NBC said it "beats with passion";* Time *magazine said it was "deeply affecting, tense and touching"; the* New York Daily News *called it "an angry, unremitting and gripping piece of political theater." One critic said* Heart *was to the AIDS epidemic what Arthur Miller's* The Crucible *had been to the McCarthy*

54

55

9. A. M. Rosenthal, "AIDS: Everyone's Business," *New York Times,* December 29, 1987, p. A19.

era. New York Magazine*'s critic John Simon, who had recently been over-*
heard saying that he looked forward to when AIDS had killed all the ho-
mosexuals in New York theater, conceded in an interview that he left the
play weeping. (p. 556)

How is it that for four years the deaths of thousands of gay men could
leave the dominant media entirely unmoved, but Larry Kramer's play
could make them weep? Shilts offers no explanation, nor is he suspicious of this momentary change of heart. *The Normal Heart* is a *pièce à
clef* about the Gay Men's Health Crisis (GMHC), the AIDS service organization Kramer helped found and which later expelled him—because, as the play tells it, he, like Shilts, insisted on speaking the truth.[10]
In one of his many fights with his fellow organizers, Ned Weeks, the
character that represents Kramer, explodes, "Why is anything I'm saying compared to anything but common sense?" (p. 100). Common sense,
in Kramer's view, is that gay men should stop having so much sex, that
promiscuity kills. But this common sense is, of course, conventional
moral wisdom: it is not safe sex, but monogamy that is the solution. The
play's message is therefore not merely reactionary, it is lethal, since
monogamy per se provides no protection whatsoever against a virus
that might already have infected one partner in a relationship.

"I am sick of guys who can only think with their cocks" (p. 57), says Ned
Weeks, and later, "Being defined by our cocks is literally killing us"
(p. 115). For Kramer, being defined by sex is the legacy of gay politics;
promiscuity and gay politics are one and the same:

*Ned [to Emma, the doctor who urges him to tell gay men to stop having
sex]: Do you realize that you are talking about millions of men who have
singled out promiscuity to be their principal political agenda, the one
they'd die before abandoning? (pp. 37–38)*

10. Larry Kramer, *The Normal Heart* (New York and Scarborough, Ontario: New American Library, 1985). Page numbers for citations are given in the text.

Bruce [the president of GMHC]: . . . the entire gay political platform is fucking. (p. 57)

Ned: . . . the gay leaders who created this sexual liberation philosophy in the first place have been the death of us. Mickey, why didn't you guys fight for the right to get married instead of the right to legitimize promiscuity? (p. 85)

These lines represent the view of someone who did not participate in the gay movement, and who has no sense of its history, its complexities, its theory and practice (was he too busy taking advantage of its gains?). Kramer's ignorance of and contempt for the gay movement are demonstrated throughout the play:

Ned: Nobody with a brain gets involved in gay politics. It's filled with the great unwashed radicals of any counterculture. (p. 37)

Mickey: You know, the battle against the police at Stonewall was won by transvestites. We all fought like hell. It's you Brooks Brothers guys who—

Bruce: That's why I wasn't at Stonewall. I don't have anything in common with those guys, girls, whatever you call them.

Mickey: . . . and . . . how do you feel about lesbians?

Bruce: Not very much. I mean, they're . . . something else.

Mickey: I wonder what they're going to think about all this? If past history is any guide, there's never been much support by either half of us for the other. Tommy, are you a lesbian? (pp. 54–55)

I want to return to gay politics, and specifically to the role lesbians have played in the struggle against AIDS, but first it is necessary to explain why I have been quoting Kramer's play as if it were not fictional, as if it could be unproblematically taken to represent Kramer's own political views. As I've already said, *The Normal Heart* is a *pièce à clef*, a form adopted for the very purpose of presenting the author's experience and views in dramatic form. But my criticism of the play is not merely that Kramer's political views, as voiced by his characters, are reactionary—though they certainly are—but that the genre employed by Kramer will dictate a reactionary content of a different kind: because the play is written within the most traditional conventions of bourgeois theater, its politics are the politics of bourgeois individualism. Like *And the Band Played On, The Normal Heart* is the story of a lonely voice of reason drowned out by the deafening chorus of unreason. It is a play with a hero, Kramer himself, for whom the play is an act of vengeance for all the wrong done him by his ungrateful colleagues at the Gay Men's Health Crisis. *The Normal Heart* is a purely personal—not a political—drama, a drama of a few heroic individuals in the AIDS movement. From time to time, some of these characters talk "politics":

Emma: Health is a political issue. Everybody's entitled to good medical care. If you're not getting it, you've got to fight for it. Do you know this is the only industrialized country in the world besides South Africa that doesn't guarantee health care for everyone? (p. 36)

But this is, of course, politics in the most restricted sense of the word. Such a view refuses to see that power relations invade and shape all discourse. It ignores the fact that the choice of the bourgeois form of drama, for example, is a political choice that will have necessary political consequences. Among these is the fact that the play's "politics" sound very didactic, don't "work" with the drama. Thus in *The Normal Heart*, even these "politics" are mostly pushed to the periphery; they become décor. In the New York Shakespeare Festival production of the play, "The walls of the set, made of construction-site plywood, were whitewashed. Everywhere possible, on this set and upon the theater walls too, facts and figures and names were painted, in black, simple lettering" (p. 19). These were such facts as

MAYOR KOCH [of New York City]: $75,000—MAYOR FEINSTEIN [of San Francisco]: $16,000,000. (For public education and community services.)

During the first nineteen months of the epidemic, the New York Times *wrote about it a total of seven times. During the first three months of the Tylenol scare in 1982, the* New York Times *wrote about it a total of 54 times. (pp. 20–21)*

No one would dispute that these facts and figures have political signifi-cance, that they are part of the political picture of AIDS. But in the con-text of *The Normal Heart,* they are absorbed by the personal drama taking place on the stage, where they have no other function than to prove Ned Weeks right, to vindicate Ned Weeks's—Larry Kramer's—rage. And that rage, the play itself, is very largely directed against other gay men.

Shilts's book and Kramer's play share a curious contradiction: they blame the lack of response to the epidemic on the misrepresentation of AIDS as a gay disease even as they themselves treat AIDS almost exclu-sively as a gay problem. Both display indifference to the other groups drastically affected by the epidemic, primarily, in the United States, IV drug users, who remain statistics for the two writers, just as gay men do for the people the two authors rail against.

The resolution of this contradiction, which is pervasive in AIDS dis-course, would appear to be simple enough. AIDS is not a gay disease, but in the United States it affected gay men first and, thus far, has af-fected us in greater proportion. But AIDS probably did not affect gay men first, even in the United States. What is now called AIDS was first seen in middle-class gay men in America, in part because of our access to medical care. Retrospectively, however, it appears that IV drug users—whether gay or straight—were dying of AIDS in New York City through-out the '70s and early '80s, but a class-based and racist health care system failed to notice, and an epidemiology equally skewed by class and racial bias failed to begin to look until 1987.[11] Moreover, AIDS has

11. In October 1987, the *New York Times* reported that the New York City Department of Health conducted a study of drug-related deaths from 1982 to 1986, which found an estimated 2,520 AIDS-related deaths that had not been reported as such. As a result,

never been restricted to gay men in Central Africa, where the syndrome is a problem of apocalyptic dimensions, but to this day receives almost no attention in the United States.

What is far more significant than the real facts of HIV transmission in various populations throughout the world, however, is the initial conceptualization of AIDS as a syndrome affecting gay men. No insistence on the facts will render that discursive construction obsolete, and not only because of the intractability of homophobia. The idea of AIDS as a gay disease occasioned two interconnected conditions in the United States: that AIDS would be an epidemic of stigmatization rooted in homophobia and that the response to AIDS would depend in very large measure on the very gay movement Shilts and Kramer decry.

The organization Larry Kramer helped found, the Gay Men's Health Crisis, is as much a part of the early construction of AIDS as were the first reports of the effects of the syndrome in the *Morbidity and Mortality Weekly Report*. Though it may be true that few of the founders of GMHC were centrally involved in gay politics, everything they were able to accomplish—from fundraising and recruiting volunteers to consulting with openly gay health care professionals and getting education out to the gay community—depended on what had already been achieved by the gay movement. Moreover, the continued life of GMHC as the largest AIDS service organization in the United States has

"AIDS-related deaths involving intravenous drug users accounted for 53 percent of all AIDS-related deaths in New York City since the epidemic began, while deaths involving sexually active homosexual and bisexual men accounted for 38 percent." Even these statistics are based on CDC epidemiology that continues to see the beginning of the epidemic as 1981, following the early reports of illnesses in gay men, in spite of widespread anecdotal reporting of a high rate of deaths throughout the 1970s from what was known as "junkie pneumonia" and was likely *Pneumocystis* pneumonia. Moreover, the study was undertaken not through any recognition of the seriousness of the problem posed to poor and minority communities, but, as New York City Health Commissioner Stephen Joseph was reported as saying, because "the higher numbers ... showed that the heterosexual 'window' through which AIDS presumably could jump to people who were not at high risk was much wider that we believed"' (Ronald Sullivan, "AIDS in New York City Killing More Drug Users," *New York Times*, October 22, 1987, p. 131).

necessarily aligned it with other, more radical grassroots AIDS organizations both in the gay community and in other communities affected by the epidemic. The Gay Men's Health Crisis, whose workforce comprises lesbians and heterosexual women as well as gay men (heterosexual men are notably absent from the AIDS movement), is now an organization that provides services for infants with AIDS, IV drug users with AIDS, women with AIDS. It is an organization that every day puts the words *gay men* in the mouths of people who would otherwise never speak them. More important, it is an organization that has put the words *gay men* in the mouths of nongay people living with the stigma attached to AIDS by those very words. The Gay Men's Health Crisis is thus a symbol, in its very name, of the fact that the gay movement is at the center of the fight against AIDS. The limitations of this movement—especially insofar as it is riven by race and class differences—are therefore in urgent need of examination.

In doing this, we must never lose sight of the fact that the gay movement is responsible for virtually every positive achievement in the struggle against AIDS during the epidemic's early years. These achievements are not only those of politically organized response—of fighting repressive measures; of demanding government funding, scientific research, and media coverage; of creating service organizations to care for the sick and to educate the well. They are also the achievements of a sexual community whose theory and practice of sex made it possible to meet the epidemic's most urgent requirement: the development of safe sex practices. But who counts as a member of this community? Who will be protected by the knowledge of safe sex? Kramer's character Mickey was right in saying that it was transvestites who fought back at Stonewall. What he did not say was that those "guys in Brooks Brothers suits" very soon hounded transvestites out of the movement initiated by Stonewall, because the "gay good citizens"[12] didn't want to be associated with "those guys, girls, whatever you call them." Now, in 1988, what AIDS

12. I borrow the phrase from Guy Hocquenghem, who used it to describe a gay movement increasingly devoted to civil rights rather than to the more radical agenda issuing from the New Left of the 1960s.

service organizations are providing transvestites with safe sex information? Who is educating hustlers? Who is getting safe sex instructions, printed in Spanish, into gay bars in Queens that cater to working-class Colombian immigrants?[13] It is these questions that cannot be satisfactorily answered by a gay community that is far from inclusive of the vast majority of people whose homosexual practices place them at risk. It is also these questions that we must ask even more insistently of AIDS education programs that are now being taken out of the hands of gay people—AIDS education programs devised by the state, outside of any existing community, whatever its limitations.

Kramer's summary dismissal of transvestites in *The Normal Heart* is followed by his assumption that lesbians will show no interest in the AIDS crisis. Not only has Kramer been proven dead wrong, but his assumption is grounded in a failure to recognize the importance of a gay *political* community that has always included both sexes. In spite of the very real tensions and differences between lesbians and gay men, our common oppression has taught us the vital necessity of forming a coalition. And having negotiated and renegotiated this coalition over a period of two decades has provided much of the groundwork for the coalition politics necessitated by the shared oppression of all the radically different groups affected by AIDS. But the question Larry Kramer and other gay men should be asking in any case is not "What are lesbians doing to help us?" but rather "What are we doing to help lesbians?" Although it is consistently claimed that lesbians, as a group, are the least vulnerable to HIV transmission, this would appear to be predicated, once again, on the failure to understand what lesbians do in bed. As Lee Chiaramonte wrote in an article entitled "The Very Last Fairy Tale,"

In order to believe that lesbians are not at risk for AIDS, or that those who have already been infected are merely incidental victims, I would have to

13. I do not want to suggest that there are no gay community organizations for or including transvestites, sex workers, or Latino immigrants, but rather that no organization representing highly marginalized groups has the funding or the power to reach large numbers of people with sensitive and specific AIDS information.

know and agree with the standards by which we are judged to be safe.
Meaning I would have to believe we are either sexless or olympically
monogamous; that we are not intravenous drug users; that we do not
sleep with men; that we do not engage in sexual activities that could
prove as dangerous as they are titillating. I would also have to believe
that lesbians, unlike straight women, can get seven years' worth of hon-
est answers from their lovers about forgotten past lives.[14]

Chiaramonte goes on to cite a 1983 *Journal of Sex Research* study in
which it was determined that lesbians have almost twice as much sex as
straight women and that their numbers of partners are greater than
straight women's by nearly fifteen to one. In a survey conducted by Pat
Califia for the *Journal of Homosexuality,* over half the lesbians questioned preferred nonmonogamous relationships.[15] And, in addition to
the risks of HIV infection, which only compound women's problems
with a sexist health care system, lesbians have, along with gay men,
borne the intensified homophobia that has resulted from AIDS.

Not surprisingly it was a lesbian—Cindy Patton—who wrote one of
the first serious political analyses of the AIDS epidemic and who has
more recently coauthored a safe sex manual for women.[16] "It is critical,"
says Patton, "that the experience of the gay community in AIDS organizing be understood: the strategies employed before 1985 or so grew out
of gay liberation and feminist theory."[17] The most significant of these
strategies was—again—the development of safe sex guidelines, which,
though clearly the achievement of the organized gay community, are
now being reinvented by "experts":

62
——
63

---

14. Lee Chiaramonte, "Lesbian Safety and AIDS: The Very Last Fairy Tale," *Visibilities* 1,
no. 1 (January–February 1988), p. 5.

15. Ibid., p. 7.

16. Cindy Patton, *Sex and Germs: The Politics of AIDS* (Boston: South End Press, 1985);
and Cindy Patton and Janis Kelly, *Making It: A Woman's Guide to Sex in the Age of
AIDS* (Ithaca: Firebrand Books, 1987).

17. Cindy Patton, "Resistance and the Erotic: Reclaiming History, Setting Strategy as We
Face AIDS," *Radical America* 20, no. 6 (Facing AIDS: A Special Issue), p. 68.

At the 1987 lesbian and gay health conference in Los Angeles, many long-time AIDS activists were surprised by the extent to which safe sex education had become the province of high level professionals. The fact that safe sex organizing began and is highly successful as a grassroots, community effort seemed to be forgotten. . . . Heterosexuals—and even gay people only beginning to confront AIDS—express panic about how to make appropriate and satisfying changes in their sex lives, as if no one had done this before them. It is a mark of the intransigence of homophobia that few look to the urban gay communities for advice, communities which have an infrastructure and a track record of highly successful behavior change.[18]

As Patton insists, gay people invented safe sex. We knew that the alternatives—monogamy and abstinence—were unsafe, unsafe in the latter case because most people do not abstain from sex, and if you only tell them "just say no," they will have unsafe sex. We were able to invent safe sex because we have always known that sex is not, in an epidemic or not, limited to penetrative sex. Our promiscuity taught us many things, not only about the pleasures of sex, but about the great multiplicity of those pleasures. It is that psychic preparation, that experimentation, that conscious work on our own sexualities that has allowed many of us to change our sexual behaviors—something that brutal "behavioral therapies" tried unsuccessfully for over a century to force us to do—very quickly and very dramatically. It is for this reason that Shilts's and Kramer's attitudes about the formulation of gay politics on the basis of our sexuality is so perversely distorted, why they insist that our promiscuity will destroy us when in fact *it is our promiscuity that will save us:* "The elaborateness of gay male sexual culture which may have once contributed to the spread of AIDS has been rapidly transformed into one that inhibits spread of the disease, still promotes sexual liberation (albeit differently defined), and is as marvelously fringe and offensive to middle America as ever."[19]

18. Ibid., p. 69.
19. Ibid., p. 72.

All those who contend that gay male promiscuity is merely sexual compulsion resulting from fear of intimacy are now faced with very strong evidence against their prejudices. For if compulsion were so easily overcome or redirected, it would hardly deserve the name. Gay male promiscuity should be seen instead as a positive model of how sexual pleasures might be pursued by and granted to everyone if those pleasures were not confined within the narrow limits of institutionalized sexuality.

Indeed, it is the lack of promiscuity and its lessons that suggests that many straight people will have a much harder time learning "how to have sex in an epidemic" than we did.[20] This assumption follows from the fact that risk reduction information directed at heterosexuals, even when not clearly anti-sex or based on false morality, is still predicated on the prevailing myths about sexuality in our society. First among these, of course, is the myth that monogamous relationships are not only the norm but ultimately everyone's deepest desire. Thus the message is often not about safe sex at all, but about how to find a safe partner.

As Art Ulene, "family physician" to the *Today Show* put it, "I think it's time to stop talking about 'safe sex.' I believe we should be talking about safe partners instead. A safe partner is one who has never been infected with the AIDS virus. With a safe partner, you don't have to worry about getting AIDS yourself—no matter what you do sexually, and no matter how much protection you use while you do it."[21]

The agenda here is one of maintaining the us/them dichotomy that was initially performed by the CDC's "risk group" classifications—"Only gay men and IV drug users get AIDS." But now that neat classifications of otherness no longer "protect" the "general population,"[22] how does

20. *How to Have Sex in an Epidemic* is the title of a forty-page pamphlet produced by gay men, including people with AIDS, as early as 1983. See Patton, "Resistance and the Erotic," p. 69.
21. Art Ulene, M.D., *Safe Sex in a Dangerous World* (New York: Vintage Books, 1987), p. 31.
22. In fact there continue to be concerted efforts to deny that everyone is at risk of HIV infection. The *New York Times* periodically prints updated epidemiological informa-

one go about finding a safe partner? One obvious way of answering this question is to urge HIV antibody testing. If you and your sex partner both test negative, you can still have unbridled fun.[23] But Dr. Ulene has an additional solution: "One way to find safer partners—though a bit impractical for most—is to move to a place where the incidence of AIDS is low. There are two states that have reported only four cases of AIDS since the disease was discovered, while others are crowded with AIDS patients. Although this near-freedom from AIDS cannot be expected to last forever, the relative differences between states like Nebraska and New York are likely to last."[24] Dr. Ulene then graciously provides a breakdown of AIDS cases by state.

Most safe sex education materials for heterosexuals, however, presume that their audience consists of people who feel themselves to be at some risk, perhaps because they do not limit themselves to a single sex part-

tion editorially presented so as to reassure its readers—clearly presumed to be middle class, white, and heterosexual—that they have little to worry about. Two recent articles that resurrect old myths to keep AIDS away from heterosexuals are Michael A. Fumento, "AIDS: Are Heterosexuals at Risk?" *Commentary,* November 1987; and Robert E. Gould, "Reassuring News about AIDS: A Doctor Tells Why You May Not Be at Risk," *Cosmopolitan,* January 1988. That such articles are based on racist and homophobic assumptions goes without saying. The "fragile anus/rugged vagina" thesis is generally trotted out to explain not only the differences between rates of infection in gays and straights, but also between blacks and whites, Africans and Americans (blacks are said to resort to anal sex as a primitive form of birth control). But Gould's racism takes him a step further. Claiming that only "rough" sex can result in transmission through the vagina, Gould writes, "Many men in Africa take their women in a brutal way, so that some heterosexual activity regarded as normal by them would be closer to rape by our standards and therefore be likely to cause vaginal lacerations through which the AIDS virus could gain entry into the bloodstream."

23. Cindy Patton tells of similar advice given to gay men by a CDC official at the 1985 International AIDS Conference in Atlanta: "He suggested that gay men only have sex with men of the same antibody status, as if gay male culture is little more than a giant dating service. This advice was quickly seen as dehumanizing and not useful because it did not promote safe sex, but renewed advice of this type is seen as reasonable within the heterosexual community of late" ("Resistance and the Erotic," p. 69).

24. Ulene, *Safe Sex,* p. 49.

ner, perhaps because they are unable to move to Nebraska. Still, in most cases, these safe sex instructions focus almost exclusively on penetrative sex and always make it a woman's job to get the condom on the cock. It appears to be a foregone conclusion that there is no use even trying to get straight men to take this responsibility themselves (the title of a recent book is *How to Persuade Your Lover to Use a Condom . . . And Why You Should*). The one exception is a segment of the video aired on PBS entitled "AIDS: Changing the Rules," in which Rubén Blades talks to men directly, though very coyly, about condoms, but shows them only how to put one on a banana. Evidently condoms have now become too closely associated with gay men for straight men to talk straight about them. In addition, they have become too closely associated with AIDS for the banana companies to approve of "Changing the Rules"'s choice of props. The following letter was sent by the president of the International Banana Association to the president of PBS; I cite it to give some idea of how hilarious—if it weren't so deadly—the condom debate can be.

Dear Mr. Christiansen,

In this program, a banana is used as a substitute for a human penis in a demonstration of how condoms should be used.

I must tell you, Mr. Christiansen, as I have told representatives of WETA, that our industry finds such usage of our product to be totally unacceptable. The choice of a banana rather than some other inanimate prop constitutes arbitrary and reckless disregard for the unsavory association that will be drawn by the public and the damage to our industry that will result therefrom.

The banana is an important product and deserves to be treated with respect and consideration. It is the most extensively consumed fruit in the United States, being purchased by over 98 percent of households. It is important to the economies of many developing Latin American nations. The banana's continued image in the minds of consumers as a healthful

and nutritious product is critically important to the industry's continued
ability to be held in such high regard by the public and to discharge its re-
sponsibilities to its Latin American hosts. . . .

Mr. Christiansen, I have no alternative but to advise you that we intend
to hold PBS fully responsible for any and all damages sustained by our
industry as a result of the showing of this AIDS program depicting the ba-
nana in the associational context planned. Further, we reserve all legal
rights to protect the industry's interests from this arbitrary, unnecessary,
and insensitive action.

Yours very truly,

Robert M. Moore

The debate about condoms, and safe sex education generally, is one of
the most alarming in the history of the AIDS epidemic thus far, because
it will certainly result in many more thousands of deaths that could be
avoided. It demonstrates how practices devised at the grassroots level
to meet the needs of people at risk can be demeaned, distorted, and ultimately destroyed when those practices are co-opted by state power.
Perhaps no portion of this controversy is as revealing as the October 14,
1987, debate over the Helms amendment.[25]

In presenting his amendment to the Senate, Senator Jesse Helms made
the offhand remark, "Now we had all this mob over here this weekend,
which was itself a disheartening spectacle." He was referring to the
largest civil rights demonstration in U.S. history, in which over half a
million people, led by people with AIDS and their friends, marched on
Washington for lesbian and gay rights. Early in the morning before the
march, the Names Project inaugurated its memorial quilt, whose panels
with the names of people who had died of AIDS occupied a space on the
Mall equivalent to two football fields. As the three-by-six-foot cloth

25. Unless otherwise indicated, all quotations of this debate are taken from the *Con-*
gressional Record, October 14, 1987, pp. S14202–S14220.

panels made by friends, family, and admirers of the dead were carefully unfurled, 1,920 names were solemnly read to a crowd of weeping spectators. Though representing only a small percentage of the people who have died in the epidemic, the seemingly endless litany of names, together with the astonishing size of the quilt, brought home the enormity of our loss so dramatically as to leave everyone stunned.

But to Helms and his ilk this was just a "mob" enacting a "disheartening spectacle." In the following month's issue of the right-wing *Campus Review*, a front-page article by Gary Bauer, assistant to President Reagan and spokesperson for the administration's AIDS policy, was accompanied by a political cartoon entitled "The AIDS Quilt." It depicts a faggot and a junkie sewing panels bearing the words *sodomy* and *IV drugs*. Bauer's article explains:

"Safe sex" campaigns are not giving students the full story about AIDS. Indeed many students are arguably being denied the information that is most likely to assist them in avoiding the AIDS virus. . . . Many of today's education efforts are what could be called "sexually egalitarian." That is, they refuse to distinguish or even appear to prefer one type of sexual practice over another. Yet medical research shows that sodomy is probably the most efficient method to transfer the AIDS virus as well as other diseases—for obvious reasons. Why is this information censored on so many campuses? Does it illustrate the growing power of gay rights activists who not only want to be tolerated, but want the culture at large to affirm and support the legitimacy of the gay lifestyle?[26]

Three days after the historic march on Washington and the inauguration of the Names Project, Jesse Helms would seek to ensure that such affirmation and support would never occur, at least in the context of AIDS. The senator from North Carolina introduced his amendment to a Labor, Health and Human Services, and Education bill allocating nearly a billion dollars for AIDS research and education in fiscal 1988. Amend-

26. Gary Bauer, "AIDS and the College Student," *Campus Review,* November 1987, pp. 1, 12.

ment no. 956 began: "Purpose: To prohibit the use of any funds provided under this Act to the Centers for Disease Control from being used to provide AIDS education, information, or prevention materials and activities that promote, encourage, or condone homosexual sexual activities or the intravenous use of illegal drugs." The "need" for the amendment and the terms of the ensuing debate (involving only two other senators) were established by Helms in his opening remarks:

About 2 months ago, I received a copy of some AIDS comic books that are being distributed by the Gay Men's Health Crisis, Inc., of New York City, an organization which has received $674,679 in Federal dollars for so-called AIDS education and information. These comic books told the story, in graphic detail, of the sexual encounter of two homosexual men.

The comic books do not encourage and change [sic] any of the perverted behavior. In fact, the comic book promotes sodomy and the homosexual lifestyle as an acceptable alterative in American society. . . . I believe that if the American people saw these books, they would be on the verge of revolt.

I obtained one copy of this book and I had photostats made for about 15 or 20 Senators. I sent each of the Senators a copy—if you will forgive the expression—in a brown envelope marked "Personal and Confidential, for Senator's Eyes Only." Without exception, the Senators were revolted, and they suggested to me that President Reagan ought to know what is being done under the pretense of AIDS education.

So, about 10 days ago, I went down to the White House and I visited with the President.

I said, "Mr. President, I don't want to ruin your day, but I feel obliged to hand you this and let you look at what is being distributed under the pretense of AIDS educational material. . . ."

The President opened the book, looked at a couple of pages, and shook his head, and hit his desk with his fist.

Helms goes on to describe, with even greater disdain, the grant application with which GMHC sought federal funds (none of which were, in any case, spent on the production of the safe-sex comics). GMHC's proposal involved what any college-level psychology student would understand as prerequisite to the very difficult task of helping people change their sexual habits. Helms read GMHC's statement of the problem: "As gay men have reaffirmed their gay identity through sexual expression, recommendations to change sexual behavior may be seen as oppressive. For many, safe sex has been equated with boring, unsatisfying sex. Meaningful alternatives are often not realized. These perceived barriers must be considered and alternatives to high-risk practices promoted in the implementation of AIDS risk-reduction education."

After reading this thoroughly unextraordinary statement, Helms fumes, "This Senator is not a goody-goody two-shoes. I have lived a long time. I have seen a lot of things. I have served 4 years in the Navy. I have been around the track. But every Christian, religious, moral ethic within me cries out to do something. It is embarrassing to stand on the Senate floor and talk about the details of this travesty."

Throughout the floor debate, Helms continued in this vein:

We have got to call a spade a spade and a perverted human being a perverted human being.

Every AIDS case can be traced back to a homosexual act.

[The amendment] will force this country to slam the door on the wayward, warped sexual revolution which has ravaged this Nation for the past quarter of a century.[27]

27. Compare Larry Kramer's character Ned Weeks's statement: "You don't know what it's been like since the sexual revolution hit this country. It's been crazy, gay or straight" (p. 36).

Artwork by Donelan
Story by Greg

Three pages from GMHC *Safer Sex Comix* #4, 1986
(artwork by Donelan, story by Greg).

I think we need to do some AIDS testing on a broad level and unless we get around to that and stop talking about all of this business of civil rights, and so forth, we will not stop the spread of AIDS. We used to quarantine for typhoid fever and scarlet fever, and it did not ruin the civil liberties of anybody to do that.

There were, all told, two responses on the Senate floor to Helms's amendment. The first came from Senator Chiles of Florida, who worried about the amendment's inclusion of IV drug users among those to whom education would effectively be prevented by the legislation—worried because this group includes heterosexuals: "I like to talk about heterosexuals. That is getting into my neighborhood. That is getting into where it can be involved with people that I know and love and care about, and that is where it is getting to children. And again, these children, when you think about a child as an AIDS victim, there is just no reason in the world that should happen. And so we have to try to do what we can to prevent it."

The ritual hand-wringing sentiments about innocent children with AIDS pervade the debate, as they pervade the discussion of AIDS everywhere. This unquestioned sentiment must be seen for what it is: *a vicious apportioning of degrees of guilt and innocence to people with AIDS.* It reflects, in addition, our society's extreme devaluation of life and experience. (The hypocrisy of this distorted set of values does not, however, translate into funding for such necessities for the welfare of children as prenatal care, child care, education, and so forth.)

Because Chiles only liked to talk about heterosexuals, it was left to Senator Weicker of Connecticut to defend safe sex education for gay men. "It is not easy to stand up in the face of language such as this and oppose it," said Weicker, "but I do." Weicker's defense was not made any easier by the fact that he knew what he was talking about: "I know exactly the material that the Senator from North Carolina is referring to. I have seen it. I think it is demeaning in every way." And later, ". . . this is as repugnant to me as it is to anybody else." Because Weicker finds innocuous little drawings of gay male sex as demeaning and repugnant as the

North Carolina senator does, he must resort to "science" to oppose Helms's "philosophy":[28] "We better do exactly what we have been told to do by those of science and medicine, which is, no. 1, put our money into research and, no. 2, put our money into education." "The comic book," says Weicker, "has nothing to do with the issue at hand."

But of course the comic book has everything to do with the issue at hand—because it is precisely the sort of safe sex education material that has been proven to work, developed by the organization that has produced the greatest amount of safe sex education material of any in the country, including, of course, the federal government.[29]

28. In the Senate debate, positions such as Helms's are referred to as philosophical. Thus Senator Weicker:

This education process has been monkeyed around with long enough by this administration. This subcommittee over 6 months ago allocated $20 million requested by the Centers for Disease Control for an educational mailer to be mailed to every household in the United States. . . . That is yet to be done. It is yet to be done not because of anybody in the Centers for Disease Control, or not anybody in Secretary [of Health and Human Services] Bowen's office, but because the philosophers in the White House decided they did not want a mailer to go to every household in the United States. So the education effort is set back. (*Congressional Record,* October 14, 1987, p. S14206)

29. As reported in *New Science:*

George Rutherford of the San Francisco Department of Public Health last year told a U.S. Congressional Committee investigating AIDS that the spread of the virus dramatically slowed in 1983, when public health education programmes directed at gay men began. The year before, 21 percent of the unexposed gay population had developed antibodies to HIV, indicating that they had been exposed to the virus over the previous three months. But in 1983, that figure plummeted to 2 percent. In 1986 it was 0.8 percent, and researchers expect that it will continue to fall. . . . The campaigns to promote safe sex among gay men, and educate them about AIDS have been almost totally successful in less than four years. Such rapid changes in behavior contrast sharply with the poor response over the past 25 years from smokers to warnings about the risks to their health from cigarettes. ("'Safe Sex' Stops the Spread of AIDS, *New Science,* January 7, 1988, p. 36)

In a study of the efficacy of various forms of safe sex education materials, commissioned by GMHC and conducted by Dr. Michael Quadland, professor of psychiatry at Mount Sinai School of Medicine, it was determined that explicit, erotic films are more effective than other techniques. Dr. Quadland was quoted as saying, "We know that in trying to get people to change risky behavior, stopping smoking, for example, or wearing seat belts, that fear is effective. But sex is different. People cannot just give

Given the degree of Senate agreement that gay men's safe sex education material was "garbage," in Helms's word, it seemed possible to compromise enough on the amendment's language to please all three participants in the debate. The amendment was thus reworded to eliminate any reference to IV drug users, thereby assuaging Senator Chiles's fears that someone he knows and cares about—or someone in his neighborhood, or at least someone he doesn't mind talking about—could be affected. Helms very reluctantly agreed to strike the word *condone,* but managed to add *directly or indirectly* after *promote or encourage* and before *homosexual sexual activity.* Thus the amendment now reads: "None of the funds made available under this Act to the Centers for Disease Control shall be used to provide AIDS education, information, or prevention materials and activities that promote or encourage, directly or indirectly, homosexual sexual activities."

74
—
75

After further, very brief debate, during which Weicker continued to oppose the amendment, a roll-call vote was taken. Two senators—Weicker and Moynihan—voted against; *ninety-four senators voted for the Helms amendment,* including all other Senate sponsors of the federal gay and lesbian civil rights bill. Senator Kennedy perhaps voiced the opinion of his fellow liberal senators when he said, "The current version [the reworded amendment] is toothless and it can in good conscience be supported by the Senate. It may not do any good, but it will not do any harm." Under the amendment, as passed, most AIDS organizations providing education and services to gay men, the group most affected and, thus far, at highest risk in the epidemic, would no longer qualify for federal funding.[30] Founded and directed by gay men, the Gay Men's

sex up" (Gina Kolata, "Erotic Films in AIDS Study Cut Risky Behavior," *New York Times,* November 3, 1987).

30. After the House of Representatives passed the amendment by a vote of 368 to 47, a full-scale lobbying effort was undertaken by AIDS organizations and gay activists to defeat it in House-Senate Conference Committee. Ultimately, the amendment was retained as written, although *indirectly* was stricken and the following rider added: "The language in the bill should not be construed to prohibit descriptions of methods to reduce the risk of HIV transmission, to limit eligibility for federal funds of a grantee or potential grantee because of its nonfederally funded activities, nor shall it be construed to limit counseling or referrals to agencies that are not federally funded."

Health Crisis is hardly likely to stop "promoting or encouraging, directly or indirectly, homosexual sexual activity." Despite the fact that GMHC is the oldest and largest AIDS service organization in the United States; despite the fact that it provides direct services to thousands of people living with AIDS, whether gay men or not; despite the fact that GMHC's safe sex comics are nothing more scandalous than simple, schematically depicted scenarios of gay male safe sex; despite the fact that they have undoubtedly helped save thousands of lives—GMHC is considered unworthy of federal funding.

When we see how compromised any efforts at responding to AIDS will be when conducted by the state, we are forced to recognize that productive practices concerning AIDS will remain at the grassroots level. At stake is the cultural specificity and sensitivity of these practices as well as their ability to take account of psychic resistance to behavioral changes, especially changes involving behaviors as psychically complex and charged as sexuality and drug use. Government officials, school board members, public health officers, and Catholic cardinals insist that AIDS education must be sensitive to "community values." But the values they have in mind are those of no existing community affected by AIDS. When "community values" are invoked, it is only for the purpose of imposing the purported values of those (thus far) unaffected by AIDS on the people (thus far) most affected. Instead of the specific, concrete languages of those whose behaviors put them at risk for AIDS, "community values" require a "universal" language that no one speaks and many do not understand. "Don't exchange bodily fluids" is nobody's spoken language. "Don't come in his ass" or "pull out before you come" is what we say. "If you have mainlined or skinpopped now or in the past you may be at risk of getting AIDS. If you have shared needles, cookers, syringes, eyedroppers, water, or cotton with anyone, you are at risk of getting AIDS."[31] This is not abstract "community values" talking. This is the language of members of the IV drug–using community. It is therefore essential that the word *community* be reclaimed by those to

31. Quoted from a pamphlet issued by ADAPT (Association for Drug Abuse Prevention and Treatment), Brooklyn, New York.

whom it belongs, and that abstract usages of such terms be vigorously contested. "Community values" are, in fact, just what we need, but they must be the values of our actual communities, not those of some abstract, universalized community that does not and cannot exist.

One curious aspect of AIDS education campaigns devised by advertising agencies contracted by governments is their failure to take into account any aspect of the psychic but fear. An industry that has used sexual desire to sell everything from cars to detergents suddenly finds itself at a loss for how to sell a condom. This paralysis in the face of sex itself on the part of our most sophisticated producers of propaganda is perhaps partially explained by the strictures placed on the industry by the contracting governments—by their notion of "community values"—but it is also to be explained by advertising's construction of its audience as a group only of largely undifferentiated consumers.

In *Policing Desire*, Watney writes of the British government's AIDS propaganda campaign, produced for them by the world's largest advertising firm, Saatchi and Saatchi: "Advertisements spelled out the word 'AIDS' in seasonal gift wrapping paper, together with the accompanying question: 'How many people will get it for Christmas?' Another advert conveys the message that 'Your next sexual partner could be that very special person'—framed inside a heart like a Valentine—with a supplement beneath which tersely adds, 'The one that gives you AIDS.' The official line is clearly anti-sex, and draws on an assumed rhetoric from previous AIDS commentary concerning 'promiscuity' as the supposed 'cause' of AIDS."[32]

Similar ploys were used for ads paid for by the Metropolitan Life Insurance Company and posted throughout the New York City subway system by the city health department. One is a blow-up of a newspaper personals section with an appealing notice circled (intended to be appealing, that is, to a heterosexual woman) and the statement "I got AIDS through the personals." The other is a cartoon of a man and woman in

32. Watney, *Policing Desire*, p. 136.

bed, each with a thought bubble saying "I hope he [she] doesn't have AIDS!" And below: "You can't live on hope."

"What's the big secret?" asked the poster that was pasted over the city's worse-than-useless warnings, "You can protect yourself from AIDS." And, below, carefully designed and worded safe sex and clean works information. This was a guerrilla action by an AIDS activist group calling itself the Metropolitan Health Association (MHA), whose members also pasted strips printed with the words *government inaction* over *the personals* or *hope* to work the changes "I got AIDS from government inaction" or "You can't live on government inaction." But saving lives is clearly less important to the city than protecting the transit authority's advertising space, so MHA's "reinformation" was quickly removed.[33]

The city health department's scare tactics were next directed at teenagers—and specifically teenagers of color—in a series of public service announcements made for television. Using a strategy of enticement followed by blunt and brutal admonishment, one of these shows scenes of heavy petting in cars and alleys over a soundtrack of the pop song "Boom Boom": "Let's go back to my room so we can do it all night and you can make me feel right." Suddenly the music cuts out and the scene changes to a shot of a boy wrapped in a blanket, looking frightened, miserable, and ill. A voiceover warns, "If you have sex with someone who has the AIDS virus, you can get it, too. So before you do it, ask yourself how bad you really want it. Don't ask for AIDS, don't get it." The final phrase serves as a title for the series: "AIDS: Don't get it." The confusion of antecedents for *it*—both sex and AIDS— is, of course, deliberate. With a clever linguistic maneuver, the health department tells kids that sex and AIDS are the same thing. But the ability of these public service announcements to shock their intended audience is based not only on this manipulative language and quick edit from scenes of sexual pleasure to the closeup of a face with Kaposi's sarcoma lesions on it—

33. I borrow the term *reinformation* from Michael Eisenmenger and Diane Neumaier, who coined it to describe cultural practices whose goal is to counter disinformation to which we are all constantly subject.

the media's standard "face of AIDS." The real shock comes because images of sexy teenagers and sounds of a disco beat are usually followed on TV by Pepsi Cola and a voice telling you to get it. One can only wonder about the degree of psychic damage that might result from the public service announcement's substitution. But AIDS will not be prevented by psychic damage to teenagers caused by ads on TV. It will be stopped only by respecting and celebrating their pleasure in sex and by telling them exactly what they need and want to know in order to maintain that pleasure.

>The ADS epidemic
>
>Is sweeping the nation
>
>Acquired dread of sex
>
>Fear and panic
>
>In the whole population
>
>Acquired dread of sex
>
>This is not a Death in Venice
>
>It's a cheap, unholy menace
>
>Please ignore the moral message
>
>This is not a Death in Venice

This is the refrain of John Greyson's music-video parody of *Death in Venice*. The plague in Greyson's version of the tale is ADS, acquired dread of sex—something you can get from, among other things, watching TV. Tadzio is a pleasure-loving blond who discovers that condoms are "his very favorite thing to wear," and Aschenbach is a middle-class bigot who, observing the sexy shenanigans of Tadzio and his boyfriend, succumbs to acquired dread of sex. Made for a thirty-six-monitor video wall in the Square One shopping mail in Mississauga, a suburb of Toronto, *The ADS Epidemic*, like the public service announcements just described, is directed at adolescents and appropriates a format they're used to, but in this case the message is both pro-sex

John Greyson, *The ADS Epidemic,* 1987.

and made for the kids most seriously at risk—sexually active gay boys. The playfulness of Greyson's tape should not obscure this immensely important fact: not a single piece of government-sponsored education about AIDS for young people, in Canada or the United States, has been targeted at a gay audience, even though governments never tire of emphasizing the statistics showing that the overwhelming numbers of reported cases of AIDS occur in gay and bisexual men.

The impulse to counteract the anti-sex messages of the advertising industry's public service announcements also informs British filmmaker Isaac Julien's *This Is Not an AIDS Advertisement.* There is no hint of a didactic message here, but rather an attempt to give voice to the complexities of gay subjectivity and experience at a critical historical moment. In Julien's case, the specific experience is that of a black gay man living in the increasingly racist and homophobic atmosphere of Thatcher's Britain.[34] Using footage shot in Venice and London, *This Is Not an AIDS Advertisement* is divided into two parts, the first elegiac, lyrical; the second, building on and repeating images from the first, paced to a Bronski Beat rock song. Images of gay male sexual desire are coupled with the song's refrain, "This is not an AIDS advertisement. Feel no guilt in your desire."

Greyson's and Julien's videos signal a new phase in gay men's responses to the epidemic. Having learned to support and grieve for our lovers and friends; having joined the fight against fear, hatred, repression, and inaction; having adjusted our sex lives so as to protect ourselves and one another—we are now reclaiming our subjectivities, our communities, our culture . . . and our promiscuous love of sex.

34. In late 1987, a Helms-style anti-gay clause was inserted in Britain's Local Government Bill. Clause 28 says, "A local authority shall not (a) promote homosexuality or publish material for the promotion of homosexuality; (b) promote the teaching in any maintained school of the acceptability of homosexuality as a pretended family relationship by the publication of such material or otherwise; and (c) give financial assistance to any person for either of the purposes referred to in paragraphs (a) and (b) above." Unlike the Helms Amendment, however, the British bill, though a more sweeping prohibition of pro-gay materials, specifically forbids the use of the bill "to prohibit the doing of anything for the purpose of treating or preventing the spread of disease."

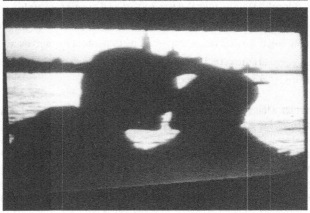

Isaac Julien, *This Is Not an AIDS Advertisement,* 1987.

4 PORTRAITS OF PEOPLE WITH AIDS

First presented at the conference "Representing AIDS:

Crisis and Criticism," University of Western Ontario,

London, Ontario, November 11–13, 1988,

and published in Cultural Studies, *ed. Lawrence*

Grossberg, Cary Nelson, and Paula Treichler

(New York: Routledge, 1992).

In the fall of 1988, the Museum of Modern Art in New York presented an exhibition of Nicholas Nixon's photographs called "Pictures of People." Among the people pictured by Nixon are people with AIDS (PWAs), each portrayed in a series of images taken at intervals of about a week or a month. The photographs form part of a larger work in progress, undertaken by Nixon and his wife Bebe, a science journalist, to, as they explain it, "tell the story of AIDS: to show what this disease truly is, how it affects those who have it, their lovers, families and friends, and that it is both the most devastating and the most important social and medical issue of our time."[1] These photographs were highly praised by reviewers, who saw in them an unsentimental, honest, and committed portrayal of the effects of this devastating illness. One photography critic wrote: "Nixon literally and figuratively moves in so close we're convinced that his subjects hold nothing back. The viewer marvels at the trust between photographer and subject. Gradually one's own feelings about AIDS melt away and one feels both vulnerable and privileged to share the life and (impending) death of a few individuals."[2] Andy Grundberg, photography critic of the *New York Times,* concurred: "The result is overwhelming, since one sees not only the wasting away of the flesh (in photographs, emaciation has become emblematic of AIDS) but also the gradual dimming of the subjects' ability to compose themselves for the camera. What each series begins as a conventional effort to pose for a picture ends in a kind of abandon; as the subjects' self-consciousness disappears, the camera seems to become invisible, and consequently there is almost no boundary between the image and ourselves."[3] In his catalog introduction for the show, MOMA curator Peter Galassi also mentions the relationship between Nixon and his sitters: "Any portrait is a collaboration between subject and photographer. Extended over time, the relationship can become richer and more intimate. Nixon has said that most of the people with AIDS he has photographed are, per-

1. Nick and Bebe Nixon, "AIDS Portrait Project Update," January 1, 1988, quoted in the press release for "People with AIDS: Work in Progress," New York, Zabriskie Gallery, 1988 (this exhibition was shown at the same time as the MOMA show).

2. Robert Atkins, "Nicholas Nixon," *7 Days,* October 5, 1988.

3. Andy Grundberg, "Nicholas Nixon Seeks a Path to the Heart," *New York Times,* September 11, 1988, p. H37.

Nicholas Nixon, *Tom Moran, East Braintree, Massachusetts,* September 1987, gelatin silver print, 7 11/16 x 9 11/16" (The Museum of Modern Art, New York. Gift of the photographer. Copy print ©2001 The Museum of Modern Art, New York).

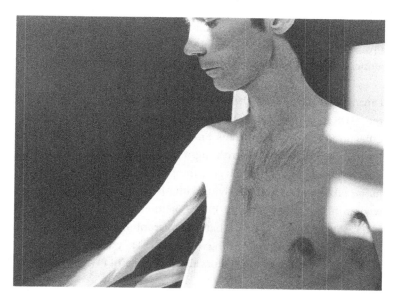

Nicholas Nixon, *Tom Moran, Boston,* October 1987, gelatin silver print, 7 11/16 x 9 11/16" (The Museum of Modern Art, New York. Gift of the photographer. Copy print © 2001 The Museum of Modern Art, New York).

haps because stripped of so many of their hopes, less masked than others, more open to collaboration."[4] And, after explaining that there can be no representative portrait of a person with AIDS, given the diversity of those affected, he concludes, "Beside and against this fact is the irreducible fact of the individual, made present to us in body and spirit. The life and death of Tom Moran [one of Nixon's subjects] were his own."[5]

I quote this standard mainstream photography criticism to draw attention to its curious contradictions. All these writers agree that there is a consensual relationship between photographer and subject that results in the portraits' effects on the viewer. But is this relationship one of growing intimacy? or is it one of the subjects' gradual tuning out, their abandonment of a sense of self? And is the result one of according the subjects the individuality of their lives and deaths? or do their lives and deaths become, through some process of identification, ours?

For those of us who have paid careful attention to media representations of AIDS, none of this would appear to matter, because what we see first and foremost in Nixon's photographs is their reiteration of what we have already been told or shown about people with AIDS: that they are ravaged, disfigured, and debilitated by the syndrome; they are generally alone, desperate, but resigned to their "inevitable" deaths.

During the time of the MOMA exhibition, a small group from ACT UP, the AIDS Coalition to Unleash Power, staged an uncharacteristically quiet protest of Nixon's portraits. Sitting on a bench in the gallery where the photographs of PWAs were hung, a young lesbian held a snapshot of a smiling middle-aged man. It bore the caption, "This is a picture of my father taken when he'd been living with AIDS for three years." Another woman held a photograph of PWA Coalition cofounder David Summers, shown speaking into a bank of microphones. Its caption read, "My friend David Summers living with AIDS." They and a small support group spoke with museum visitors about pictures of PWAs and handed out a flier that read, in part:

4. Peter Galassi, "Introduction," in *Nicholas Nixon: Pictures of People* (New York: Museum of Modern Art, 1988), p. 26.

5. Ibid., p. 27.

NO MORE PICTURES WITHOUT CONTEXT

We believe that the representation of people with AIDS affects not only how viewers will perceive PWAs outside the museum, but, ultimately, crucial issues of AIDS funding, legislation, and education.

In portraying PWAs as people to be pitied or feared, as people alone and lonely, we believe that this show perpetuates general misconceptions about AIDS without addressing the realities of those of us living every day with this crisis as PWAs and people who love PWAs.

FACT:

Many PWAs now live longer after diagnosis due to experimental drug treatments, better information about nutrition and health care, and due to the efforts of PWAs engaged in a continuing battle to define and save their lives.

FACT:

The majority of AIDS cases in New York City are among people of color, including women. Typically, women do not live long after diagnosis because of lack of access to affordable health care, a primary care physician, or even basic information about what to do if you have AIDS.

The PWA is a human being whose health has deteriorated not simply due to a virus, but due to government inaction, the inaccessibility of affordable health care, and institutionalized neglect in the forms of heterosexism, racism, and sexism.

We demand the visibility of PWAs who are vibrant, angry, loving, sexy, beautiful, acting up and fighting back.

STOP LOOKING AT US; START LISTENING TO US.

As against this demand—stop looking at us—the typical liberal position has held, from very early in the epidemic, that one of the central problems of AIDS, one of the things we needed to combat, was bureaucratic abstraction. What was needed was to "give AIDS a face," to "bring AIDS home." And thus the portrait of the person with AIDS had become something of a genre long before a famous photographer like Nicholas Nixon entered the field. In the catalog for an exhibition of another well-known photographer's efforts to give AIDS a human face—Rosalind Solomon's *Portraits in the Time of AIDS*—Grey Art Gallery director Thomas Sokolowski wrote of their perceived necessity: "As our awareness of [AIDS] grew through the accumulation of vast amounts of numerically derived evidence, we still had not seen its face. We could count it, but not truly describe it. Our picture of AIDS was a totally conceptual one. . . ."[6] Sokolowski's catalog essay is entitled "Looking in a Mirror," and it begins with an epigraph quoted from the late George Whitmore, which reads, "I see Jim—and that could be me. It's a mirror. It's not a victim-savior relationship. We're the same person. We're just on different sides of the fence." With Sokolowski's appropriation of these sentences from a man who himself had AIDS, we are confronted once again—as with the texts written in response to the Nixon photographs—with a defense mechanism, which denies the difference, the obvious sense of otherness, shown in the photographs by insisting that what we really see is ourselves.

A remarkably similar statement begins a CBS *Sixty Minutes* newsmagazine devoted to AIDS, in which a service organization director says, "We know the individuals, and they look a lot like you, they look a lot like me." The program, narrated by CBS news anchor Dan Rather, is entitled "AIDS Hits Home." Resonating with the assertion that PWAs look like you and me, the "home" of the show's title is intended to stand in for other designations: white, middle class, middle American, but primarily *heterosexual*. For this program was made in 1986, when, as Paula Treichler has written, "the big news—what the major U.S. news

6. Thomas Sokolowski, preface to *Rosalind Solomon: Portraits in the Time of AIDS* (New York: Grey Art Gallery and Study Center, New York University, 1988), np.

magazines were running cover stories on—was the grave danger of AIDS to heterosexuals."[7]

"AIDS Hits Home" nevertheless consists of a veritable catalog of broadcast television's by-then typical portraits of people with AIDS, for example, the generic or collective portraits, portraits of so-called risk groups: gay men in their tight 501s walking arm in arm in the Castro district of San Francisco; impoverished Africans; prostitutes, who apparently always work on streets; and drug addicts, generally shown only metonymically as an arm with a spike seeking its vein. Also included in this category of the generically portrayed in "AIDS Hits Home," however, are "ordinary" heterosexuals—ordinary in the sense that they are white and don't shoot drugs—since they are the ostensible subject of the show. But the heterosexual in AIDS reportage is not quite you and me. Since television routinely assumes its audience as heterosexual and therefore unnecessary to define or explain, it had to invent what we might call the heterosexual of AIDS. As seen on *Sixty Minutes,* the heterosexual of AIDS appears to inhabit only aerobics classes, discos, and singles bars, and is understood, like *all* gay men are understood, as always ready for, or readying for, sex. In addition, in spite of the proportionately much higher rate of heterosexually transmitted AIDS among people of color, the heterosexuals portrayed on *Sixty Minutes* are, with one exception, white.

"AIDS Hits Home"'s gallery of portraits also includes individuals, of course. These are the portraits that Dan Rather warns us of in the beginning of the program, when he says, "The images we have found are brutal and heartbreaking, but if America is to come to terms with this killer, they must be seen." For the most part, though, they are not seen, or only partially seen, for these are portraits of the ashamed and dying. As they are subjected to callous interviews and voice-overs about the particularities of their illnesses and their emotions, they are obscured

7. Paula Treichler, "AIDS, Homophobia, and Biomedical Discourse: An Epidemic of Signification," in *AIDS: Cultural Analysis/Cultural Activism,* ed. Douglas Crimp (Cambridge: MIT Press, 1988), p. 39.

by television's inventive techniques. Most often they appear, like terror-
ists, drug kingpins, and child molesters, in shadowy silhouette, backlit
with light from their hospital room windows. Sometimes the PWA is
partially revealed, as doctors and nurses manipulate his body while his
face remains off-camera, although in some cases, we see *only* the face,
but in such extreme close-up that we cannot perceive the whole visage.
And in the most technologically dehumanizing instance, the portrait of
the PWA is disguised with added pixelation. This is the case of the
feared and loathed bisexual, whose unsuspecting suburbanite wife has
died of AIDS. He is shown—or rather not shown—responding to an
interlocutor who says, "Forgive me asking you this question, it's not
easy, but do you feel in some way as if you murdered your wife?"

As we continue to move through the *Sixty Minutes* portrait gallery, we
come eventually to those whose faces can see the light of day. Among
these are a few gay men, but most are women. They are less ashamed,
for they are "innocent." They or the narrator explain how it is that these
perfectly normal women came to be infected with HIV: one had a
boyfriend who used drugs, another had a brief affair with a bisexual,
and another had a bisexual husband; none of them suspected the sins
of their partners. And finally there are the most innocent of all, the
white, middle-class hemophiliac children. They are so innocent that
they can even be shown being comforted, hugged, and played with.

Among the gay men who dare to show their faces, one is particularly
useful for the purposes of *Sixty Minutes,* and interestingly he has a
counterpart in an ABC *20/20* segment of a few years earlier. He is the
identical twin whose brother is straight. The double portrait of the sick
gay man and his healthy straight brother makes its moral lesson so clear
that it needs no elaboration.[8]

Indeed, the intended messages of "AIDS Hits Home" are so obvious that
I don't want to belabor them, but only to make two further points about

8. For both *Sixty Minutes* and *20/20,* the ostensible reason for showing the twins is to
discuss an experimental bone marrow transplant therapy, which requires an identical twin donor. It does not, of course, require that the donor twin be straight.

Portraits of People with AIDS

the program. First, there is the reinforcement of hopelessness. Whenever a person with AIDS is allowed to utter words of optimism, a voice-over adds a caveat such as: "Six weeks after she said this, she was dead." Following this logic, the program ends with a standard device. Dan Rather mentions the "little victories and the *inevitable* defeats," and then proceeds to tell us what has happened to each PWA since the taping of the show. This coda ends with a sequence showing a priest—his hand on the KS-lesion-covered head of a PWA—administering last rights. Rather interrupts to say, "Bill died last Sunday," and the voice of the priest returns: "Amen."

My second point is that the privacy of the people portrayed is both brutally invaded and brutally maintained. Invaded, in the obvious sense that these people's difficult personal circumstances have been exploited for public spectacle, their most private thoughts and emotions exposed. But at the same time, maintained: The portrayal of these people's personal circumstances never includes an articulation of the public dimension of the crisis, the social conditions that made AIDS a crisis and continue to perpetuate it as a crisis. People with AIDS are kept safely within the boundaries of their private tragedies. No one utters a word about the politics of AIDS, the mostly deliberate failure of public policy at every level of government to stem the course of the epidemic, to fund biomedical research into effective treatments, provide adequate health care and housing, and conduct massive and ongoing preventive education campaigns. Even when the issue of discrimination is raised—in the case of children expelled from school—this too is presented as a problem of individual fears, prejudices, and misunderstandings. The role of broadcast television in creating and maintaining those fears, prejudices, and misunderstandings is, needless to say, not addressed.

It is, then, not merely faceless statistics that have prevented a sympathetic response to people with AIDS. The media has, from very early in the epidemic, provided us with faces. Sokolowski acknowledges this fact in his preface to the Rosalind Solomon catalog:

Popular representations of AIDS have been devoid of depictions of people living with AIDS, save for the lurid journalistic images of patients in extremis, *published in the popular press where the subjects are depicted as decidedly* not *persons* living *with AIDS, but as victims. The portraits in this exhibition have a different focus. They are, by definition, portraits of individuals with AIDS, not archetypes of some abstract notion of the syndrome. Rosalind Solomon's photographs are portraits of the human condition; vignettes of the intense personal encounters she had with over seventy-five people over a ten-month period. "I photographed everyone who would let me, who was HIV-positive, or had ARC, or AIDS. . . . they talked to me about their lives."*

The resulting seventy-five images that comprise this exhibition provide a unique portrait gallery of the faces of AIDS.[9]

The brute contradiction in this statement, in which "portraits of individuals with AIDS, not archetypes of some abstract notion" is immediately conflated with "portraits of the human condition"—as if that were not an abstract notion—is exacerbated in Sokolowski's introductory text, where he applies to the photographs interpretations that read as if they were contrived as parodies of the art historian's formal descriptions and source mongering. In one image, which reminds Sokolowski of Watteau's *Gilles,* we are asked to "contemplate the formal differences between the haphazard pattern of facial lesions and the thoughtful placement of buttons fastened to the man's pullover."[10] He completes his analysis of this photograph by comparing it with an "early fifteenth-century *Imago Peitatis* of the scourged Christ." Other photographs suggest to him the medieval *Ostentatio Vulneris,* the *Momento Mori,* the *Imago Clipeata,* and the image of the *Maja* or Venus.

Clearly, when viewing Solomon's photographs most of us will not seek to place them within art historical categories. Nor will we be struck by their formal or compositional interest. Rather, many of us will see in these images, once again, and in spite of Sokolowski's insistence to the contrary, the very representations we have grown accustomed to in the

9. Sokolowski, preface to *Rosalind Solomon: Portraits in the Time of AIDS.*

10. Sokolowski, "Looking in a Mirror," in *Rosalind Solomon: Portraits in the Time of AIDS.*

mass media. William Olander, a curator at New York's New Museum of Contemporary Art who died of AIDS on March 18, 1989, saw precisely what I saw:

The majority of the sitters are shown alone; many are in the hospital; or at home, sick, in bed. Over 90% are men. Some are photographed with their parents, or at least their mothers. Only four are shown with male lovers or friends. For the photographer, "The thing that became very compelling was knowing the people—knowing them as individuals. . . ." For the viewer, however, there is little to know other than their illness. The majority of sitters are clearly ravaged by the disease. (No fewer than half of those portrayed bear the most visible signs of AIDS—the skin lesions associated with Kaposi's sarcoma.) Not one is shown in a work environment; only a fraction are depicted outside. None of the sitters is identified. They have no identities other than as victims of AIDS.[11]

But giving the person with AIDS an identity as well as a face can also be a dangerous enterprise, as is clear from the most extended, and the most vicious, story of a person with AIDS that American television has thus far presented: the notorious episode of PBS *Frontline* "AIDS: A National Inquiry." "This is Fabian's story," host Judy Woodruff informs us, "and I must warn you it contains graphic descriptions of sexual behavior." One curious aspect of this program, given its ruthlessness, is its unabashed self-reflexivity. It begins with the TV crew narrating about itself, apparently roaming the country in search of a good AIDS story: "When we came to Houston, we didn't know Fabian Bridges. He was just one of the faceless victims." After seeing the show, we might conclude that Fabian would have been better off if he'd remained so. "AIDS: A National Inquiry" is the story of the degradation of a homeless black gay man with AIDS at the hands of virtually every institution he encountered, certainly including PBS. Fabian Bridges was first diagnosed with AIDS in a public hospital in Houston, treated, released, and given a one-way ticket out of town—to Indianapolis, where his sister and brother-

11. William Olander, "'I Undertook This Project as a Personal Exploration of the Human Components of an *Alarming Situation*,' 3 Vignettes (2)," *New Observations* 61 (October 1988), p. 5 (the quote used as a title is Rosalind Solomon's).

in-law live. They refuse to take him in, because they're afraid for their young child, about whom the brother-in-law says, "He doesn't know what AIDS is. He doesn't know what homosexuality is. He's innocent." Arrested for stealing a bicycle, Fabian is harassed and humiliated by the local police, who are also under the illusion that they might "catch" AIDS from him. After a prosecutor drops the charges against him, Fabian is once again provided with a one-way ticket out of town, this time to Cleveland, where his mother lives. But in Indianapolis, a police reporter picked up the story, and, as the *Frontline* crew informs us, "It was Kyle Niederpreun's story that first led us to Fabian. It was a story about the alienation and rejection that many AIDS victims suffer"—an alienation and rejection that the crew seemed all too happy to perpetuate.

Frontline finally locates its "AIDS victim" in a cheap hotel room in Cleveland. "We spent several days with Fabian," the narrator reports, "and he agreed to let us tell his story." Cut to Fabian phoning his mother in order that her refusal to let him come home can be reenacted for the video camera. "He said he had no money," the crew goes on, "so sometimes we bought him meals, and we had his laundry done. One day Fabian saw a small portable radio he liked, so we bought it for him." The narration continues, "He spent time in adult bookstores and movie houses, and he admitted it was a way he helped support himself." Then, in what is surely one of the most degrading invasions of privacy ever shown on TV, Fabian describes, on camera, one of his tricks, ending with the confession, "I came inside him . . . accident . . . as I was pulling out, I was coming." "After Fabian told us he was having unsafe sex, we faced a dilemma," the narrator explains. "Should we report him to authorities or keep his story confidential, knowing that he could be infecting others? We decided to tell health officials what we knew."

At this point begins the story *Frontline* has really set out to tell, that of the supposed conflict between individual rights and the public welfare.[12] It is a story of the futile attempts of health officials, policemen,

12. The fascination of the media with the supposed threat of "AIDS carriers" was dramatically revealed in the response to Randy Shilts's *And the Band Played On,* which focused almost exclusively on Shilts's story of the so-called Patient Zero (see "How

and the vice squad to lock Fabian up, protected as he is by troublesome civil rights. A city council member in Cleveland poses the problem: "The bottom line is we've got a guy on the street here. The guy's got a gun and he's out shootin' people. . . . What do we say collectively as a group of people representing this society?" But while the city council contemplates its draconian options, the disability benefits Fabian had applied for several months earlier arrive, and after a nasty sequence involving his sadly ill-counseled mother, who has momentarily confiscated the money in order to put it aside for Fabian's funeral, Fabian takes the money and runs.

By now *Time* magazine has published a story on what it calls this "pitiful nomad," and the local media in Houston, where Fabian has reappeared, have a sensational story for the evening news. The *Frontline* crew finds him, homeless and still supporting himself as a hustler, so, they report, "We gave him $15 a night for three nights to buy a cheap hotel room. We gave him the money on the condition that he not practice unsafe sex and that he stay away from the bathhouses." Pocketing the generous gift of $45, Fabian continues to hustle, and the vice squad moves in to enforce an order by the Houston health department, issued in a letter to Fabian, that he "refrain from exchanging bodily fluids." But now the vice squad, too, faces a dilemma. "Catch 22," one of the officers says. How do you entrap someone into exchanging bodily fluids without endangering yourself? They decide to get Fabian on a simple solicitation charge instead, to "get him to hit on one of us," as they put it, but Fabian doesn't take the bait.

Ultimately a leader of the local gay community decides on his own to try to help Fabian, and a lawyer from the Houston AIDS Foundation offers him a home, developments about which the Houston health commis-

to Have Promiscuity in an Epidemic," this volume). The fascination has clearly not abated. At the Sixth International Conference on AIDS in San Francisco, June 20–24, 1990, members of the media took part in a panel discussion entitled "AIDS and the Media: A Hypothetical Case Study." The hypothetical case was that of an American soldier stationed in the Philippines accused of infecting forty prostitutes. The soldier's "past" had him frequenting prostitutes in Uganda and bathhouses in the Castro district of San Francisco.

sioner blandly remarks, "It would never have occurred to me to turn to the gay community for help." But *Frontline* has now lost its story. As the narrator admits, "The gay community was protecting him from the local press and from us." There is, nevertheless, the usual coda: "The inevitable happened. Fabian's AIDS symptoms returned. Just one week after he moved into his new home, he went back into the hospital. This time, he stayed just over a month. Fabian died on November 17. His family had no money to bury him, so after a week he was given a pauper's funeral and buried in a county grave."

Judy Woodruff had introduced this program by saying, "The film you are about to see is controversial; that's because it's a portrait of a man with AIDS who continued to be promiscuous. In San Francisco and other cities, the organized gay community is protesting the film, because they say it is unfair to persons with AIDS." This strikes me as a very ambiguous reason to protest, and I have no doubt that the organized gay community's position against the film was articulated more broadly. How is it unfair to persons with AIDS? What persons with AIDS? Isn't the film unfair, first and foremost, to Fabian Bridges? The true grounds on which I imagine the gay community protested are the dangerous insinuations of the film: that the public health is endangered by the free movement within society of people with AIDS, that gay people with AIDS irresponsibly spread HIV to unsuspecting victims. They might also have protested the film's racist presumptions and class biases, its exploitation not only of Fabian Bridges but of his entire family. In addition, it seems hard to imagine a knowledgeable person seeing the film who would not be appalled at the failure of PBS to inform its audience of the extraordinary misinformation about AIDS conveyed by virtually every bureaucratic official in the film. And finally I imagine the gay community protested the film because it is so clear that the filmmakers were more interested in getting their footage than in the psychological and physical welfare of their protagonist, that instead of leading him to social service agencies or AIDS service organizations that could have helped him and his family, they lured him with small bribes, made him dependent on them, and then betrayed him to various authorities. A particularly revealing sequence intercut toward the end of the film takes us back to Fabian's hotel room in Cleveland. "We remembered something he'd said to us earlier," the narrator says, and Fabian then intones in his affectless voice, "Let me go down in history as being . . . I am somebody, you know, somebody that'll be respected, somebody who's appreciated, and somebody who can be related to, because a whole lot of people just go, they're not even on the map, they just go."

Here we have explicitly the terms of the contract between the *Frontline* crew and Fabian Bridges. *Frontline* found in Fabian, indeed, the "alienation and rejection" that many people with AIDS suffer, and offered him the false means by which our society sometimes pretends to grant transcendence of that condition, a moment of glory in the mass media. They said to this lonely, ill, and scared young man, in effect, "We're gonna make you a star."

After witnessing this contract, we may wish to reconsider the various claims made for photographers Nicholas Nixon and Rosalind Solomon that the difference of their work from ordinary photojournalism's exploitation of people with AIDS resides in the pact they have made with their sitters. "The rather unique situation of Rosalind Solomon's portraits, done in the time of AIDS," writes Thomas Sokolowski, "is that the subjects have been asked."[13] The claim for Nixon is made less directly by his curatorial apologist. When introducing Nixon for a lecture at the Museum of Modern Art, Peter Galassi said, "Mr. Nixon was born in Detroit in 1947. It seems to me that's all you really need to know, and the part about Detroit isn't absolutely essential. What is relevant is that Nixon has been on the planet for about forty years and has been a photographer for about half of that time. It's also relevant that for about the past fifteen years he has worked with a large, old-fashioned view camera which stands on a tripod and makes negatives measuring eight by ten inches."[14] The point about the size of Nixon's equipment, of course, is that it is so obtrusive that we can never accuse him of catching his

---

13. Sokolowski, preface to *Rosalind Solomon: Portraits in the Time of AIDS*.

14. This introduction by Peter Galassi and the following statements by Nicholas Nixon are transcribed from Nixon's talk at the Museum of Modern Art, October 11, 1988.

subjects unawares; he has to win their confidence. According to a friend of Nixon quoted in the *Boston Globe*, "The reason people trust him is that he has no misgivings about his own motivations or actions."[15] Or, as Nixon himself put it in his talk at MOMA, "I know how cruel I am, and I'm comfortable with it."

My initial reaction on seeing both the Nixon and Solomon exhibitions was incredulity. I had naively assumed that the critique of this sort of photography, articulated over and over again during the past decade, might have had some effect. I will cite just one paragraph from a founding text of this criticism as an indication of the lessons not learned. It comes from Allan Sekula's "Dismantling Modernism, Reinventing Documentary (Notes on the Politics of Representation)," written in 1976: "At the heart of [the] fetishistic cultivation and promotion of the artist's humanity is a certain disdain for the 'ordinary' humanity of those who have been photographed. They become the 'other,' exotic creatures, objects of contemplation. . . . The most intimate, human-scale relationship to suffer mystification in all this is the specific social engagement that results in the image; the negotiation between photographer and subject in the making of a portrait, the seduction, coercion, collaboration, or rip off."[16]

Here is one indication of the photographer's disdain while negotiating with his sitter: Showing one of his serial PWA portraits, Nixon explained,

I started taking his picture in June of '87, and he was so resistant to the process—even though he kept saying "Oh no, I love it, I want to do it"— every other part of him was so resistant that after three times I kind of kicked him out and said, "When you really want to do this, call me up, you don't really want to do this." Then one day in December he called me

15. Neil Miller, "The Compassionate Eye," *Boston Globe Magazine,* January 29, 1989, p. 36.
16. Allan Sekula, "Dismantling Modernism, Reinventing Documentary (Notes on the Politics of Representation)," in *Photography against the Grain* (Halifax: Press of the Nova Scotia College of Art and Design, 1984), p. 59.

up and said, "I'm ready now," and so I went, of course, and this picture doesn't kill me, but, I'll tell you, it's miles better than anything I'd gotten from him before. I really felt like he was ready when I saw it. He was paralyzed from the waist down. That was part of the challenge, I guess.

An audience member asked Nixon to explain what he meant when he said the subject was resistant, and he replied, "He wasn't interested. He was giving me a blank wall. He was saying, 'Yes, I think this is something I'm interested in, but I don't like this process, I don't like this big camera, I don't like it close to me, I don't like cooperating with you, I don't like the fact that your being here reminds me of my illness, I'm uncomfortable.' But at the same time he kept on going through the motions. I had to drive forty minutes to his house. I'm not interested in somebody just going through the motions. Life's too short."

How, then, might this intimate, human-scale relationship that Sekula cautions us about be constructed differently?

We can perhaps agree that portraits of people with AIDS created by the media and art photographers alike are demeaning, and that they are overdetermined by a number of prejudices that precede them about the majority of the people who have AIDS—about gay men, IV drug users, people of color, poor people. Not only do journalism's (and art's) images create false stereotypes of people with AIDS, they depend on already existing false stereotypes about the groups most significantly affected by AIDS. Much of the PBS discussion with "experts" that followed its airing of Fabian's story involved the fear that Fabian would be seen as the stereotype of the homosexual with AIDS. The reaction of many of us when we see homosexuality portrayed in the media is to respond by saying, "That's not true. We're not like that" or "I'm not like that" or "we're not all like that." But what *are* we like? What portrait of a gay person, or of a PWA, would we feel comfortable with? Which one would be representative? how could it be? and why should it be? One problem of opposing a stereotype, a stereotype that Fabian Bridges was indeed intended to convey, is that we tacitly side with those who would distance themselves from the image portrayed, we tacitly agree that it is other, whereas our foremost responsibility in this case is to *defend* Fabian Bridges, to acknowledge that he is one of us. To say that it is unfair to represent a gay man or a PWA as a hustler is tacitly to collaborate in the media's ready condemnation of hustlers, to pretend along with the media that prostitution is a moral failing rather than a choice based on economic and other factors limiting autonomy. Or, to take another example, do we really wish to claim that the photographs by Nicholas Nixon are untrue? Do we want to find ourselves in the position of denying the horrible suffering of people with AIDS, the fact that very many PWAs become disfigured and helpless, and that they die? Certainly we can say that these representations do not help us, and that they probably hinder us, in our struggle, because the best they can do is elicit pity, and pity is not solidarity. We must continue to demand and create our own counterimages, images of PWA self-empowerment, of the organized PWA movement and of the larger AIDS activist movement, as the ACT UP demonstrators insisted at MOMA. But we must also recognize that every image of a PWA is a *representation,* and formulate our activist demands not in relation to the "truth" of the image, but in relation to the conditions of its construction and to its social effects.

I want to conclude this discussion, therefore, with a work that does not seek to replace negative images with positive ones, that does not substitute the good PWA for the bad, the apparently healthy for the visibly ill, the active for the passive, the exceptional for the ordinary. My interest in the videotape *Danny,* made by Stashu Kybartas,[17] does not derive from its creation of a countertype, but rather from its insistence on a particular stereotype, one that is referred to among gay men, whether endearingly or deprecatingly, as the clone.

Without, I think, setting out deliberately or programmatically to articulate a critique of media images of PWAs, *Danny* nevertheless constitutes one of the most powerful critiques that exists to date. This is in part because it duplicates, in so many of its features, the stereotypes of PWA portraiture, but at the same time reclaims the portrait for the commu-

17. *Danny,* 1987, is distributed by Video Data Bank, Chicago.

nity from which it emerges, the community of gay men, who have thus far been the population most drastically affected by AIDS in the United States. *Danny* accomplishes this through one overriding difference: the formulation of the relationship between artist and subject not as one of empathy or identification, but as one of explicit sexual desire, a desire that simultaneously accounts for Kybartas's subjective investment in the project and celebrates Danny's own sense of gay identity and hard-won sexual freedom.

A great many of the conventions of media portraits of the PWA appear in *Danny,* but their meanings are reinvested or reversed. *Danny* begins, for example, where virtually every other television portrait ends: with the information about the death of the video's subject, here matter-of-factly announced in a rolling text before we have even seen an image. Thus, although the video ends at the second recounting of Danny's death, it does not come as a coda to tell us what has happened to the subject after the tape was made. Indeed, as we discern from the apostrophizing voice-over, the tape was made as a work of mourning, the artist's working through of his loss of a friend in the AIDS movement. The retrospective voice is reinforced by a refusal of the live video image's movement. Using videotape that he shot with Danny during their brief friendship, Kybartas compiled it as a series of stills, which also serves to make it equivalent to the still photographs taken of Danny prior to his illness, when he lived in Miami.

The first words uttered by Danny, in his somewhat difficult-to-understand voice, are the following: "He doesn't refer to me as his son. Instead of saying, 'My son'll be up to get it,' 'The boy'll be up to get it.' Whadaya mean the boy? It makes me feel like Tarzan and the jungle. Me boy." The statement remains somewhat opaque until we come to those fragments of dialogue in which Kybartas queries Danny further about his father. When Danny talks of his decision to return to his parents' home in Steubenville, Ohio, at the moment when he learned he'd have to begin chemotherapy for his Kaposi's sarcoma, he mentions the difficulty of telling his mother, who nevertheless accepted the fact. Kybartas asks, "Were you worried about your dad?" "Yeah," says Danny, "I was wondering how he was going to take having a gay son, and one with AIDS on top of it, but she never told him. I have to watch what I say around him, or if anything about AIDS is on television, my mom flicks it off. She doesn't want him to hear about it."

We are left to imagine Danny's home life, as his father watches his son die and never bothers to ask why. Then, in the final conversation between the two friends before the tape ends, Danny says, "What I should have done this week was to have contacted the funeral home, because I would like to feel secure knowing that I could be buried there, instead of their getting the body and saying, 'No, we can't handle that body,' and my father saying, 'Why?' 'Because he has AIDS.' That's not a time that he needs to be faced with that, not after my dying." Kybartas probes, "Why are you concerned about his reaction to that?" and Danny answers, "Trying to spare his feelings, I guess." "Why?" Kybartas persists. "I guess as much as I dislike him, I don't want to hurt him either." "Why not?" Kybartas chides, and the dialogue fades out.

It is this gruesome family scene, so typical—perhaps even stereotypical—of gay men's relations with their fathers, that is denied in sentimental media stories of gay men going home to die in the caring fold of the family, something they often do as a last resort when medical insurance has run out or disability benefits won't cover the rent. In the mainstream media, though, this scenario tells of the abandonment of gay men by their friends in the dark and sinful cities they inhabit, and the return to comfort and normality in some small town in the midwest. But in Kybartas's tape it is the small hometown, a steel town near Pittsburgh, that is dark and sinister, "slowly dying," as Danny puts it, whereas the metropolis to which Danny fled to find his sexual freedom is the very opposite of dark, though it may, in conventional moralizing terms, be sinful—that, of course, is its appeal.

This reversal of mainstream media pieties about hometown USA and the biological family serves to delimit the space of the sexual for gay men, for if Danny's father has not discerned that his son is gay and dying of AIDS, it is because Danny's identity as a sexual being must be disavowed. Kybartas articulates this in the tape by saying, "I wanted you to come and live with us. We'd take care of you. We could go to the gay bars in Pittsburgh, dance, and watch the go-go boys."

Danny's image as a kid who lived for sex is complicated in the video by another subtle reversal. Mainstream coverage of AIDS is padded with portentous pictures of medical procedures—IV needles being inserted, doctors listening through stethoscopes, tinkering in laboratories. Parallel imagery in *Danny* refers not to Danny's disease, but to his profession as a medical technician, showing the procedure of the carotid angiogram that he performed. But just because Danny is a full human being with a respectable profession doesn't mean he's heroized by Kybartas. Immediately following Danny's reminiscence about his job is the "Miami Vice" sequence, in which Kybartas uses footage from that program's credits as Danny talks about shooting cocaine with shared needles back in 1981, before anyone knew the transmission risks. The result is that still another media myth is interfered with: the one that makes gay men (always presumed to be white and middle class) and IV drug users (presumed to be poor people of color) separate "risk groups."

A standard media device for constructing AIDS as a morality tale uses before-and-after images of people with AIDS. Stuart Marshall's *Bright Eyes*, made for Britain's Channel 4 in 1984, performed a brilliant analysis on the British tabloid *Sunday People*'s use of PWA Kenny Ramsaur to that end. In 1983, ABC's *20/20* also used Kenny Ramsaur to show the effects of AIDS in one of the earliest and most lurid television newsmagazine stories on the subject, narrated by none other than Giraldo Rivera. ABC's camera first shows Ramsaur's face, horribly swollen and disfigured; then snapshots of the handsome, healthy Kenny as hedonistic homosexual appear, after which we return to the live image as the camera pans down to Kenny's arm to see him pull up his sleeve to reveal his KS lesions. Kybartas reworks this ploy in *Danny*. We see snapshots of a young and healthy hedonist in Miami as Danny talks with relish of his life, of how he would spend the day on the beach, return home and let

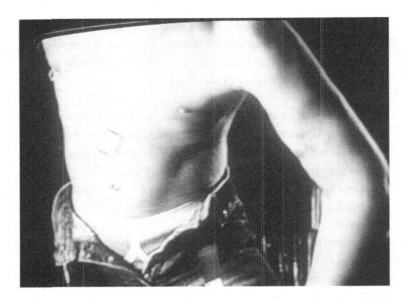

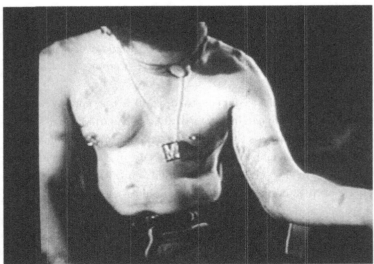

Stashu Kybartas, *Danny*, 1987.

the suntan oil sink in, and then shower. After douching in the shower, he tells us, he would shave his balls and the side of his cock, put on his tight 501s, and go out and cruise. Close-ups of Danny putting in his nipple ring are intercut with a close-up of his nipple surrounded by KS lesions, taken in Kybartas's studio in Pittsburgh during Danny's illness. And when we move from a second series of early snapshots of Danny to the video images of his face, shot after he has returned to Steubenville, it is bloated from chemotherapy. He is nevertheless still fully sexualized. Kybartas, narrating over the image of the face, laments, "Danny, when I look at all these pictures of you, I can see that the chemotherapy caused your appearance to change from week to week. One day when you walked into the studio, I thought you looked like a longshoreman who had just been in a fight.[18] [pause] The only time I saw you cry was on Christmas Eve, when your doctor told you that the chemotherapy was no longer working."

This movement back and forth from the tough to the tender, from desiring to grieving in relation to the entire series of images constitutes the major text of the tape, and it may be said to encompass something of the range of gay men's sexuality as well as our present condition. The theme is most often elaborated in the revelation of the KS lesions, as time and again we see stop-motion footage of Danny removing his shirt, or as still images show fragments of his chest and arms covered with lesions. But, like scars or tattoos, the lesions are always seen as marking the body as sexually attractive, a sexiness that is indicated by Kybartas at one point when he says, "Danny, do you remember the first night we were shooting the film at my studio? You'd taken off your shirt and we were looking at all your lesions. Later, as I was rubbing your back and you were telling me about the problems you were having with relationships and sex, something happened. It was suddenly very quiet in the studio, and my heart was beating fast. I don't know what it was . . . the heat, your body. The only sound was the steam hissing out of the radiator. . . ."

18. The sexual attractiveness of the gay clone was constructed through stylistic reference to clichéd hypermasculine professions such as the cowboy, policeman, sailor, and, indeed, the longshoreman.

After seeing *Danny,* it occurred to me that there is a deeper explanation for portrayals of PWAs, and especially of gay men with AIDS, as desperately ill, as either grotesquely disfigured or as having wasted to fleshless, ethereal bodies. These are not images that are intended to overcome our fear of disease and death, as is sometimes claimed. Nor are they meant only to reinforce the status of the PWA as victim or pariah, as we often charge. Rather, they are, precisely, *phobic* images, images of the terror at imagining the person with AIDS as still sexual. In the *Frontline* special the Houston public health commissioner says, with patent fear and loathing, "Fabian was only diagnosed last April. He might live another two years, and furthermore this person is in remission now. He's not demonstrating any *signs* of illness!" The unwillingness to show PWAs as active, as in control of their lives, as acting up and fighting back, is the fear that they might also still be sexual, or as Judy Woodruff said of Fabian Bridges, that "he was a man with AIDS who continued to be promiscuous."

The comfortable fantasy that AIDS would spell the end of gay promiscuity, or perhaps of gay sex altogether, has pervaded American and Western European culture for almost a decade now. But we will fail to understand its pervasiveness and its representational effects if we think it only occupies the minds of the likes of Jesse Helms and Patrick Buchanan. I want to end, therefore, with a quotation that will bring this phobic fantasy closer to home in the context of cultural studies. In an interview published in the German art magazine *Kunstforum,* Jean Baudrillard appears sanguine about William Burroughs's (and Laurie Anderson's) dictum that "language is a virus":

Language, particularly in all areas of information, is used in a more and more formulaic way, and thereby gets sicker and sicker from its own formulas. One should no longer speak of sickness, however, but of virality, which is a form of mutation. . . . Perhaps the new pathology of virality is the last remedy against the total disintegration of language and of the body. I don't know, for example, whether a stock market crash such as that of 1987 should be understood as a terrorist process of economy or as a form of viral catharsis of the economic system. Possibly, though, it is like AIDS, if we understand AIDS as a remedy against total sexual liberation, which is sometimes more dangerous than an epidemic, because the latter always ends. Thus AIDS could be understood as a counterforce against the total elimination of structure and the total unfolding of sexuality.[19]

19. "Virtuelle Katastrophen" (interview with Jean Baudrillard by Florian Rötzer), *Kunstforum,* January–February 1990, p. 266. Thanks to Hans Haacke for bringing this interview to my attention.

5 GOOD OLE BAD BOYS

First presented at "AIDS, Art, and Activism:

A Conference on the Culture of AIDS,"

Ohio State University, Columbus,

March 10–12, 1989.

I want here to address art's—and art criticism's—most vilified position, the position that is referred to as "politically correct." I feel well qualified to discuss this position, because I am—or more accurately OCTOBER, the journal of which I am an editor, is—so often thought to demand it. The most virulent expression of this opinion occurred in a profile of OCTOBER editor Rosalind Krauss published in the trade journal *Avenue Magazine* (the avenue in question is Madison), where an unnamed art critic was quoted as saying of the OCTOBER editors, "They're all Stalinists, and I hope they die." More recently, more indirectly, and explicitly regarding the issue of OCTOBER on AIDS that I edited, Gary Indiana wrote in the *Village Voice* concerning a new East Village queer zine called *Comrade/Sister!:* "It carries none of the deadening spiritual influence of various middle-aged, late-blooming gay leaders who feel they've been put in charge of homosexuality. There is no polemical ax grinding in the background, no prevailing sense of 'correctness.' It is a nice reminder that every generation provides a fresh batch of sexually diverse people all by itself, eager to do their own and each other's things without the slightest theoretical training from the senior staff of OCTOBER."

I guess Indiana's venom was motivated in this instance by his association, as contributor to the catalog, with the exhibition *Against Nature,* organized by Dennis Cooper and Richard Hawkins and mounted in early 1988 at Los Angeles Contemporary Exhibitions. Apparently I was cast as this exhibition's opponent, since, rumor has it, *Against Nature* was conceived from the beginning as a rebuttal of the "politically correct" demands made in the AIDS issue of OCTOBER.[1] And, as John Greyson wrote in the catalog for *AIDS: The Artists' Response, Against Nature* was "certainly not politically correct."

Good Ole Bad Boys

1. This rumor is hinted at in John Greyson's contribution to the show's catalog, "Parma Violets: A Video Script," in *Against Nature: A Show by Homosexual Men,* ed. Dennis Cooper and Richard Hawkins (Los Angeles: Los Angeles Contemporary Exhibitions, 1988), pp. 11–12.

But what is meant by the rubric "politically correct"? Or more accurately, since I have never heard anyone use the term except as an accusation of someone else's demand for it, what is meant by the statement, "I refuse to be politically correct"? What, for example, did John Greyson mean when he wrote that *Against Nature* was "certainly not politically correct"? Let me give you the whole sentence: "The curators sought work that referenced AIDS from [an] ironic, campy perspective—work that was biting, irreverent, self-consciously decorative, elegiac, impolite, bad boy, certainly not politically correct."[2] Let's leave aside the fact that most of the work in the show hardly lived up to the provocation Greyson attributed to it, that the main problem with the art was that it tended toward the tame and academic. But let's look instead at the curators' wish to be incorrect, for although their wish cannot always be discerned in the work exhibited, it can be seen in certain details of the show's apparatus. Take, for example, the exhibition's subtitle: "A show by homosexual men." Throughout the catalog, the word *homosexual* is consistently used, rarely the word *gay*. I take this to be an example of refusing to be politically correct, since the correct term is now generally understood to be *gay*. Why else did gay men and lesbians wage a prolonged battle with the *New York Times* to substitute *gay* for *homosexual*, a battle that was partially won only in 1988? Using *homosexual men* in the subtitle of this show would be roughly equivalent to a show by black men referring to themselves as Negro men, or a show by people with AIDS referring to themselves as AIDS victims.

I think I can locate the very passage from the AIDS issue of *October* in which the perceived demand for the politically correct term appears. It comes from Simon Watney's essay "The Spectacle of AIDS": "The very notion of a 'homosexual body' only exposes the more or less desperate ambition to confine mobile desire in the semblance of a stable object, calibrated by its sexual aim, regarded as a 'wrong choice.' The 'homo-

2. John Greyson, "Parma Violets for Wayland Flowers," in *AIDS: The Artists' Response,* ed. Jan Zita Grover (Columbus: Hoyt L. Sherman Gallery, Ohio State University, 1989), p. 12.

sexual body' would thus evidence a fictive collectivity of perverse sexual performances, denied any psychic reality and pushed out beyond the furthest margins of the social. This, after all, is what the category of 'the homosexual' (which we *cannot* continue to employ) was invented to do in the first place."[3]

When Watney insists that we cannot continue to use the term *homosexual*, he does so in the course of an argument that shows very precisely how that term is being used against us with renewed vehemence in the face of AIDS. His argument is made within the context of a history of resisting the medicalizing terminology in the work of, among many others, Jeffrey Weeks and Michel Foucault, and also in Stuart Marshall's videotape *Bright Eyes*, one of the first important videos about AIDS, which provides a sustained analysis of the origins, the history, and the present murderous deployment of the term.[4] Why then has it returned in the subtitle of *Against Nature*? Is it because the show's literary conceit, evidenced in the title appropriated from J.-K. Huysmans's symbolist novel, returns us to the historical moment when the pathologizing term *homosexual* came into use in the literature of sexology? Unfortunately, it is difficult to say, because, unlike Watney or Weeks or Foucault or Marshall, the curators of *Against Nature* make no arguments for their positions, and we are therefore left to surmise that to call the exhibition "a show by homosexual men" is merely a means of registering the refusal to be politically correct.[5] Even to have used terms like *queer* or *fag*

3. Simon Watney, "The Spectacle of AIDS," in *AIDS: Cultural Analysis/Cultural Activism*, ed. Douglas Crimp (Cambridge: MIT Press, 1988), p. 79 (italics in original).

4. See Martha Gever, "Pictures of Sickness: Stuart Marshall's *Bright Eyes*," in *AIDS: Cultural Analysis*, pp. 109–126.

5. The show's curators include the following statement in the catalog, which I quote in its entirety:

We constructed *Against Nature* along personal lines. Who are we? We're gay male artists obsessed with the ways in which sexual desire informs, distances and empowers the recent history of art made by guys like us. We're thinking of, say [a little self-aggrandizement here?], Kenneth Anger, Jean Genet, William Burroughs, Marc Almond, Denton Welch . . . just to start. These artists share at least two concerns— a finely-tuned irreverence for the cultural and moral standards imposed by and for heterosexuals, and a reverence and desire for, mixed with anxiety about the male would have been understood to be in a politically viable line of appropriations of terms of oppression by the oppressed themselves, to say "Yeah, we're faggots, so what?" *Homosexual*, however, has a very different resonance, because, as Watney argued, it is the term of a confining essentialism. It has always been deployed to claim that there is an essential homosexual character or identity, which resides in our inherent sickness.

John Greyson wrote of *Against Nature* that its strength is that it sparked a significant debate, but I'm not so sure. The curators resolutely refused a public discussion of the exhibition, just as they refused to stake out a clear position in the catalog. Although the director of LACE, the head of the Critical Studies Program at the California Institute of the Arts, John Greyson himself, and many others in the L.A. art community pleaded for a public discussion of the show, the curators refused to hold one. And thus we will probably never know why *homosexual* instead of *gay*, why "a show by homosexual men" instead of a show dealing with all the populations disporportionately affected by AIDS, for it was a show about AIDS that the curators were asked by LACE to organize.[6]

For this latter omission I can suggest an answer, an answer that concerns the local contours of the epidemic. Los Angeles recently surpassed San Francisco among U.S. cities for absolute numbers of people diagnosed with AIDS, with nearly 6,000 cases as of the end of 1988. Of these, 89 percent are among gay and bisexual men. The curators refrained from providing this information, however, information that might have partially explained why, in L.A., one might want to focus an

body, their own, friends', strangers', stars'. It's a limiting esthetic, maybe, but the results speak for themselves. We suspect that the works in this show do too. This catalogue is a component of *Against Nature*, and not its tracing. ("About *Against Nature*," in *Against Nature*, p. 4)

6. In her introduction to the catalog, LACE's director hints at the institution's worries: "At first we were concerned that this show could possibly be antithetical to our original intent to promote AIDS activism in an all-encompassing context. However, the Exhibition Committee was willing to take a chance based on our confidence and trust in the curators' knowledge of and commitment to both AIDS activism and gay activism" (Joy Silverman, "Introduction/Acknowledgments," in *Against Nature*, p. 3).

exhibition about AIDS on the aesthetic responses of gay men, presumably because such an explanation might have made them appear to be trying to be politically correct.

Now, I want to consider some of the confusions that result from this example of refusing to be politically correct. First, the most general and dangerous confusion, that of designating as authoritarian—even Stalinist—arguments or artworks that are in fact made as resistance to authority. Let's stay with our example. To say that you are refusing to be politically correct is to hold up your refusal as an assertion of freedom in the face of a demand, seen as rigid, proscriptive, authoritarian. The demand in this case is the one made by Simon Watney that we not continue to employ the term *homosexual*. But Watney urges us to do this not in order to exercise his authority over us, but in solidarity with us as he joins us in our acts of resistance. For *homosexual* is the term deployed by all those authorities—medical, scientific, governmental—who use it to deny us our self-identifications, our rights, our pleasures, and now our very lives, and against whom we therefore struggle.

A second, related problem resulting from the refusal to be politically correct is that of confusing genuine authority, the authority of persuasive argument, with authoritarianism. What is generally characterized as a demand to be politically correct is nothing other than a political argument, one that identifies itself as such and one that is *authoritative.* This is just the opposite of *authoritarian,* which involves the arbitrary exercise of power, and which usually pretends to be apolitical. The authoritative argument that is repudiated in the refusal to be politically correct is, in fact, made as *resistance* to this arbitrary exercise of power. One can, as we've seen, make an authoritative argument against using the term *homosexual,* but those in power will nevertheless exercise their authority arbitrarily in the face of that argument and continue to use *homosexual*—witness the *New York Times* in the twenty years following the Stonewall rebellion.

What happens, then, when Dennis Cooper and Richard Hawkins also choose to use the term? Are they resisting authority or are they acceding to authority? And when they do this, are they not themselves exercising power—albeit limited power? Were the artists in *Against Nature* asked if they wanted to be referred to as "homosexual men" or were they arbitrarily subjected to the label by the power of the show's curators?

Finally, in this case at least, I think the claim of a refusal to be politically correct is merely a deceitful way of carrying on the art world's business-as-usual, of pretending to be bad when what you're really doing is being good. The confusion of the authoritative argument with authoritarianism results in acceding to the status quo of relations of power. In the *OCTOBER* AIDS issue I did not wish to make a proscriptive argument for what art dealing with AIDS should be. Rather I wanted to show how confining was the standard art-world view of how artists might address AIDS: first through participation in charity auctions, thereby contributing to the volunteerism that the Reagan and Bush administrations pretend is the solution to the government's own refusal to do anything to fight the epidemic, and second through conventional representations of loss that would "outlast" and "transcend" the epidemic. I argued that the exclusive attention to these kinds of responses—determined by traditional conceptions of art as universal and timeless (and as worth a lot of money)—masked another possibility, the possibility of art practices directly engaged in the struggle to end the epidemic. I did not specify what these should be, but I gave a few examples of existing practices. Happily, such practices have proliferated since I made the argument, but the institutions of real power in the art world are very slow to recognize them. When, for example, the Museum of Modern Art last year mounted the exhibition *Committed to Print*,[7] showing activist art in the print medium since the 1960s, there was not one example of AIDS activist work; when asked about this omission by a *Village Voice* writer, the show's curator claimed that none of any interest existed. Evidently she had never seen a poster with a pink triangle that said "Silence=Death." And when, this year, MOMA did mount an exhibition including AIDS as a subject—Nicholas Nixon's *Pictures of People*—it was so offensive to

---

7. Deborah Wye, *Committed to Print: Social and Political Themes in Recent American Printed Art* (New York: Museum of Modern Art, 1988).

people with AIDS and AIDS activists that ACT UP staged a protest. In the meantime, the charity auctions continue, as AMFAR has gone on the road with *Art against AIDS*.

The point of all this is simply to say that the position against which I argued remains the dominant position, against which we must still struggle, both with our work and with our arguments. But we must also be prepared, when our work and our arguments are persuasive, to be accused of demanding political correctness.

Gregg Bordowitz said in our conversation published in the catalog for *AIDS: The Artists' Response*, "What I contest is the dominant art world's view that you can make anything except overtly politicized art. There's still this idea that you can do anything in the art world except make an overt statement. Didacticism is the only vulgar thing you can do in the art world! And that's what I've been interested in since art school—that No-no. . . ."[8] How many times have we heard that political art is always bad art, that it is merely propaganda? This is the most sacred art-world dogma of all, and it is one to which Dennis Cooper and Richard Hawkins, in their stance against political correctness, cling. Their greatest fear seems to be that what they do might be dismissed as propaganda. Bordowitz has also made the statement that serves as the perfect rejoinder to the timidity of their position. When he once referred to himself during a lecture as a propagandist, someone in the audience asked whether that didn't open him to the charge of trying to convert others to homosexuality. "If I thought a representation could make someone gay," he responded, "that's the kind of representation I'd be making." These are not the words of an abject homosexual, these are the words of a fierce faggot. I leave it to you to decide whether they are politically correct.

8. "Art and Activism: A Conversation between Douglas Crimp and Gregg Bordowitz," in *AIDS: The Artists' Response*, p. 9.

6 RANDY SHILTS'S MISERABLE FAILURE

First presented at the panel discussion "And the

Band Played On: *History as Mini-Series?" as part of*

the Ethics and Evidence in Gay and Lesbian Studies

series at the Center for Lesbian and Gay Studies,

City University of New York, April 13, 1989, and

published, with a postscript, in A Queer World:

The Center for Lesbian and Gay Studies Reader,

ed. Martin Duberman (New York: New York

University Press, 1997).

During the first week of April 1989, a young Dutchman on his way to the National Lesbian and Gay Health Conference and AIDS Forum in San Francisco was detained at the airport in Minneapolis—St. Paul when customs officials discovered he had AIDS. He was then incarcerated on the basis of a law barring entry to foreigners with contagious diseases, a category in which AIDS is now included. The Immigration and Naturalization Service ruled against a waiver for the Dutchman, stating, "The risk of harm by an AIDS-infected alien in the absence of humanitarian reasons for the temporary admission of aliens far outweighs the privilege of an alien to enter the United States to participate in a conference."[1] I think we all know how ludicrous this is, and how dangerous are its consequences. With one of the highest number of cases of AIDS of any country in the world, the United States is nevertheless one of only a very few countries that, against the recommendations of the World Health Organization, has enacted such a law. The law is based on a whole series of myths—that AIDS is contagious, that people with AIDS are ruthless, deliberate spreaders of disease, and that, in any case, people need not *routinely* take precautions against becoming infected or infecting others with HIV. These extremely pervasive myths result, directly, not only in bad laws, but in bad policy, discrimination, and violence, and, indirectly, in the deaths of thousands of people who are not being properly treated or educated.

The March 1989 issue of *Esquire* carries an article by Randy Shilts that, while very largely a piece of self-puffery, purports to be about something more significant: the supposedly incomprehensible fact that although his book *And the Band Played On* made *him* a media celebrity, it nevertheless failed to affect the way AIDS is perceived by the populace, reported in the media, and dealt with at the levels of policy and funding. As Shilts put it, "Never before have I succeeded so well; never before have I failed so miserably."[2] He goes on to regale us with stories of his success interwoven with examples of his failure. The principal failure is the scandal of the National Institutes of Health's stonewalling

1. "Alien with AIDS Is Ordered Freed," *New York Times,* April 8, 1989, p. A9.
2. Randy Shilts, "Talking AIDS to Death," *Esquire,* March 1989, p. 124.

about the hopelessly stalled development of drug treatments and the media's inability to see a story in this scandal. At the international AIDS conference in Stockholm, Shilts provided the hot tip of this story to his fellow journalists, since he himself was too busy with his book promotion tour to cover it. "One reporter responded to my tip," Shilts writes, "with the question: 'But who's going to play *you* in the miniseries?'"[3] "Clinical trials were not sexy," Shilts complains. "Clinical trials were boring."[4]

A second anecdote concerns Shilts's appearance on the Morton Downey Jr.
show, where, in spite of assurances that this was an issue Downey was not going to play games with because his brother had AIDS, he nevertheless—hardly surprisingly—turned the show into a referendum on quarantine and fueled the flames of his audience's homophobia. Shilts gives his astute analysis of this situation: "For Morton Downey Jr., talking about AIDS was not an act of conscience; it was a ratings ploy."[5]

Story three is about a Palm Springs fundraiser with various movie stars and socialites, where Shilts would receive an award for his valiant fight against AIDS. When receiving the award, Shilts launched into the series of AIDS jokes he'd been telling on the lecture circuit. These are all about Shilts's clever repartee with the yahoos who call in to talk shows with their absurd questions about how you "catch" AIDS. But this time, when he told the one about the woman who called in and asked, "What if a gay waiter took my salad back into the kitchen and ejaculated into my salad dressing?" a silence fell over the audience. Shilts explains, "Fears that I dismissed as laughable were the genuine concerns of my audience, I realized."[6]

The stories that Shilts tells reduce basically to two: the story of irrational fears of AIDS and loathing of those who have it and the media's sense of

3. Ibid., p. 128.
4. Ibid., p. 126.
5. Ibid., p. 128.
6. Ibid., p. 130.

the fascination of its audience with "sexy" stories about AIDS. What Shilts is thus describing are reactions to AIDS that I think we must recognize as unconscious, and therefore extremely intractable, incapable of being rectified by what Shilts calls "the truth," or objective reporting of the facts.

I want to suggest here that it is only by taking account of reactions to AIDS that operate at the level of the unconscious and by unpacking Shilts's unproblematized notion of "the truth" or of "objectivity" that we can understand why *And the Band Played On* is so deeply flawed.

Many people have written about why Shilts's book is, by his own admission, a miserable failure, or have addressed criticisms directly to Shilts when they encountered him on his celebrity tour. Needless to say, this is an aspect of being a celebrity that Shilts fails to report in his *Esquire* article. In spite of Shilts's own sense of failure, he arrogantly dismisses the questions raised by his critics. He still appears to feel that he has written the perfect book, the book that really tells the *true* story of the epidemic's first five years.

Let me give you just one example, taken from the transcripts of Shilts's book-promotion appearance at the Institute of Contemporary Arts in London. Shilts was asked in some detail about his book's most widely criticized passages, those dealing with the story of Patient Zero, in an exchange with the writer Adam Mars-Jones.

"At what stage did you decide to give [the Patient Zero story] so much prominence?" Mars-Jones asked.

"Well, I don't think it is that prominent in the book . . . , but I thought it was a fascinating story. . . . I think it represents very good investigative journalism."

"There are passages describing how [Patient Zero] would have sex with people in bathhouses, then turn the lights on and say, 'I'm going to die and so are you.'"

"Which he did! At the time he was doing that, I was hearing about it."

"But those were rumors."

"No, it wasn't rumors, I talked to people he did this to. . . . I mean, he was doing it quite a bit. The fact is it all happened. The facts are not disputed."

"William Darrow of the CDC does repudiate them."

"No, he does not. The fact is that William Darrow saw every word that was written about him and about the study [the 1982 CDC cluster study involving the so-called Patient Zero], and he approved every word of it. Now we're getting into very fine points of argument, and they're not very substantial."[7]

This exchange refers, in part, to a review of *And the Band Played On* that had just been published by Duncan Campbell in the *New Statesman*.[8] Campbell reports a telephone conversation with Darrow in which Darrow explained that the CDC cluster study, which sought to determine whether AIDS was caused by sexual transmission of an infectious agent, was based on speculation that the duration between infection and onset of symptoms was nine to eleven months. Having later learned, as all of us, including Shilts, did, that the period probably averages about eight *years*, Darrow claimed that he made it very clear to Shilts that the Patient Zero story was nonsense. He furthermore said that he pleaded with Shilts not to publish the name of Patient Zero, Gaeton Dugas, fearing that Dugas's family would suffer (and indeed the family later faced death threats).

Shilts canceled an interview with Campbell when he learned what the *New Statesman* review would entail, and later attacked Campbell in an interview with the gay newspaper *Coming Up*, complaining that this

7. See Tim Kingston, "Controversy Follows Shilts and 'Zero' to London," *Coming Up*, April 1988, p. 11.

8. Duncan Campbell, "An End to the Silence," *New Statesman*, March 4, 1988, pp. 22–23.

was the "typical crap I get from certain segments of the gay press. . . . I go way back on working on this [epidemic]—and to get it from Campbell, who just came out of his comfortable closet a year ago. . . . I think he has ideological reasons. He's out front, he says it makes gay people look bad. The fact is Patient Zero did exist. . . . It's a brilliant book, superb. . . . [The review is] more snide than *The Bay Area Reporter*. It's a nasty, vindictive attack. It's the only place I've gotten a bad review; the mainstream press loved my book."[9]

Indeed, the mainstream press did love Shilts's book. What Shilts does not say, but what he nevertheless makes clear, is that he returns their love. Ultimately he dismisses the Campbell review by saying that the *New Statesman* (a British equivalent to the *Nation* in the United States) is insignificant, a marginal publication. Shilts's book is in every way a product of his identification with the dominant media and their claim to objectivity. It is this claim that allows Shilts, along with the *New York Times*, for example, to disregard the demands of people with AIDS that they not be called AIDS victims. Not to do so would be to give in to a special interest group, a group with an ideological bias. Other groups with ideological biases meriting Shilts's disdain, for which there is ample evidence in *And the Band Played On*, are gay community leaders and AIDS activists.

"Personally, I'm not an ideological person," Shilts said at the ICA. "I don't think you can be a journalist and really have a political ideology, because you tend to see the fallacies in all ideologies." Speaking from this dangerously naive or cynically disingenuous ideological position that calls itself "objective," Shilts explains that "the whole problem of AIDS from the start was that liberals were trying to be sweet and not tell the whole story, and conservatives did not want to tell the whole story, and I felt what I wanted to do was get the whole story out. At some point I just have to say, I think my work has integrity. I think my work is honest."

9. Quoted in Kingston, "Controversy Follow Shilts," p. 11.

Shilts's defense of the Patient Zero story hinges entirely upon this naive notion of truth, on the fact, simply, that the story actually happened. But truth is never unproblematic, never a simple matter of empirical facts; it is always selective, always a particular construction, and always exists within a specific context. By the time the narrative of *And the Band Played On* ends, officially 6,079 people had died of AIDS in the United States. Shilts might have selected any one of those people's stories to tell. Among the very few he did select was that of Gaeton Dugas, which makes his story about one six-thousandth of the "truth."

Shilts selected Dugas's story, as he said at the ICA, because it was "fascinating." But what does it mean in the context of AIDS to be *fascinated*? What are the *unconscious* mechanisms that would account for this very selective will to truth? Is this not precisely what Shilts means when he says of the media that they are interested in sexy stories? Is this not, in fact, the recounting of a story that we already know? the story of Typhoid Mary? the story of the murderously irresponsible, sexually voracious gay man? Is this not the story of Fabian Bridges, as told on the 1986 PBS *Frontline* special "AIDS: A National Inquiry," in which a black homeless gay man with AIDS, who was forced to support himself by hustling, was bribed by the PBS crew in order to get their story and then reported to the authorities? Is it not the story of the bisexual deliberately infecting "innocent women" in the *Midnight Caller* episode of December 13, 1988, whose producers defended themselves against the protests of the San Francisco gay community by citing the Patient Zero story as proof that such things really do happen?[10] Is it not the story of Rock Hudson, as it was recounted before a jury who would award his ex-lover millions of dollars in damages? Is it not the story of prostitutes and junkies as the media portrays them every day? Is it not ultimately the story of all people with AIDS as they haunt the imaginations of those

10. "Mr. DiLello noted that Randy Shilts, in his acclaimed book about AIDS, 'And the Band Played On,' wrote about Gaetan Dugas, the man who may have brought AIDS to San Francisco and who continued to have a multitude of sexual partners even after learning that he was ill" (Stephen Farber, "AIDS Groups Protest Series Episode," *New York Times,* December 8, 1988, p. C24).

whose fear and loathing Shilts is so unable to comprehend? Is it not, finally, in the eyes of the INS, the story of Hans Paul Verhoef, the Dutchman they feared would spread AIDS at the Lesbian and Gay Health Conference?

The problem with the Patient Zero story is not whether or not it is true. We now know, in any case, that it is not, at least insofar as we know that Gaeton Dugas had sex with the other men in the CDC cluster study after they had already been infected. Nor is it merely the problem that this story was selected by Shilts's publishers as the story that would sell the book, and that they therefore gave it pride of place in their publicity and had it serialized in *California Magazine*.[11] The real problem with Patient Zero is that he already existed as a phobic fantasy in the minds of Shilts's readers before Shilts ever wrote the story. And, thanks in part to *And the Band Played On*, that fantasy still haunts us—as it still haunts Shilts— today. "I had written a book to change the world," Shilts says in *Esquire*.[12] What he forgot was that this is a world in which people's fantasies about homosexuality include gay waiters running into the kitchen to ejaculate in the salad dressing, or of gay foreigners attending health conferences with no other purpose than to infect their fellow conferees with a deadly virus. Patient Zero is just such a fantasy, and it matters not one whit whether his story is true or not.

1996 Postscript: History as Musical Comedy?

The question posed to this CLAGS panel, "*And the Band Played On: History as Mini-Series?*" arose, no doubt, for two reasons, first, because *And the Band Played On* had been widely acclaimed as the definitive history of the epidemic up to 1985, and second, because the rights to *And the Band Played On* had been purchased by Esther Shapiro, producer of the popular nighttime television soap opera *Dynasty*. Shilts's

11. October 1987 issue.
12. Shilts, "Talking AIDS to Death," p. 124.

book faithfully adopted the episodic form of the television series, itself a derivative of the Victorian serialized novel. Each of the stories Shilts's book recounts is interwoven with many others, and each passage of its telling leaves off at just the point where something especially dramatic is portended. Television's series format, in which each segment ends with the demand that we "tune in next time," is scrupulously followed by Shilts, keeping us in a constant state of suspenseful excitement.

When *And the Band Played On* finally made it to the television screen, however, it was not a mini-series but an HBO special movie in yet another TV format, the docudrama. Perhaps this pseudo-documentary formula seemed to the team of scriptwriters a more appropriate form of historical reporting. In any case, the fact that the film was still made after such a long delay, and that it met with great success, is testimony to the durability of Shilts's version of events of the early years of the AIDS epidemic. My undergraduate students often cite the HBO film as their most important source of information about AIDS.

The HBO movie greatly reduces the dramatis personae of Shilts's book, and it revolves around a single hero, Don Francis, an honorable and dedicated CDC epidemiologist. Patient Zero is still there, but less prominent and less sensationally portrayed than he is in the book. His function now is that of the reluctant but finally cooperative, if arrogant, participant in the CDC's cluster study (the accuracy and relevance of whose findings are left uncontested in the film), just one of many moments in the story of a heroic scientist as he relentlessly pursues the truth about AIDS against the obstacles thrown in his way by tightfisted government bureaucrats, other scientists with more ego than integrity, profiteering blood-bank executives, and gay activists who care only about preserving their overheated sex lives. Shilts acted as a consultant for the film.

At about the same time that *And the Band Played On* aired on national television, another version of the Patient Zero story appeared on movie screens to provide an off-beat but eloquent critique of Shilts's account. *Zero Patience,* independent Canadian filmmaker John Greyson's wacky musical comedy, stars a ghost named Zero and a Toronto Natural History Museum taxidermist named Dick. The only living being who can see and hear Zero, Dick is the Victorian orientalist and explorer Sir Richard Francis Burton, famous for his translation of *The Thousand and One Nights*. As the narrator explains, Burton's unfortunate encounter with the Fountain of Youth in 1892 extended his lifespan indefinitely. Now engaged in constructing a "Hall of Contagion" at the museum, Burton seizes on the story of "the man who brought AIDS to North America" as the crowning set piece of his exhibit. Zero's story is to be presented as a spectacular music video funded by a pharmaceutical company called Gilbert and Sullivan.

In preparing his video, Burton edits his filmed interviews in such a way as to distort his interlocutors' words, thus making them conform to his preconceived idea of Zero as a sexually insatiable gay "serial killer." Faced with Zero's mother's adamant refusal to be interviewed, Burton cajoles, "Think about how it could help someone else, another young man, another mother." Burton's camera surreptitiously records Madame Zero's reply: "That's just what the journalist said. Ever so smoothly, and I believed him. Well, he made it sound like Zero was the devil, bringing his boyfriends home, flaunting his life style under our noses. Zero never did that, not once." The beleaguered woman's words reappear in the edited tape: ". . . Zero was the devil, bringing his boyfriends home, flaunting his life style under our noses. . . ."

"Sometimes the facts have to be rearranged to get at the real truth," argues Burton when Zero confronts him. But, contrary perhaps to our expectations, Greyson's critique of Shilts does not consist of this charge of rearranging and misrepresenting the facts. Unquestionably, Greyson does intend to clear Zero's name. He makes his protagonist sexy, charming, and adorable, and never more so than at the moment when, having learned the truth about the CDC cluster study from none other than "Miss HIV," he proclaims with a broad grin, "I'm innocent. I'm *not* the first, but I'm still the best." Not only do we, the film's viewers, fall in love with Zero, but so does Burton, who decides in the end to refashion his exhibit to clear Zero's name. Recording a new narration for his video, he says, "Patient Zero should be proclaimed a hero of the epidemic. Through his cooperation in the 1982 cluster study, he helped prove that AIDS was sexually transmitted. Thus Zero should be lauded as the slut who inspired safer sex."

"Thanks for nothing," Zero responds. "This has nothing to do with me, with what I was, with what I want. . . . This is just another of your lies." What Zero really desires, Burton cannot give him: Zero wants his life back.

The point is that whatever spin Burton puts on the events, it's never Zero's story, it's Burton's. This is the real thrust of Greyson's critique of Shilts, for unlike Shilts, Greyson makes us aware at every moment that his film is, after all, only a story. Not for nothing is the fate of Scheherazade the film's framing conceit: "Tell a story, save a life, just like Scheherazade," sings Zero in the opening Esther Williams–style water ballet. What might seem wildly eccentric in *Zero Patience* is in fact strategic. That the story's protagonists are a ghost and a nineteenth-century figure still alive in the present; that their story is told through musical numbers that include a pair of singing assholes, a song-and-dance performance whose characters are animals from the natural history museum's dioramas suddenly sprung to life, and an HIV virus portrayed by Michael Callen in drag and singing falsetto in a Busby Berkeley–style routine seen through a microscope—what could more fully alert us to the *artifice*, the *invention* of this version of the Patient Zero story?

While every storytelling is a construction relying on the codes of its chosen genre, certain genres seek to obscure their conventions, to naturalize them, in order to pose as direct, transparent accounts of the facts, to provide what might be called a truth-effect. This is the case of most mainstream journalism and documentary filmmaking, but surely it is less germane to so-called creative nonfiction and TV docudrama. The latter fuses documentary and dramatic techniques to tell a story indistinguishable from fiction film, except that it is supposedly "a true story." The former derives its conventions from bourgeois fiction. Nevertheless, regarding the "creative" qualities of *And the Band Played On*, Shilts

John Greyson, *Zero Patience,* 1993 (photo: Rafy).

writes, "There has been no fictionalization. For purposes of narrative flow, I reconstruct scenes, recount conversations and occasionally attribute observations to people with such phrases as 'he thought' or 'she felt.'"[13] Thus, for Shilts, conventions meant to produce a truth-effect, even those clearly adopted from fiction, are mistaken for truth itself. His own labor to construct that "truth" is disavowed, and his only defense reinforces the disavowal: "The fact is, it all happened." "It was a fascinating story."

Zero Patience, too, tells a sexy story, but one that "happened" only through John Greyson's vivid imagination, political consciousness, and deft manipulation of filmic conventions. But our fascination with *this* story does not return us to one we already know. This story asks us to question what we think we know, how we come to know, what and how else we might know. For Shilts, history is the story of what actually happened. For Greyson, history is what we make by telling a story.

13. Randy Shilts, *And the Band Played On* (New York: St. Martin's Press, 1987), p. 607. Shilts adopted the novelistic form for his biography of Harvey Milk, *The Mayor of Castro Street* (1982), and used it consistently right through *Conduct Unbecoming* (1993).

7 MOURNING AND MILITANCY

First presented at the "Gay Men in Criticism" session

of the English Institute, Harvard University,

Cambridge, Massachusetts, August 24–27, 1989,

and published in OCTOBER *51 (winter 1989).*

In a contribution to a special issue of the *South Atlantic Quarterly* on "Displacing Homophobia," Lee Edelman applies the lessons of Derridian deconstruction to the AIDS activist movement slogan SILENCE= DEATH. Claiming that our slogan calls for a discourse of facts marshaled against a demagogic rhetoric, Edelman concludes that the equation unknowingly produces the literal as a figure, and thereby betrays its ideological entanglement in the binary logic of Western discourse.

Precisely because the defensive appeal to literality in a slogan like Silence=Death must produce the literal as a figure of the need and desire for the shelter of certain knowledge, such a discourse is always necessarily a dangerously contaminated defense—contaminated by the Derridian logic of metaphor so that its attempt to achieve a natural or literal discourse beyond rhetoricity must reproduce the suspect ideology of reified (and threatened) identity marking the reactionary medical and political discourse it would counteract. The discursive logic of Silence=Death thus contributes to the ideologically motivated confusion of the literal and the figural, the proper and the improper, the inside and the outside, and in the process it recalls the biology of the human immunodeficiency virus as it attacks the mechanism whereby the body is able . . . to distinguish between "Self and Not-Self." [1]

I do not think Edelman's deconstruction of the "text" of SILENCE= DEATH is necessarily wrong, but he seems to have very little sense of how the emblem functions for the movement. First, it is precisely as a figure that it does its work: as a striking image appearing on posters, placards, buttons, stickers, and T-shirts, its appeal is primarily graphic, and hardly therefore to be assimilated to a privileging of the logos. Second, it desires not a discourse of facts but direct action, the organized, militant enunciation of demands within a discursive field of *contested* facts. And finally, a question of address: for whom is this application of literary theory intended other than those within the academy who will

1. Lee Edelman, "The Plague of Discourse: Politics, Literary Theory, and AIDS," *South Atlantic Quarterly* 88, no. 1 (winter 1989), pp. 313–314.

find it, simply, interesting?[2] SILENCE=DEATH was produced and is employed for collective political struggle, and it entails altogether different problems for the community of AIDS activists. Taking our symbol literally holds for us a danger that goes unnoticed in Edelman's textual analysis: We ourselves are silent precisely on the subject of death, on how deeply it affects us.

I, too, will have something to say about the distinction between self and not-self, about the confusion of the inside and the outside, but I am impelled to do this *for us,* for my community of AIDS activists. Writing about mourning and militancy is for me both necessary and difficult, for I have seen that mourning troubles us; by "us" I mean gay men confronting AIDS. It should go without saying that it is not only gay men who confront AIDS, but because we face specific and often unique difficulties, and because I have some familiarity with them, I address them here exclusively. This essay is written for my fellow activists and friends, who have also informed it with their actions, their suggestions and encouragement—and in this I include many women as well. The conflicts I address are also my own, which might account for certain of the essay's shortcomings.

I will begin then with an anecdote about my own ambivalent mourning, though not of an AIDS death. In 1977, while I was visiting my family in Idaho, my father died unexpectedly. He and I had had a strained and increasingly distant relationship, and I was unable to feel or express my grief over his death. After the funeral I returned to New York for the opening of an exhibition I'd organized and resumed my usual life. But within a few weeks a symptom erupted which to this day leaves a scar near my nose: my left tear duct became badly infected, and the result-

2. For a retrospective corrective to this statement, see footnote 24 to the introduction of this volume. For a different critique of the slogan SILENCE=DEATH, see Stuart Marshall, "The Contemporary Use of Gay History: The Third Reich," in *How Do I Look? Queer Film and Video,* ed. Bad Object Choices (Seattle: Bay Press, 1991), pp. 65–102. See also Douglas Crimp, with Adam Rolston, *AIDS Demo Graphics* (Seattle: Bay Press, 1990).

ing abscess grew to a golf-ball sized swelling that closed my left eye and completely disfigured my face. When the abscess finally burst, the foul-smelling pus oozed down my cheek like poison tears. I have never since doubted the force of the unconscious. Nor can I doubt that mourning is a psychic process that must be honored. For many AIDS activists, however, mourning is not respected; it is suspect: "I look at faces at countless memorial services and cannot comprehend why the connection isn't made between these deaths and going out to fight so that more of these deaths, including possibly one's own, can be staved off. Huge numbers regularly show up in cities for Candlelight Marches, all duly recorded for the television cameras. Where are these same numbers when it comes to joining political organizations . . . or plugging in to the incipient civil disobedience movement represented in ACT UP?" These sentences are taken from a recent essay by Larry Kramer,[3] against whose sense of the quietism represented by AIDS candlelight marches I want to juxtapose the words of the organizer of this year's candlelight vigil on Christopher Street, addressed from the speaker's platform to the assembled mourners: "Look around!" he said, "This is the gay community, not ACT UP!"[4]

The presumption in this exhortation that no AIDS activists would be found among the mourners—whose ritual expression of grief is at the same time taken to be truer to the needs of the gay community—confidently inverts Kramer's rhetorical incomprehension, an incomprehension also expressed as antipathy: "I do not mean to diminish these sad rituals," Kramer writes, "though indeed I personally find them slightly ghoulish."[5]

Public mourning rituals may of course have their own political force, but they nevertheless often seem, from an activist perspective, indul-

3. Larry Kramer, "Report from the Holocaust," in *Reports from the Holocaust: The Making of an AIDS Activist* (New York: St. Martin's Press, 1989), pp. 264–265.
4. The remark of Red Maloney was the subject of a letter written by Naphtali Offen to *Outweek* 4 (July 17, 1989), p. 6.
5. Kramer, "Report from the Holocaust," p. 264.

gent, sentimental, defeatist—a perspective only reinforced, as Kramer implies, by media constructions of us as hapless victims. "Don't mourn, organize!"—the last words of labor movement martyr Joe Hill—is still a rallying cry, at least in its New Age variant, "Turn your grief to anger," which assumes not so much that mourning can be forgone as that the psychic process can simply be converted.[6] This move from prohibition to transformation only *appears*, however, to include a psychic component in activism's response, for ultimately both rallying cries depend on a definite answer to the question posed by Reich to Freud: "Where does the misery come from?" Activist antagonism to mourning hinges, in part, on how AIDS is interpreted, or rather, where the emphasis is laid, on whether the crisis is seen to be a natural, accidental catastrophe—a disease syndrome that has simply struck at this time and in this place—or as the result of gross political negligence or mendacity—an epidemic that was allowed to happen.

But leaving aside, only for the moment, the larger political question, I want to attend to the internal opposition of activism and mourning. That the two are incompatible is clear enough in Freud's description of the work of mourning, which he calls "absorbing." "Profound mourning," Freud writes in "Mourning and Melancholia," involves a "*turning away from every active effort* that is not connected with thoughts of the dead. It is easy to see that this inhibition and circumscription in the ego is the expression of an *exclusive* devotion to its mourning, *which leaves nothing over for other purposes or other interests.*"[7] Although Freud's

---

6. Joe Hill's statement is also quoted by Michael Bronski in an essay that takes up some of the issues discussed here; see his "Death and the Erotic Imagination," in *Taking Liberties: AIDS and Cultural Politics,* ed. Erica Carter and Simon Watney (London: Serpent's Tail in association with the ICA, 1989), pp. 219–228. The pop psychological/ metaphysical notions of New Age "healers"—such as the particularly repulsive idea that people choose illness to give meaning to their lives—are considered by Allan Bérubé in "Caught in the Storm: AIDS and the Meaning of Natural Disaster," *Outlook* 1, no. 3 (fall 1988), pp. 8–19.

7. Sigmund Freud, "Mourning and Melancholia," in John Rickman, ed., *A General Selection from the Works of Sigmund Freud* (New York: Anchor Books, 1989), pp. 125–126 (emphasis added).

account of this process is well known, I want to repeat it here in order to underscore its exclusive character:

The testing of reality, having shown that the loved object no longer exists, requires forthwith that all the libido shall be withdrawn from its attachments to this object. Against this demand a struggle of course arises—it may be universally observed that man never willingly abandons a libido-position, not even when a substitute is already beckoning to him. This struggle can be so intense that a turning away from reality ensues, the object being clung to through the medium of a hallucinatory wish-psychosis. The normal outcome is that deference for reality gains the day. Nevertheless its behest cannot be at once obeyed. The task is now carried through bit by bit, under great expense of time and cathectic energy, while all the time the existence of the lost object is continued in the mind. Each single one of the memories and hopes which bound the libido to the object is brought up and hyper-cathected, and the detachment of the libido from it accomplished.[8]

In an important paper about mourning in the time of AIDS, which turns on a reading of Walt Whitman's "Drum-Taps" poems, Michael Moon argues that Freud's view of mourning presents a difficulty for gay people, insofar as it promises a return to a normalcy that we were never granted in the first place: "As lesbians and gay men," Moon writes, "most of us are familiar with the experience of having been categorically excluded from 'normalcy' at critical junctures in our lives. Having been through as much as most of us have in both our personal and collective struggles to get our own needs recognized, acknowledged, accepted, sometimes fulfilled, the Freudian model of mourning may well look fundamentally normalizing and consequently privative, diminishing the process and foreclosing its possible meaning rather than enriching it or making it more accessible to understanding."[9]

8. Ibid., p. 126.
9. Michael Moon, "Memorial Rags," paper presented in a session entitled "AIDS and the Profession" at the 1988 MLA convention, manuscript. Thanks to Michael Moon for making this paper available to me.

Probably no gay man or lesbian can have an untroubled response to Freud, but we must nevertheless take care to maintain a crucial distinction: the ambition to normalize, to adapt, belongs not to Freud but to his later "egocentric" revisionists, to whom gay people owe a good portion of our oppression. This is not to say that there is no vision of normalcy in Freud, only that there is also no such thing as ever fully achieving it, *for anyone.* Freud *does* refer to mourning as a "grave departure from the normal attitude to life,"[10] but what that normal attitude is in this context can be learned easily enough by reading his characterization of the state to which we return after the work of mourning is accomplished: very simply, "deference for reality gains the day," and "the ego becomes free and uninhibited again."[11]

So rather than looking beyond "Mourning and Melancholia" for other possibilities—Moon proposes fetishism, but a fetishism rescued from Freud's 1927 account by making it a *conscious* means of extending our homoerotic relations, even with the dead—I want to stay with Freud's earlier text, to read it in relation to the conflicts many of us now experience. First, two preliminary caveats: "Mourning and Melancholia" is not a theory of mourning as such, but of pathological mourning, that is, of melancholia. Moon is therefore right when he says that Freud's view of mourning only repeats conventional wisdom; it purports to do no more than describe mourning's dynamic process. Second, Freud can tell us very little about our grieving rituals, our memorial services and candlelight marches. Of our communal mourning, perhaps only the Names Project quilt displays something of the psychic work of mourning, insofar as each individual panel symbolizes—through its incorporation of mementos associated with the lost object—the activity of hyper-cathecting and detaching the hopes and memories associated with the loved one. But as against this often shared activity, mourning, for Freud, is a solitary undertaking. And our trouble begins here, for, from the outset, there is already a social interdiction of our private efforts. In the opening pages of *Policing Desire,* Simon Watney recounts a funeral

10. Freud, "Mourning and Melancholia," p. 125.
11. Ibid., pp. 126, 127.

service similar to those many of us have experienced, an event that made him decide "then and there" that he would write his book on AIDS:

[Bruno's] funeral took place in an ancient Norman church on the outskirts of London. No mention was made of AIDS. Bruno had died, bravely, of an unspecified disease. In the congregation of some forty people there were two other gay men besides myself, both of whom had been his lover. They had been far closer to Bruno than anyone else present, except his parents. Yet their grief had to be contained within the confines of manly acceptability. The irony of the difference between the suffocating life of the suburbs where we found ourselves, and the knowledge of the world in which Bruno had actually lived, as a magnificently affirmative and life-enhancing gay man, was all but unbearable.[12]

Because Watney's anecdote is meant to explain his determination to write a polemic, it also suggests what has happened to mourning. It is not only that at this moment of society's demand for hypocrisy the three gay men had to conceal their grief, but also that their fond memories of Bruno as a gay man are thereby associated with the social opprobrium that attaches to them. When these memories are then recalled, hyper-cathexis may well be met with a defense, a need to preserve Bruno's world intact against the contempt in which it is commonly held. "My friend was not called Bruno," Watney adds. "His father asked me not to use his real name. And so the anonymity is complete. The garrulous babble of commentary on AIDS constructs yet another 'victim.' It is this babble which is my subject matter, the cacophony of voices which sounds through every institution of our society on the subject of AIDS."[13]

Thus one of our foremost international AIDS activists became engaged in the struggle; no further memories of Bruno are invoked. It is probably no exaggeration to say that each of us has a story like this, that during the AIDS crisis there is an all but inevitable connection between the mem-

12. Simon Watney, *Policing Desire: Pornography, AIDS, and the Media* (Minneapolis: University of Minnesota Press, 1987), p. 7.
13. Ibid., p. 8.

ories and hopes associated with our lost friends and the daily assaults on our consciousness. Seldom has a society so savaged people during their hour of loss. "We look upon any interference with [mourning] as inadvisable or even harmful," warns Freud.[14] But for anyone living daily with the AIDS crisis, ruthless interference with our bereavement is as ordinary an occurrence as reading the *New York Times*.[15] The violence we encounter is relentless, the violence of silence and omission almost as impossible to endure as the violence of unleashed hatred and outright murder. Because this violence also desecrates the memories of our dead, we rise in anger to vindicate them. For many of us, mourning *becomes* militancy. Freud does not say what might happen if mourning is interfered with, but insofar as our conscious defenses direct us toward social action, they already show the deference to reality that Freud attributes to mourning's accomplishment. Nevertheless we have to ask just how, against what odds, and with what unconscious effects this has been achieved.

The activist impulse may be reinforced by a second conflict within the process of mourning. "Reality," Freud explains, "passes its verdict—

14. Freud, "Mourning and Melancholia," p. 125.
15. The *New York Times*'s reporting of AIDS issues—or rather its failure to report them accurately or at all—is probably the most persistent scandal of the AIDS epidemic. Larry Kramer gave a detailed accounting of the scandal on a panel discussion of AIDS in the print media organized by the PEN American Center in New York City on May 11, 1989. In the summer of 1989, the *Times* ran an editorial that both typified its position throughout the history of the epidemic and reached new heights of callousness. Implicitly claiming once again that *its* presumed readers had little to worry about, since "the disease is still very largely confined to specific risk groups," the writer went on to say, cheerily, "Once all susceptible members [of these groups] are infected, the numbers of new victims will decline." The newspaper's simple writing off of the lives of gay men, IV drug users, their sex partners and children—a mere 200,000–400,000 people *already* estimated to be HIV-infected in New York City alone—triggered an ACT UP demonstration, which was in turn thwarted by perhaps the largest police presence at any AIDS activist demonstration to date. ACT UP stickers saying "Buy Your Lies Here. The *New York Times* Reports Half the Truth about AIDS" still adorn newsstands in New York City, while the coin slots of *Times* vending machines are covered with stickers that read "*The New York Times* AIDS Reporting is OUT OF ORDER." The *Times* editorial is reproduced as part of a Gran Fury project entitled "Control" in *Artforum* 27, no. 2 (October 1989), p. 167.

that the object no longer exists—upon each single one of the memories and hopes through which the libido was attached to the lost object, and the ego, confronted as it were with the decision whether it will share this fate, is persuaded by the sum of its narcissistic satisfactions in being alive to sever its attachment to the non-existent object."[16] But this confrontation with reality is especially fraught for gay men mourning now, since our decision whether we will share this fate is so unsure. For people with AIDS, the HIV-infected, and those at significant risk whose sero-status is unknown to them, narcissistic satisfactions in *still* being alive *today* can persuade us, will undoubtedly persuade us in our unconscious, to relinquish our attachments. But how are we to dissociate our narcissistic satisfactions in being alive from our fight to stay alive? And, insofar as we *identify* with those who have died, how can our satisfactions in being alive escape guilt at having survived?[17]

Upholding the memories of our lost friends and lovers and resolving that we ourselves shall live would seem to impose the same demand: resist! Mourning feels too much like capitulation. But we must recognize that our memories and our resolve also entail the more painful feelings

16. Freud, "Mourning and Melancholia," pp. 136–137.
17. The decision not to share the fate of the lost object, as well as guilt at having survived, are certainly problems of mourning for everyone. Clearly insofar as any death brings us face to face with our own mortality, identification with the lost object is something we all feel. Thus this difficulty of mourning is certainly not gay men's alone. I only wish to emphasize its exacerbation for gay men to the extent that we are directly and immediately implicated in the particular cause of these deaths, and implicated, as well, through the specific nature of our deepest pleasures in life—our gay sexuality. Simon Watney has urged that this very implication be taken as the reason for forming consensus among gay men about AIDS activism: "I believe that the single, central factor of greatest significance for all gay men should be the recognition that the current HIV antibody status of everyone who had unprotected sex in the long years before the virus was discovered is a matter of *sheer coincidence.* . . . Every gay man who had the good fortune to remain uninfected in the decade or so before the emergence of safer sex should meditate most profoundly on the whim of fate that spared him, but not others. Those of us who chance to be seronegative have *an absolute and unconditional responsibility* for the welfare of seropositive gay men" (Simon Watney, "'The Possibilities of Permutation': Pleasure, Proliferation, and the Politics of Gay Identity in the Age of AIDS," in *Fluid Exhanges: Artists and Critics in the AIDS: Crisis,* ed. James Miller [Toronto: University of Toronto Press, 1992]).

of survivor's guilt, often exacerbated by our secret wishes, during our lovers' and friends' protracted illnesses, that they would just die and let us get on with our lives.

We can then partially revise our sense—and Freud's—of the incompatibility between mourning and activism and say that, for many gay men dealing with AIDS deaths, militancy might arise from conscious conflicts *within* mourning itself, the consequence, on the one hand, of "inadvisable and even harmful interference" with grief and, on the other, of the impossibility of deciding whether the mourner will share the fate of the mourned. But because mourning is a psychic process, conscious reactions to external interference cannot tell the whole story. What is far more difficult to determine is how these reactions are influenced by already existing unconscious strife. Only by recognizing the role of the unconscious, however, will we be able to understand the relationship between the external obstacles to our grief and our own antagonism to mourning. But I want to be clear: It is because our impatience with mourning is burdensome for the movement that I am seeking to understand it. I have no interest in proposing a "psychogenesis" of AIDS activism. The social and political barbarism we daily encounter requires no explanation whatsoever for our militancy. On the contrary, what may require an explanation, as Larry Kramer's plaint suggested, is the quietism.

At the weekly ACT UP meetings in New York, regularly attended by about 400 people, I am struck by the fact that only a handful are of my generation, the Stonewall generation. The vast majority are post-Stonewall, born hardly earlier than the gay liberation movement itself, and their losses differ in one significant respect from ours. Last year one of these young men said something to me that said it all. A group of us had seen an early '70s film at the Gay and Lesbian Experimental Film Festival and went out for drinks afterwards. The young man was very excited about what seemed to me a pretty ordinary sex scene in the film, but then he said, "I'd give anything to know what cum tastes like, somebody else's that is." That broke my heart, for two reasons: for him because he didn't know, for me because I do.

Freud tells us that mourning is the reaction not only to the death of a loved person, but also "to the loss of some abstraction which has taken the place of one, such as fatherland, liberty, an ideal. . . ."[18] Can we be allowed to include, in this "civilized" list, the ideal of perverse sexual pleasure itself rather than one stemming from its sublimation? Alongside the dismal toll of death, what many of us have lost is a culture of sexual possibility: back rooms, tea rooms, bookstores, movie houses, and baths; the trucks, the pier, the ramble, the dunes. Sex was everywhere for us, and everything we wanted to venture: golden showers and water sports, cocksucking and rimming, fucking and fist fucking. Now our untamed impulses are either proscribed once again or shielded from us by latex. Even Crisco, the lube we used because it was edible, is now forbidden because it breaks down the rubber. Sex toys are no longer added enhancements; they're safer substitutes.

For those who have obeyed civilization's law of compulsory genital heterosexuality, the options we've lost might seem abstract enough. Not widely acknowledged until the advent of the AIDS crisis, our sex lives are now publicly scrutinized with fascination and envy, only partially masked by feigned incredulity (William Dannemeyer, for example, entered into the *Congressional Record* of June 26, 1989 the list of pleasures I just enumerated). To say that we miss uninhibited and unprotected sex as we miss our lovers and friends will hardly solicit solidarity, even tolerance. But tolerance is, as Pier Paolo Pasolini said, "always and purely nominal," merely "a more refined form of condemnation."[19] AIDS has further proved his point. Our pleasures were never tolerated anyway; we took them. And now we must mourn them too.

When, in mourning our ideal, we meet with the same opprobrium as when mourning our dead, we incur a different order of psychic distress, since the memories of our pleasures are already fraught with ambivalence. The abject repudiation of their sexual pasts by many gay men tes-

18. Freud, "Mourning and Melancholia," p. 125.
19. Pier Paolo Pasolini, "Gennariello," in *Lutheran Letters,* trans. Stuart Hood (Manchester: Carcanet New Press, 1983), pp. 21–22.

tifies to that ambivalence, even as the widespread adoption of safe sex practices vouches for our ability to work through it. Perhaps we may even think of safe sex as the substitute libido-position that beckoned to us as we mourned our lost sexual ideal. But here, I think, the difference between generations of gay men makes itself felt most sharply. For men now in their twenties, our sexual ideal is mostly just that—an ideal, the cum never swallowed. Embracing safe sex is for them an act of defiance, and its promotion is perhaps the AIDS activist movement's least inhibited stance. But for many men of the Stonewall generation, who have also been the gay population thus far hardest hit by AIDS, safe sex may seem less like defiance than resignation, less like accomplished mourning than melancholia. I don't want to suggest that there is anything pathological about this disposition, but it does comprise many features of melancholia as Freud describes it, especially if considered in the context of its causes.

"The occasions giving rise to melancholia," Freud writes, "for the most part extend beyond the clear case of a loss by death, and include all those situations of being wounded, hurt, neglected, out of favor, or disappointed, which can . . . reinforce an already existing ambivalence."[20] Although Freud's theory concerns an object relationship, if we transpose these situations to the social sphere, they describe very perfectly the condition of gay men during the AIDS crisis, as regards both our rejection and our self-doubt. In Freud's analysis, melancholia differs from mourning in a single feature: "a fall in self-esteem":[21] "In grief the world becomes poor and empty; in melancholia it is the ego itself [which becomes poor and empty]."[22] And this lowering of self-esteem, Freud insists, is "predominantly moral";[23] it is a "dissatisfaction with the self on moral grounds."[24] "The patient represents his ego to us as worthless, incapable of any effort, and morally despicable; he reproaches himself,

20. Freud, "Mourning and Melancholia," p. 132.
21. Ibid., p. 125.
22. Ibid., p. 127.
23. Ibid., p. 128.
24. Ibid., p. 129.

vilifies himself, and expects to be cast out and chastised."[25] "In his exacerbation of self-criticism he describes himself as petty, egoistic, dishonest, lacking in independence, one whose sole aim has been to hide the weaknesses of his own nature. . . ."[26] Moreover, the melancholiac "does not realize that any change has taken place in him, but extends his self-criticism back over the past and declares that he was never any better."[27]

This moralizing self-abasement is only too familiar to us in the response of certain gay men to AIDS— *too* familiar especially because the media have been so happy to give them voice as our spokesmen. Randy Shilts comes readily to mind, and though I've dealt with him elsewhere,[28] it is worth mentioning in this context that he was chosen as our representative to address the closing ceremonies of the Fifth International AIDS Conference in Montreal, where he obliged his hosts with an attack on the militancy of international AIDS activists attending the conference. But there is a recent example that is even more groveling: the book *After the Ball*, an aptly titled sequel to Shilts's *And the Band Played On*, whose authority it cites approvingly, and whose "Patient Zero" continues here to play his unhappy role. This flyleaf-described "gay manifesto for the nineties," published by Doubleday, is the dirty work of two Harvard-trained social scientists, one of whom now designs aptitude tests for people with high IQs, while the other is a Madison Avenue PR consultant whose specialty is creating "positive images" for what the two of them call "'silent majority' gays." Informed by the latest trends in sociobiology, Marshall Kirk and Hunter Madsen have devised a program to eradicate homophobia—which they prefer to call homo-hatred so as to deny its unconscious force. Their proposal centers on a media campaign whose basis is the denial of difference. "A good beginning would be to take a long look at Coors beer . . . commercials," they suggest.[29]

25. Ibid., p. 127.
26. Ibid., p. 128.
27. Ibid., pp. 127–128.
28. See "How to Have Promiscuity in an Epidemic," this volume.
29. Marshall Kirk and Hunter Madsen, *After the Ball: How America Will Conquer Its Fear and Hatred of Gays in the '90s* (New York: Doubleday, 1989), p. 154.

But copying Coors ads does not stop with creating "positive" images. We have to "clean up our act," they say, and live up to those images.[30] This means purging our community of "'fringe' gay groups"—drag queens, radical fairies, pederasts, bull dykes, and other assorted scum.

Clearly we can take this book seriously only as a symptom of malaise— in its excoriation of gay culture, it bears every distinguishing characteristic of melancholia Freud specifies. Moreover, its accusations are also self-accusations: "*We,* the authors, are every bit as guilty of a lot of the nastiness we describe as are other gays," the Harvard boys confess. "This makes us not less qualified to inveigh against such evils but, if anything, even more so."[31] The authors' indictments of gay men are utterly predictable: We lie, deny reality, have no moral standards; we are narcissistic, self-indulgent, self-destructive, unable to love or even form lasting friendships; we flaunt it in public, abuse alcohol and drugs; and our community leaders and intellectuals are fascists.[32] Here are a few sample statements:

When we first delved into the gay urban demimonde, *we assumed that they held, if not our values, a least* some *values. We were quickly disabused of this notion.*

As the works of many students of sociopathic personality assert, a surprisingly high percentage of pathological liars are, in fact, gay.

The gay bar is the arena of sexual competition, and it brings out all that is most loathsome in human nature. Here, stripped of the facade of wit and cheer, gays stand nakedly revealed as single-minded, selfish sexual predators.[33]

30. "Cleaning Up Our Act" is actually a subheading of the book's final chapter, which concludes with "A Self-Policing Code."
31. Kirk and Madsen, *After the Ball,* p. 278.
32. These accusations appear in chapter 6: "The State of Our Community: Gay Pride Goeth before a Fall."
33. Kirk and Madsen, *After the Ball,* pp. 292, 283, 313.

Therefore, "straights hate gays not just for what their myths and lies *say* we are, but also for what we *really* are."[34] This is the only line in the book with which I agree; and it is a statement that, if taken seriously, means that no sociological account of homophobia will explain or counteract it. Kirk and Madsen's reliance on homophobic myths to describe what we really are demonstrates, in any case, not their understanding of homophobia, but their complete identification with it.

Although melancholia, too, depends on the psychic process of identification and introjection, I will not press the point. No matter how extreme the self-hatred, I am loath for obvious reasons to accuse gay men of any *pathological* condition. I only want to draw an analogy between pathological mourning and the sorry need of some gay men to look on our imperfectly liberated past as immature and immoral. But I will not resist a final word from Freud on melancholia, taken this time from "The Ego and the Id": "What is now holding sway in the super-ego is, as it were, a pure culture of the death-instinct."[35]

ACT UP, the AIDS Coalition to Unleash Power, was founded in March of 1987 in response to a speech at New York's Gay and Lesbian Community Center by Larry Kramer. In his inimitable manner of combining incomprehension and harangue, Kramer chided, "I sometimes think we have a death wish. I think we must want to die. I have never been able to understand why for six long years we have sat back and let ourselves literally be knocked off man by man—without fighting back. I have heard of denial, but this is more than denial; this *is* a death wish."[36]

Nearly two years later, in a mean-spirited, divisive attack on AIDS activism published by the *Nation,* Darrell Yates Rist accused ACT UP— entirely falsely—of ignoring any gay issue but AIDS. After recalling a visit to San Francisco's Tenderloin district, in which he encountered teenage gay runaways and hustlers, Rist continued, "I had just spent a night

34. Ibid., p. 276.
35. Sigmund Freud, *The Ego and the Id* (New York: W.W. Norton, 1962), p. 43.
36. Kramer, "Report from the Holocaust," p. 128.

among those abandoned adolescents when, at a dinner in the Castro, I listened to the other guests talk about nothing but AIDS, the dead, the dying—which to their minds included every gay man in the city: fashionable hysteria. 'This,' one of the them actually said, 'is the only thing worth fighting for.' Not long before, I'd heard Larry Kramer, playwright and AIDS activist, say something like that too, and had felt, in that suffocating moment, that finally we'd all gone suicidal, that we'd die of our own death wish."[37] It is between these two allegations of a death-wish—one because we were not yet AIDS activists, the other because we now are—that I want to frame the remainder of my discussion.

It might appear from what I've outlined so far that gay men's responses to the enormous losses suffered in the AIDS epidemic are predictable. This is far from the case, and is only the result of my schematic reading of "Mourning and Melancholia" against what I know of our experiences. I have accounted for neither the full depth and variety of our conflicts nor the multiplicity of their possible outcomes. What I offer to rectify this inadequacy is simply a list, to which anyone might add, of the problems we face.

Most people dying of AIDS are very young, and those of us coping with these deaths, ourselves also young, have confronted great loss entirely unprepared. The numbers of deaths are unthinkable: Lovers, friends, acquaintances, and community members have fallen ill and died. Many have lost upwards of a hundred people. Apart from the deaths, we contend with the gruesome illness itself, acting as caretakers, often for very extended periods, making innumerable hospital visits, providing emotional support, negotiating our wholly inadequate and inhuman health care and social welfare systems, keeping abreast of experimental treatment therapies. Some of us have learned as much or more than most doctors about the complex medicine of AIDS. Added to the caretaking

37. Darrell Yates Rist, "The Deadly Costs of an Obsession," *Nation,* February 13, 1989, p. 181. For the response of ACT UP, among others, see the issues of March 20 and May 1, 1989. For an impassioned discussion of the entire debate, see also Watney, "'The Possibilities of Permutation.'"

and loss of others is often the need to monitor and make treatment decisions about our own HIV illness, or face anxiety about our own health status.[38]

Through the turmoil imposed by illness and death, the rest of society offers little support or even acknowledgment. On the contrary, we are blamed, belittled, excluded, derided. We are discriminated against, lose our housing and jobs, denied medical and life insurance. Every public agency whose job it is to combat the epidemic has been slow to act, failed entirely, or been deliberately counterproductive. We have therefore had to provide our own centers for support, care, and education and even to fund and conduct our own treatment research. We have had to rebuild our devastated community and culture, reconstruct our sexual relationships, reinvent our sexual pleasure. Despite great achievements in so short a time and under such adversity, the dominant media still pictures us only as wasting deathbed victims; we have therefore had to wage a war of representation, too.

Frustration, anger, rage, and outrage, anxiety, fear, and terror, shame and guilt, sadness and despair—it is not surprising that we feel these things; what is surprising is that we often don't. For those who feel only a deadening numbness or constant depression, militant rage may well be unimaginable, as again it might be for those who are paralyzed with fear, filled with remorse, or overcome with guilt. To decry these responses—our own form of moralism—is to deny the extent of the violence we have all endured; even more important, it is to deny a fundamental fact of psychic life: violence is also self-inflicted.

The most contested theoretical concept in the later work of Freud is the drive to death, the drive that competes with the life instincts and com-

38. It seems to me particularly telling that throughout the epidemic the dominant media has routinely featured stories about anxieties provoked by AIDS—the anxieties of health-care workers and cops exposed to needle sticks, of parents whose children attend schools with a child who has been infected with HIV, of straight women who once upon a time had a bisexual lover . . . but I have never once seen a story about the millions of gay men who have constantly lived with these anxieties since 1981.

prises both aggression and self-aggression. It was over this concept that Reich broke with Freud, insisting that with the death drive Freud definitively side-stepped the social causes of human misery. But, against Reich's objection, and that of other early proponents of a political psychoanalysis, Jacqueline Rose argues that it is *only* through the concept of the death drive that we can understand the relationship between psychic and social life, as we seek to determine "where to locate the violence."[39] As opposed to Darrell Yates Rist's pop-psychology assertion that activists have a death wish, I want to suggest on the contrary that we do not acknowledge the death drive. That is, we disavow the knowledge that our misery comes from within as well as without, that it is the result of psychic as well as of social conflict—or rather, as Rose writes, our misery "is not something that can be located on the inside or the outside, in the psychic or the social . . . , but rather something that appears as the effect of the dichotomy itself."[40] By making all violence external, pushing it to the outside and objectifying it in "enemy" institutions and individuals, we deny its psychic articulation, deny that we are effected, as well as affected, by it.

Perhaps an example will clarify my point. The issue of HIV antibody testing has been a central concern for AIDS activists from the moment the movement was formed. We have insisted, against every attempt to implement mandatory or confidential testing, on the absolute right of voluntary *anonymous* testing. At the International AIDS Conference in Montreal in June of 1989, Stephen Joseph, health commissioner of New York City, called for confidential testing with mandatory contact tracing, based on the fact that immune-system monitoring and early treatment intervention for those who are HIV-positive could now prolong and perhaps save their lives. We immediately raised all the proper objections to his cynical proposal: that only if anonymity is guaranteed will people get tested, that New York has too few testing sites to accom-

39. Jacqueline Rose, "Where Does the Misery Come From?" in *Feminism and Psychoanalysis,* ed. Richard Feldstein and Judith Roof (Ithaca: Cornell University Press, 1989), p. 28.
40. Ibid.

modate the people wishing to be tested as it is, and that the services necessary to care for people who test positive cannot even accommodate the current caseload. Agreeing that testing, counseling, monitoring, and early treatment intervention are indeed crucial, we demanded instead an increase in the number of anonymous testing sites and a system of neighborhood walk-in HIV clinics for monitoring and treatment. We were entirely confident of the validity of our protests and demands. We know the history of Stephen Joseph's provocations, we know the city government's dismal failure to provide health care for its huge infected population, and we know not only the advantages of early intervention but also exactly what the treatment options are.

But with all this secure knowledge, we forget one thing: our own ambivalence about being tested, or, if seropositive, about making difficult treatment decisions. For all the hours of floor discussion about demanding wide availability of testing and treatment, we do not always avail *ourselves* of them, and we seldom discuss our anxiety and indecision.[41] Very shortly after Joseph's announcement in Montreal and our successful mobilization against his plan,[42] Mark Harrington, a member of ACT UP's Treatment and Data Committee, made an announcement at a Monday-night meeting: "I personally know three people in this

41. I do not wish to claim that the "right" decision is to be tested. AIDS activists insist quite properly only on choice, and on the viability of that choice through universally available health care. But problems of HIV testing are not only sociopolitical; they are also psychic. In "AIDS and Needless Deaths: How Early Treatment Is Ignored," Paul Harding Douglas and Laura Pinsky enumerate a series of barriers to early intervention in HIV disease, including lack of advocacy, lack of media coverage, lack of services, and, crucially, "The Symbolic Meaning of Early Intervention for the Individual." This final section of their paper provides a much-needed analysis of psychic resistance to taking the HIV antibody test. I wish to thank Paul Douglas and Laura Pinsky for making their paper available to me.

42. The successes of the AIDS activist movement are, unfortunately, never secure. In the late fall of 1989, during the transition from Ed Koch's mayoralty to that of David Dinkins, Stephen Joseph resigned his position as health commissioner. But not without a parting insult to those of us who had opposed his policies all along: Once again, and now with the full support of the New York City Board of Health, Joseph asked the state health department to collect the names of people who test positive to HIV and to trace and contact their sex partners and those with whom they shared needles.

group who recently came down with PCP [*Pneumocystis carinii* pneumonia]," he said. "We have to realize that activism is not a prophylaxis against opportunistic infections; it may be synergistic with aerosolized pentamidine [a drug used prophylactically against PCP], but it won't on its own prevent you from getting AIDS."

By referring to Freud's concept of the death drive, I am not saying anything so simple as that a drive to death directly prevents us from protecting ourselves against illness. Rather I am saying that by ignoring the death drive, that is, by making all violence external, we fail to confront ourselves, to acknowledge our ambivalence, to comprehend that our misery is also self-inflicted. To return to my example: It is not only New York City's collapsing health-care system and its sinister health commissioner that affect our fate. Unconscious conflict can mean that we may make decisions—or fail to make them—whose results may be deadly too. And the rage we direct against Stephen Joseph, justified as it is, may function as the very mechanism of our disavowal, whereby we convince ourselves that we are making all the decisions we need to make.

Again I want to be very clear: The fact that our militancy may be a means of dangerous denial in no way suggests that activism is unwarranted. There is no question but that we must fight the unspeakable violence we incur from the society in which we find ourselves. But if we understand that violence is able to reap its horrible rewards through the very psychic mechanisms that make us part of this society, then we may also be able to recognize—along with our rage—our terror, our guilt, and our profound sadness. Militancy, of course, then, but mourning too: mourning *and* militancy.

8 THE BOYS IN MY BEDROOM

First presented at the panel discussion

"Postmodernisn and Its Discontents," Whitney

Museum of American Art, New York, November 5,

1989, and published in Art in America, *February*

1990. This is a revised version first published in The

Lesbian and Gay Studies Reader, *ed. Henry Abelove,*

Michèle Aina Barale, and David M. Halperin (New

York: Routledge, 1993).

In 1983, I was asked to contribute to the catalog of an exhibition about the postmodernist strategy of appropriation organized by the Institute of Contemporary Art in Philadelphia—a museum now placed on probation by the National Endowment for the Arts.[1] I chose as a negative example—an example, that is, of old-fashioned *modernist* appropriation—the photography of Robert Mapplethorpe. Here is part of what I wrote:

Mapplethorpe's photographs, whether portraits, nudes or still lifes (and it is not coincidental that they fall so neatly into these traditional artistic genres), appropriate the stylistics of prewar studio photography. Their compositions, poses, lighting, and even their subjects (mondain personalities, glacial nudes, tulips) recall Vanity Fair and Vogue at that historical juncture when such artists as Edward Steichen and Man Ray contributed to those publications their intimate knowledge of international art photography. Mapplethorpe's abstraction and fetishization of objects thus refer, through the mediation of the fashion industry, to Edward Weston, while his abstraction of the subject *refers to the neoclassical pretenses of George Platt Lynes.*[2]

In contrast to Mapplethorpe's conventional borrowings, I posed the work of Sherrie Levine:

When Levine wished to make reference to Edward Weston and to the photographic variant of the neoclassical nude, she did so by simply rephotographing Weston's pictures of his young son Neil—no combinations, no transformations, no additions, no synthesis. . . . In such an undisguised theft of already existing images, Levine lays no claim to conven-

1. As punishment for having organized *Robert Mapplethorpe: The Perfect Moment* with funding approved by the National Endowment for the Arts, the ICA was subjected, through an amendment to a 1989 congressional appropriations measure, to a five-year probationary period during which its activities would be specially scrutinized by the NEA.

2. Douglas Crimp, "Appropriating Appropriation," in *Image Scavengers: Photography* (Philadelphia: Institute of Contemporary Art, 1982), p. 30.

The Boys in My Bedroom

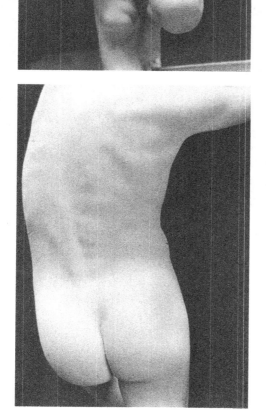

Sherrie Levine, *Untitled (After Edward Weston)*, 1981.

Robert Mapplethorpe, *Michael Reed*, 1987

(© The Estate of Robert Mapplethorpe.Used with permission).

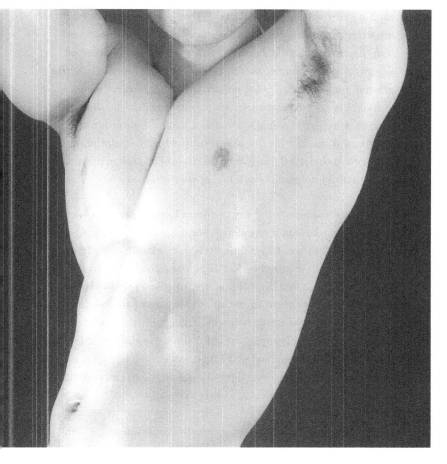

Robert Mapplethorpe, *Torso,* 1985

(© The Estate of Robert Mapplethorpe. Used with permission).

tional notions of artistic creativity. She makes use of the images, but not to constitute a style of her own. Her appropriations have only functional value for the particular historical discourses into which they are inserted. In the case of the Weston nudes, that discourse is the very one in which Mapplethorpe's photographs naively participate. In this respect, Levine's appropriation reflects on the strategy of appropriation itself—the appropriation by Weston of classical sculptural style; the appropriation by Mapplethorpe of Weston's style; the appropriation by the institutions of high art of both Weston and Mapplethorpe, indeed of photography in general; and finally, photography as a tool of appropriation.[3]

For several years I had hanging in my bedroom Levine's series of Weston's young male nudes. On a number of occasions, a certain kind of visitor to my bedroom would ask me, "Who's the kid in the photographs?" generally with the implication that I was into child pornography. Wanting to counter that implication, but unable easily to explain what those photographs meant to *me,* or at least what I *thought* they meant to me, I usually told a little white lie, saying only that they were photographs by a famous photographer of his son. I was thereby able to establish a credible reason for having the pictures without having to explain postmodernism to someone I figured—given the nature of these encounters—wouldn't be particularly interested anyway.

But some time later I was forced to recognize that these questions were not so naive as I'd assumed. The men in my bedroom were perfectly able to read—in Weston's posing, framing, and lighting the young Neil so as to render his body a classical sculpture—the long-established codes of homoeroticism. And in making the leap from those codes to the codes of kiddie porn, they were stating no more than what was enacted, in the fall of 1989, as the law governing federal funding of art in the United States. That law—proposed by right-wing senator Jesse Helms in response to certain of Mapplethorpe's photographs—directly equated homoeroticism with obscenity and with the sexual exploita-

3. Ibid., p. 30.

tion of children.[4] Of course, all of us know that neither Weston's nor Mapplethorpe's photographs would be declared obscene under the supreme court's *Miller v. California* ruling, to which the appropriations bill pretended to defer; but we also know that NEA grant applications do not come before a court of law.[5] For those considering whether to fund arts projects, it is the equation itself that would matter. As Jesse Helms himself so aptly said of his victory: "'Old Helms will win every time' on cutting Federal Money for art projects with homosexual themes."[6] And indeed he will. As I hope everyone remembers, in 1987, when gay men still constituted over 70 percent of all reported cases of AIDS in the United States, 94 senators voted for the Helms amendment to prevent safe sex information directed at us from being funded by Congress.[7]

Given these assaults on our sexuality and indeed on our lives, what are we to say now of the ways we first theorized postmodernism? To stay with the parochial debate with which I began, what does the strategy of

4. The compromise language of the notorious Helms amendment to the NEA/NEH appropriations bill read:

None of the funds authorized to be appropriated for the National Endowment for the Arts or the National Endowment for the Humanities may be used to promote, disseminate, or produce materials which in the judgment of the National Endowment for the Arts or National Endowment for the Humanities may be considered obscene, including but not limited to, depictions of sadomasochism, homo-eroticism, the sexual exploitation of children, or individuals engaged in sex acts and which, when taken as a whole, do not have serious literary, artistic, political or scientific value. (*Congressional Record—House,* October 2, 1989, p. H6407)

5. Moreover, in flagrant disregard of their own inclusion of the *Miller* language, the new law declared a Sense of the Congress, clearly referring to photographs by Mapplethorpe and Andres Serrano, "that recently works have been funded which are without artistic value but which are criticized as pornographic and shocking by any standards" (*Congressional Record—House,* October 2, 1989. p. H6407). For an illuminating discussion of *Miller* in relation to the Right's attack on the NEA, see Carole S. Vance, "Misunderstanding Obscenity," *Art in America* 78, no. 5 (May 1990), pp. 39–45.

6. Maureen Dowd, "Jesse Helms Takes No-Lose Position on Art," *New York Times,* July 28, 1989, p. A1.

7. See my discussion of this other notorious Helms amendment in "How to Have Promiscuity in an Epidemic," this volume.

appropriation matter now? My answer is that we only now know how it might really matter.

In October of 1989, the third annual conference of the Lesbian and Gay Studies Center at Yale began with violence unleashed on the participants by the Yale and New Haven police forces.[8] The trouble started with the arrest of Bill Dobbs, a lawyer and member of Art Positive, a group within New York's AIDS Coalition to Unleash Power (ACT UP) that was formed in response to the Helms amendment. Dobbs was presumed to be responsible for putting up a series of what the police claimed were obscene posters around the sites of the conference. The 11x17 xerox posters—showing various images of and texts about sex appropriated from such sources as old sex education manuals, sexology texts, and pulp novels, and accompanied by the words "Sex Is" or "Just Sex"—were produced by the anonymous San Francisco collective Boy with Arms Akimbo, also formed to fight the Helms amendment. The collective's goal was to get as many people as possible involved in placing in public places imagery showing various cultural constructions of sexuality. Four thousand of the "Sex Is" posters were wheatpasted around San Francisco, and they also appeared in Sacramento, on various Bay Area college campuses, in Boston, New York, Tel Aviv, and Paris, as well as, of course, New Haven. For the month prior to the Yale lesbian and gay conference, the "Sex Is" xeroxes were shown in the city-sponsored San Francisco Arts Commission Gallery, situated across from San Francisco City Hall, in an exhibition entitled "What's Wrong with This Picture? Artists Respond to Censorship."

But it is precisely the censorial intent of the Helms amendment, to which Boy with Arms Akimbo's pictures were intended to call attention at the Yale conference, that was effaced in the reporting of the events of that weekend. While charges against others arrested in the fracas were quickly dropped, those against Dobbs were not. And Yale president

8. The conference, entitled "Outside/Inside," was held on the weekend of October 27–29, 1989. The police-instigated violence occurred on Friday evening, October 27.

Benno Schmidt adopted an uncompromising stance. Rather than apologize for the homophobic actions of his police, he sought to exonerate them through an "impartial" investigation, conducted as usual by the police themselves, to adjudicate the obscenity call and to consider possible police misconduct.[9] Moreover, Schmidt was quoted in the *New Haven Register* as saying that he thought at least one of the posters would be considered obscene using the supreme court's definition. The court's caveat regarding "serious literary, artistic, political or scientific value" was simply disregarded by this so-called expert in First Amendment law, since the serious *political* value of Boy with Arms Akimbo's posters—that they constitute a form of political speech about Helms's equation of homoeroticism with obscenity—was never even admitted as an issue.[10]

9. On November 30, the *New York Times* reported that "charges against Mr. Dobbs were eventually dropped," and that "two Yale police officers will be disciplined for using 'poor judgment.'" Thus, for the violence many of us protesting the intial arrests experienced at the hands of both Yale and New Haven police, the officers' disciplining will consist of a reprimand for one and three days without pay for the other. This accords perfectly with a number of recent cases in which the police have investigated their own abuses, as well as with a general failure to take attacks against gay men and lesbians seriously.

10. I wrote an open letter of protest to President Schmidt, the text of which I reproduce here:

As the keynote speaker for the third annual conference sponsored by the Lesbian and Gay Studies Center at Yale last weekend, I am writing you to express my outrage at the homophobic violence unleashed against us on Friday evening, violence initiated by the Yale police and escalated by the New Haven police. In addition, I write to protest the Yale administration's wholly inadequate response to this violence. When we gathered for that response on Saturday morning, we were treated to a series of insults: first, that you did not consider homophobic violence against us as requiring your presence; second, that the very people who suffered or witnessed this violence were told that "the facts were not yet known"; and finally, that the violence itself could not even be named. We were told merely that Yale University supports freedom of expression—a vague and easy claim—and that an impartial investigation would take place.

Gay men and lesbians have very little reason to have faith in "impartiality" in these matters, especially after having experienced the atmosphere at Yale. Throughout the weekend, conference members were subjected to homophobic remarks wherever we went. My own speech Saturday night was deliberately disrupted by students

Boy with Arms Akimbo is only one example of how the postmodernist strategy of appropriation has been transformed through its shift from a grounding in art-world discourse to a grounding in movement politics.

squealing their car tires outside the Whitney Humanities Center. Since apparently no one in an official capacity at Yale attended my speech, I want to reconstruct for you some of my opening remarks.

Participants in the Lesbian and Gay Studies Conference this past weekend included some of the most distinguished and committed gay and lesbian scholars and activists working today. Among them were members of the international community of people fighting against the AIDS epidemic, including people living with AIDS. It is my opinion that until all of us are satisfied with Yale University's support of our work, including substantial financial commitments to the Center for Lesbian and Gay Studies, we should no longer lend credibility to Yale's pretense of upholding free expression by our presence at Yale. The University's claim to respect free speech will remain hollow until you, as president, issue an unambiguous public statement condemning all forms of homophobia—named as such. This condemnation must also extend to labeling representations of our sexualities as obscene. Moreover, we expect a statement of positive support for all forms of expression by gay men and lesbians of our sexualities.

I was deeply impressed and moved by the Yale students and faculty who organized and participated in the Lesbian and Gay Studies conference. They deserve all the credit for the success of the conference—success in the face of the university's variously expressed contempt for us. In the past you have belittled the strong presence at Yale of a gay and lesbian community by catering to, rather than countering, homophobic charges and fears. In light of that injury, and of the added insults of this past weekend, it is now imperative that your gay and lesbian scholars be given not only protection in a clearly homophobic environment, but every encouragement to carry on with their courageous work. This is not to be accomplished by your occasional chats with an openly gay professor, but rather by meeting directly with the full gay constituency at Yale to hear their grievances and to follow their guidance, and by taking a strong public position.

The international community of lesbian and gay scholars and activists will not let this matter rest until the demands issued at the conference are met to the letter.

After a version of the present essay appeared in *Art in America,* Benno Schmidt wrote a letter to the editor, to which I was given the chance to reply. After seeing my response, Schmidt withdrew his letter, claiming that it had not been meant for publication. I include here the text of my letter, from which some of the contents of Schmidt's letter may be inferred:

Benno Schmidt's letter only reiterates his uncompromising stance regarding homophobic actions at Yale during the third annual Lesbian and Gay Studies Conference

The Boys in My Bedroom

Within the AIDS activist movement, and especially within ACT UP New York, a certain savvy about this narrow aspect of postmodernist theory has been especially enabling. The graphic work of the Silence=Death Project, Gran Fury, and many others, the video activism of DIVA TV (for Damned Interfering Video Activist Television) grows very directly out of propositions of postmodernist theory. Assaults on authorship have led to

last October. He confirms my charge that he sought to exonerate his police force by ordering them to investigate themselves (if he could not anticipate the conclusions, he must be ignorant of the usual results of self-investigations by police in this country). Schmidt's order was in flagrant disregard of the demand by the conferees that "the university panel reviewing the actions of the Yale police include significant representation of the university's lesbian, gay and bisexual community." Moreover, Schmidt fails to mention that, even under the biased circumstances of the investigation, two police officers were disciplined for infractions of procedures and serious errors of judgment. Schmidt also withholds the information that a Yale graduate student has officially challenged the accuracy of the police investigation and that the Yale Police Advisory Board has commenced an independent investigation.

What Schmidt refers to as the "views of the conference organizers" are in fact only the views of five Yale faculty members (all of them male)—explicitly so stated: "the 'we' of this letter should be understood only to include the undersigned faculty members." A very different position is held by other conference organizers, especially graduate students, who did the bulk of the work. Schmidt appears to be indifferent to their views. And what of the views of those of us subjected to the police violence? Not a single one of the demands drawn up by conference goers in response to the actions of the Yale and New Haven police has been met.

If Schmidt thinks "judgments in the area of obscenity are notoriously subtle and difficult to make," why was he so easily able to assert the probable obscenity of "at least one of the posters," as was reported in the press?

It seems odd, too, that postering in a university building where conference sessions would take place the following day, and this at 8:30 in the evening, should seem to Schmidt an obvious security threat. Rather the police action is to be explained by the remarks of the Yale law professor who phoned the police to complain about what she called "gay and lesbian crap"—this from the police transcript of the phone call.

Benno Schmidt's attitude toward gays and lesbians at Yale was made clear in 1987, when he wrote a letter to Yale alumni reassuring them that Yale was not nearly as gay a place as they might have read in the press. In other words, gays and lesbians are for him a public relations problem. When, as keynote speaker of the conference, I wrote Schmidt a letter abhorring the homophobia variously expressed against us, including the disruption of my own speech by students squealing their car tires outside the lecture hall, I received no response. Only now that I've written in a more public forum does the president have the "courtesy" to reply.

anonymous and collective production. Assaults on originality have given rise to dictums like "if it works, use it"; "if it's not yours, steal it." Assaults on the institutional confinement of art have resulted in seeking means of reaching affected and marginalized communities more directly.[11]

But finally, I want to say something about what was excluded from postmodernist theory, which made it considerably less enabling—excluded not only from the aesthetic theory I've been addressing, but also from more global theories. My own blindness in the Mapplethorpe/Levine comparison is symptomatic of a far greater blindness. My failure to take account of what those men in my bedroom insisted on seeing was a failure of theory generally to consider what we are now only beginning to be able to consider—what, in fact, was being variously considered at the Yale lesbian and gay studies conference: the dangerous, even murderous, ways in which homophobia structures every aspect of our culture. Sadly, it has taken the horror of AIDS and the virulent backlash against gays and lesbians that AIDS has unleashed to teach us the gravity of this theoretical omission. What must be done now—if only as a way to begin rectifying our oversight—is to *name* homophobia, the very thing that Yale's President Schmidt so adamantly refused to do, the very thing that the entire membership of Congress refuses to do.

Returning once again to the comparison with which I began, but this time taking into consideration what the boys in my bedroom saw, the photographs by Mapplethorpe and Levine no longer seem definitional of postmodernism through their opposition. Appropriating Weston's photographs of Neil, Levine claimed them as her own. Seen thus in the possession of a woman, the nude pictures of the young boy no longer appear, through their deployment of a classical vocabulary, as universal aesthetic expression. Because Levine has "taken" the photographs, we recognize the contingency of gender in looking at them. Another consequence of that contingency is made explicit by Mapplethorpe. Appropriating Weston's style, Mapplethorpe puts in the place of Weston's child

11. See Douglas Crimp, with Adam Rolston, *AIDS Demo Graphics* (Seattle: Bay Press, 1990).

the fully sexualized adult male body. Gazing at that body, we can no longer overlook its eroticism. That is to say, we must abandon the formalism that attended *only* to the artwork's style. In both cases, then, we learn to experience Weston's modernist photographs not as universal images, but as images of the universal constituted by disavowing gender and sexuality; and it is such deconstructions of modernism's claims to universality—as well as its formalism—that qualify as postmodernist practices.

What made Boy with Arms Akimbo's posters a provocation to the Yale police and its president was perhaps after all not their imputed obscenity, but rather their *variety*, their proliferation of different ways of showing *Sex Is . . . Just Sex*. Or rather, as Jesse Helms has made clear, difference, in our culture, *is* obscenity. And it is this with which postmodern theory must contend.

9 A DAY WITHOUT GERTRUDE

First presented at the panel discussion "Art, Activism,

and AIDS: Into the Second Decade," held in

conjunction with A Day without Art, Soho Photo

Gallery, New York, November 30, 1990.

In the introduction to *AIDS: Cultural Analysis/Cultural Activism,* I wrote that "my intention was to show . . . that there was a critical, theoretical, activist alternative to the personal, elegiac expressions that appeared to dominate the art-world response to AIDS. What seemed to me essential was a vastly expanded view of culture in relation to crisis." I took some flak for that statement, because it was interpreted as saying that personal expressions of loss are unacceptable, that *only* activist responses are legitimate. That was not what I meant, and for several reasons. The first is, as I tried to make clear in writing an essay about the activist hostility to mourning, that I think our sense of personal loss must be honored absolutely. And if this includes artistic expressions of mourning, then they are to be honored, too. The second is that I think it is dangerous to essentialize activism, to presume to know in advance what constitutes activism and what does not.

Having said that, I think what I wrote in 1987 is still true of the art world generally. Even though a certain amount of attention has recently been paid to activist practices, that attention is limited—limited mostly to the collective Gran Fury, which the art world seems to have designated as the AIDS activist cultural group that can represent activist practice *tout court.* But what I'd like to recall, and to speak about briefly, is the second sentence of my original statement: "What seemed to me essential was a vastly expanded view of culture in relation to crisis." It isn't merely a question of the accommodation of certain aesthetic practices by the institutions of art—a videotape by DIVA TV shown here, a performance by Gang there.[1] Rather it is crucial that art institutions recognize that representation is not restricted to discrete symbolic gestures, events, or works, but rather that everything they do functions as representation. It is not a matter of occasionally allowing a political representation of the AIDS crisis; rather, institutions constantly make political representations, directly or indirectly, of the crisis.

"A Day without Art" is an example of what I mean. A Day without Art is itself a vast representation, and it can be read as such. A Day without Art

1. DIVA TV (for Damned Interferring Video Activist Television) and Gang were two activist art collectives formed from within ACT UP New York.

has become somewhat more complex in this, its second year, taking on a more activist cast than it did last year—by providing education, raising money for service organizations, providing forums for discussions of AIDS activism and spaces for exhibitions of AIDS activist art. But it still signifies mostly in two ways: first, by showing that the art world has borne heavy losses to the epidemic that it wishes to mourn, and second, by being willing to set aside *one day* to draw attention to the devastation, if not always to the political mendacity that bears much of the blame for this devastation. It still seems necessary to interpret this sense of loss as a privileged one, that is, that the loss of artists' lives is somehow greater than the loss of other lives. This is what I mean by the fact that A Day without Art is itself a representation, and in this sense, a regrettable one.

But more important, what A Day without Art represents, in its very name, is that the art world is willing in various ways to participate in the struggle against AIDS for *one day* each year. If art institutions were to recognize what I called a vastly expanded view of culture in relation to crisis, it seems obvious that they would consider 364 more days a year during which they might act as if they knew a crisis existed. If, for example, an art museum is willing to display AIDS information on A Day without Art, why not display that information every day of the year?

Here's another way of posing this question: Last year, the Metropolitan Museum's participation in A Day without Art involved removing for the day Picasso's famous portrait of Gertrude Stein, a gesture that seemed particularly obscure to many people. If we were to ask the museum to remove that picture until the end of the AIDS crisis, what do you suppose their response would be? Something, I suppose, on the order of "What purpose would such deprivation serve?" And our answer would have to be: "The same purpose as removing it for one day, only with a permanence more commensurate with the losses that we are actually experiencing." My real problem with the Met's gesture, which is being repeated this year with other paintings, is that it is meaningless, or if not meaningless, then meaningful only in ways that art institutions understand representation generally—that is, as hermetic, necessary to interpret.

I'll make a stab at interpreting the Met's gesture from last year's Day without Art: It is meant to signify lesbian invisibility—not just lesbian invisibility generally, but the invisibility of lesbians in the AIDS epidemic. And my suggestion for how the Met might make their representation more meaningful is that they replace Picasso's portrait of Gertrude Stein with a text about the refusal of the Centers for Disease Control to include lesbian transmission in its epidemiology, and to explain further that this refusal regarding lesbians might stand symbolically for the CDC's wider refusal to include the diseases that HIV-infected women get among the diseases that determine the definition of AIDS. In other words, what I would ask of art institutions is that they consider the concrete representational politics of AIDS. For the CDC, too, is involved in representational practices, in this case representational practices that systematically undercount the number of women with AIDS in the United States.

ACT UP will demonstrate at the CDC this week to try to force them to change their epidemiology to include women. ACT UP, too, is fighting a war of representation. ACT UP's understanding of representation is the understanding I had in mind when I said that we needed a vastly expanded view of culture in relation to crisis. And I still think the art world needs to pay heed to this expanded view.

10 RIGHT ON, GIRLFRIEND!

First presented as a Twenty-Fifth Anniversary Symposium Lecture at the University of California, Irvine, April 10, 1991, and published in Social Text *33 (1992).*

At Vito Russo's memorial service in December of 1990, the first speaker was New York's mayor David Dinkins. It had been reported in the gay press that Dinkins paid a hospital visit a few days before Vito died, and that Vito had mustered the strength to sit up and say, "In 1776, Edmund Burke of the British Parliament said about the slavery clause, 'A politician owes the people not only his industry but his judgment, and if he sacrifices his judgment to their opinions, he betrays them.'"[1] Those of us who are queer and/or AIDS activists knew very well what Vito was alluding to, because Mayor Dinkins had by then already sacrificed what we took to be his judgment when we voted for him. He failed to make a public issue of the rising tide of violence against gays and lesbians, refusing to march with us in Staten Island to protest the homophobically motivated murder of a disabled gay man, and unwilling to press for labeling as bias-related the murder of a gay Latino in a Jackson Heights cruising area.[2] He appointed Woodrow Myers health commissioner over the vehement objections of AIDS activists; he canceled New York's pilot needle-exchange program, initiated by Myers's predecessor but opposed by the city's conservative black leadership; he allowed thousands of homeless people infected with HIV to remain in warehouse shelters, where they are vulnerable to opportunistic diseases, especially to the terrifying new epidemic of multi-drug-resistent strains of tuberculosis; and he drastically cut funding for health services even as the city's health-care system faced collapse from underfinancing. Still, when Dinkins eulogized Vito Russo, he quoted what Vito had said to him in the hospital and, with no apparent sense of irony, professed that he would always remember it.

1. Arnie Kantrowitz, "Milestones: Vito Russo," *Outweek* 73 (November 21, 1990), p. 37.
2. Several months later, however, Dinkins took a courageous stand against anti-gay and lesbian prejudice by marching with the Irish Gay and Lesbian Organization (IGLO) in New York's St. Patrick's Day parade. He did this in order to broker a compromise between IGLO and the Ancient Order of Hibernians, the parade organizers who had refused IGLO's application to participate. The result was that Dinkins was subjected to torrents of abuse from the crowd and a cold shoulder from Cardinal O'Connor, which led the mayor to compare his experience to civil rights marches in the South in the 1960s. See Duncan Osborne, "The Cardinal, the Mayor and the Balance of Power," *Outweek* 92 (April 3, 1990), pp. 30–37.

As soon as he had delivered his short speech, the mayor and his entourage left the memorial service, accompanied by a small chorus of boos. The next speaker was Vito's old friend Arnie Kantrowitz, who began by saying that just in case we thought we had learned something new about Vito—that he was a student of American history—we should know that the lines he'd quoted to Dinkins came from the movie version of the Broadway musical *1776*. Our laughter at Arnie's remark brought back the Vito we knew and loved, the fierce activist who was very funny and very queer, a very funny queer who knew and loved movies, who knew better than anybody how badly the movies treated queers, but still loved them. Those qualities were captured yet again in another of Arnie's remarks. Reminiscing about Vito's pleasure in showing movies at home to his friends and about his unashamed worship of Judy Garland, Arnie summed up Vito's brand of gay militancy (or perhaps I should say, his gay brand of militancy): "In Vito's house," Arnie quipped, "either you respected Judy . . . or you left."

A very different chord was struck later in the service by Larry Kramer. "The Vito who was my friend was different from the one I've heard about today," the Hollywood screenwriter said. "Since I hate old movies, I wasn't in his home-screening crowd."[3] Kramer went on to ask, rhetorically, "Who killed Vito?" And his answer? "As sure as any virus killed him, we killed him. Everyone in this room killed him. Twenty-five million people outside this room killed him. Vito was killed by twenty-five million gay men and lesbians who for ten long years of this plague have refused to get our act together. Can't you see that?"

The "can't you see that?" was the refrain of Kramer's speech, which went on to name names—mostly those of closeted gay men and lesbians in the entertainment industry. The last names mentioned were those associated with an AIDS fundraiser: "There's going to be a benefit screening of a movie called *Silence of the Lambs*. The villain is a gay man who mass-murders people. AmFAR is holding the benefit. Thanks a lot,

3. Larry Kramer, "Who Killed Vito Russo?" *Outweek* 86 (February 20, 1990), p. 26.

Mathilde Krim [Mathilde Krim is, as is well known, the chairperson of the American Foundation for AIDS Research]. Thanks a lot, Arthur Krim, for financing the film [Arthur Krim, Mathilde's husband, is the founder of Orion Pictures]. Thanks a lot, Jodie Foster, for starring in it [Jodie Foster is . . . well, we know who Jodie Foster is . . .]."

Some other people at the memorial service disagreed with Larry about who killed Vito. As several hundred of Vito's friends and admirers arrived at the service, we were handed a xeroxed flier signed "Three Anonymous Queers," which began:

On the same night last month, Vito Russo died from AIDS and Jesse Helms was reelected to another six years of power. . . . I believe with all my heart that Jesse Helms killed Vito Russo. And I believe without question that when I was queer-bashed, Helms was as responsible for my injuries as if he had inflicted the wounds with his own hands. I fully imagine in a meeting with Helms, he would have the blood and flesh of dead dykes and fags dripping from his hands and mouth. And I hate him and I believe he is a threat to my very existence and I have every right to defend myself against him with any amount of force I choose.

The flier closed with two questions: "If I am ever brave enough to murder Jesse Helms, will you hand me the gun to carry out the deed? Will you hide me from the law once it is done?"

Most queers will recognize, in these two rhetorical answers to the question, Who killed Vito? positions taken on debates in contemporary queer politics, debates about "outing" and "bashing back." My interest here is not so much to take sides in these debates as to describe both the political conjuncture within which they take place and some of the cultural interventions within them. I also want to attend to their relevance for AIDS activism, the movement that to some degree brought them to the fore and in which they are sometimes played out. It is not coincidental that they surfaced at Vito Russo's memorial service, for in many ways Vito was the quintessential gay activist turned AIDS activist.

Vito's death was more than a personal loss to his friends and admirers. It was also a great symbolic loss to ACT UP. The Three Anonymous Queers put it this way: "Vito is dead and everything remains the same. I thought I might go to sleep the night after his death and wake up to find the city burned to the ground." Such a fantasy, which recalls spontaneous riots in the wake of murdered civil rights leaders of the 1960s, arises, I think, not only because Vito was a cherished leader, but because he held out hope in a very particular way, hope that he voiced in his famous Albany speech from ACT NOW's Nine Days of Protest in the spring of 1988.[4] The speech began: "A friend of mine has a half-fare transit card which he uses on busses and subways. The other day when he showed his card, the token attendant asked what his disability was. He said, 'I have AIDS,' and the attendant said, 'No you don't. If you had AIDS, you'd be home, dying.' I'm here to speak out today as a PWA who is not dying from, but for the last three years quite successfully living with, AIDS." Vito ended the speech by saying, "After we kick the shit out of this disease, I intend to be alive to kick the shit out of this system, so that this will never happen again."

Vito's death painfully demonstrated to many AIDS activists that the rhetoric of hope we invented and depended on—a rhetoric of "living with AIDS," in which "AIDS is not a death sentence," but rather "a chronic manageable illness"—that rhetoric was becoming difficult to sustain. I don't want to minimize the possibility that anyone's death might result in such a loss of hope for someone, and, moreover, within a two-week period of Vito's death, four other highly visible members of ACT UP New York also died, a cumulative loss for us that was all but unbearable. But I think many of us had a special investment in Vito's survival, not only because he was so beloved, but because, as a long-term survivor, as a resolute believer in his own survival, and as a highly visible and articulate fighter for his and others' survival, he fully embodied that hope.

4. See Douglas Crimp, with Adam Rolston, *AIDS Demo Graphics* (Seattle: Bay Press, 1990), pp. 53–69.

Vito's death coincided with the waning not only of our optimism but also of a period of limited but concrete successes for the AIDS activist movement. During that period—roughly, the first two and a half years after the founding of ACT UP in the spring of 1987—we had succeeded in focusing greater public attention on AIDS, in shifting the discussion of AIDS from one dominated by a punitive moralism to one directed toward combating a public health emergency, and in affecting policy in concrete ways, particularly drug development policy.

During the past two years, however, we have experienced only disappointments and setbacks. We have seen almost no new drugs to combat AIDS, whether antivirals or treatments for, or prophylaxes against, opportunistic infections (OIs). The results of ddI and ddC studies have been less than encouraging, and the few potentially effective treatments for OIs are either held up in the FDA's approval process or, when granted marketing approval, subject to record-breaking price gouging. We have had to return to other battles we had thought were behind us, such as the call for mandatory testing of health-care professionals in the wake of hysteria caused by the possible transmission of HIV from a dentist to his patients; after having worked tirelessly to get the voices of people with AIDS heard, the media and Congress finally listened sympathetically to one, that of Kimberly Bergalis, who in fact spoke not as a person with AIDS ("I didn't do anything wrong," she protested), but as the "victim" of people with AIDS ("My life has been taken away").[5] We have seen the leveling off or shrinking of spending on AIDS at local, state, and federal levels, a particularly disheartening example of which was the passage, with great fanfare, of the Ryan White Emergency CARE bill providing disaster relief to the hardest hit cities, and then, at budget time, the failure to provide most of the funding for it. At the same time, case loads continue to spiral upwards, new HIV infections continue to multiply, and the epidemic becomes more entrenched in populations already burdened with other poverty-related problems, populations with no primary health care, no health insurance, often no housing.

5. Quoted in the *New York Times,* September 27, 1991, p. A12.

Perhaps even more demoralizing than the cumulative effects of these setbacks, we are faced with a new kind of indifference, an indifference that has been called the "normalization of AIDS." If, for the first eight years of the epidemic—the term of Ronald Reagan's presidency—indifference took the form of callously ignoring the crisis, under George Bush, AIDS has been "normalized" as just one item on a long list of supposedly intractable social problems. How often do we hear the list recited?—poverty, crime, drugs, homelessness, and AIDS. AIDS is no longer an emergency. It's merely a permanent disaster. One effect of this normalization process is the growing credence granted the claim that AIDS has received a disproportionate amount of federal funding for medical research. This claim overlooks the fact that AIDS is a new disease syndrome, that it primarily threatens the lives of the young, that it is not merely an illness but a bewildering array of illnesses, and, most important, that it is an epidemic still out of control. The saddest irony is that, now that our optimism has turned to grim realism, our old rhetoric is appropriated to abet the process of normalization and defunding. Hence our ambivalence at Magic Johnson's powerful example of "living with HIV," since we now know that, particularly among people of color, Johnson's ability to "fight the virus," as he puts it, will be exceptional, and that the sense that AIDS is already manageable will only relax efforts to make it so.

This is a very sketchy background against which new tactics have been embraced by queers. More important, it is the background against which AIDS activism is being painfully transformed. The interrelation between the two—queer activism and AIDS activism—is complex, shifting, sometimes divisive. As a means of analyzing the transformations and the divisions, I want to return to Larry Kramer's finger-pointing at Vito Russo's memorial service.

Before coming to Jodie Foster and *The Silence of the Lambs,* a short archeology of "outing."[6] All queers have extensive experience with the

---

6. For a detailed account of outing, including historical background and analysis of the contemporary debates as well as an appendix of essential articles from the media,

closet, no matter how much of a sissy or tom boy we were as children, no matter how early we declared our sexual preferences, no matter how determined we are to be openly gay or lesbian. The closet is not a function of homosexuality in our culture, but of compulsory and presumptive heterosexuality. I may be publicly identified as gay, but in order for that identity to be acknowledged, I have to declare it on each new occasion. By "occasion," I mean something as simple as asking a cab driver to take me to a bar like the Spike, or kissing my friend Jeff good-bye on a crowded subway when he gets off two stops before me on our way home from the gym. Fearing for my safety, I might choose not to kiss Jeff, thereby hiding behind our fellow riders' presumption that we're straight.[7]

As part of our experience with the closet, which was for most of us the only safe place to be as adolescents, we also know what it's like to keep the closet door firmly shut by pretending not only to be heterosexual but also to be homophobic—since in many circumstances the mark of one's heterosexuality is the open expression of hatred toward queers. Thus most of us have the experience, usually from our youth, of oppressing other queers in order to elude that same oppression. Eve Sedgwick writes in *Epistemology of the Closet* that "it is entirely within the experience of gay people to find that a homophobic figure in power has . . . a disproportionate likelihood of being gay and closeted."[8] I'm not so sure. I don't think there is much likelihood at all that Jesse Helms, Cardinal O'Connor, and Patrick Buchanan, for example, are gay and closeted. We do have experience with homophobia dictated by the closet, but that experience is as much of ourselves as of others. And it is often the projection of that experience that makes us suspicious of the homophobic figure in power.

see Larry Gross, *The Contested Closet: The Politics and Ethics of Outing* (Minneapolis: University of Minnesota Press, 1993).

7. It's not that Jeff and I are so butch as to be unreadable as gay; indeed many people might presume that we *are* gay, but our not behaving "overtly" allows them to act precisely as if the operative presumption is that everyone is straight unless openly declaring themselves not to be.

8. Eve Kosofsky Sedgwick, *Epistemology of the Closet* (Berkeley and Los Angeles: University of California Press, 1990), p. 81.

Such suspicions, enhanced by rumors, have sometimes led us to im-
pugn the heterosexuality of our oppressors. A celebrated case is that of
former New York City mayor Ed Koch. A confirmed bachelor, Koch required a former beauty queen for a "beard" to win his first mayoral primary, since the opposition's slogan was "Vote for Cuomo, not the homo."
The "homo" won the election, and thereby gained control of the city
that would soon have the highest number of AIDS cases of any city in
the world. During the time when attention to AIDS implied attention to
a gay disease, Koch paid no attention, and many interpreted his need to
dissociate himself as a form of self-defense, the defense of his closet.
The spectacular conclusion, some years later, was Koch's open admission on a radio talk show of his *hetero*sexuality, which, after many years
of insisting that his sexuality was nobody's business, made the front
page of *New York Newsday*. For ACT UP's *Target City Hall* demonstration in March 1989, an affinity group pasted that *Newsday* cover to
placards. Its banner headline—"KOCH: I'M HETEROSEXUAL"—answered with "Yeah, and I'm Carmen Miranda." The *Newsday* headline
also inspired a tongue-twister chant for the day: "Why's New York AIDS
care ineffectual? Ask Ed Koch, the heterosexual." *Target City Hall* was
an outing with a queer sense of humor.

The tendency to suspect a closeted homosexual behind a lack of commitment to fighting AIDS migrated, in the figure of Michelangelo Signorile, from ACT UP to *Outweek,* New York's short-lived gay and lesbian
weekly. In charge of ACT UP's media committee during *Target City Hall*
and later *Outweek's* features editor, Signorile also wrote a column called
"Gossip Watch," a queer variation on media watches that restricted its
purview to gossip columns. Using the blunt instruments of all-caps,
four-letter-word invective and the AIDS crisis as an excuse for righteous
indignation, Signorile's "Gossip Watch" chastised gossip columnists—
often themselves closeted homosexuals—for, among other things, in-
venting beards for closeted celebrities who had done nothing publicly
about the AIDS crisis.

This circumscribed context of what came to be called outing has important bearing on the ensuing debate. Signorile appeared initially to want

to say something about the privileged position of gossip in our culture's management of *the* open secret. Outing is not (at least not at first) the revelation of that secret, but the revelation that the secret was no secret at all. That was the scandal of *Outweek*'s Malcolm Forbes cover story, for which *Time* and *Newsweek*—not *Outweek*—invented the term "outing."[9] The dominant media heaped its fear and loathing upon Signorile, *Outweek*, and queers generally, not because Forbes's homosexuality had been revealed, but because their own complicity in concealing it had been revealed. Forbes was not "outed," the media's homophobia was.

From the moment "outing" was named, however, the straight media set the terms of debate, and we queers foolishly accepted those terms by seeking to justify an act of which we had not been guilty. We resorted then to our two, mutually contradictory excuses: that our oppressors are disproportionately likely to be gay and closeted and that we need them as role models. In adopting our paradoxical defense, we ignored the ways in which both of these positions are turned against us, especially in the context of AIDS. AIDS has often resulted in a peculiarly public and unarguable means of outing. Day after day, as we read the obituary section of the *New York Times,* we are faced with incontrovertible proof—in their survival by "long-time companions" (a term invented by the *Times*)—of the homosexuality of artists, actors, and dancers; of fashion designers, models, and interior decorators; of doctors, lawyers, and stockbrokers. The tragic irony is that it has taken AIDS to prove our Stonewall slogan: "We are everywhere."[10]

But the two most notorious outings by AIDS should give us pause about the benefits of such revelations. Responses to the deaths of Rock Hudson and Roy Cohn have a perverse symmetry. Hudson was locked in

9. William Henry III, "Forcing Gays Out of the Closet," *Time,* January 29, 1990, p. 67; David Gelman, "'Outing': An Unexpected Assault on Sexual Privacy," *Newsweek,* April 30, 1990, p. 66.

10. This was not always the case. It took intense pressure from queers and AIDS activists to force the *Times* to list surviving lovers of gay men. Even now, the *Times* only mentions a "companion" in the course of an obituary story, not as one of the survivors, who are still limited to blood relatives and legal spouses.

Hollywood's '50s closet, hiding from, among other things, a McCarthyism that equated commies and queers. Cohn was the closeted McCarthyite. Hudson personified decency to a majority of Americans, and his homosexuality was seen as a betrayal. He became "the hunk who lived a lie."[11] Roy Cohn came belatedly to represent indecency to most Americans; *his* homosexuality was seen as fidelity to his very being. He was the McCarthyite queer, the evil homosexual who lied about everything.[12] The revelation of the secret—the secret that was, of course, no secret in either case—became in both cases the revelation that homosexuals are liars and traitors. Nothing new about that.

In this scenario, who is the oppressor and who the role model? As I read the homophobic press accounts, Hudson is the oppressor—guilty of oppressing himself and all the innocent fans who believed him—and Cohn the role model—absolutely faithful to the truth of homosexuality in his duplicity and cowardice. Our outing fantasy—that the revelation of homosexuality would have a transformative effect on homophobic discourse—was only a fantasy after all, and a dangerous one at that. As Sedgwick counsels in *Epistemology of the Closet:*

We have too much cause to know how limited a leverage any individual revelation can exercise over collectively scaled and institutionally em-

11. See Richard Meyer, "Rock Hudson's Body," in *Inside/Out: Lesbian Theories, Gay Theories,* ed. Diana Fuss (New York and London: Routledge, 1991), pp. 259–288.

12. See, e.g., Robert Sherrill, "King Cohn," *Nation,* May 21, 1988, pp. 719–725. Beginning with the sentence, "Cohn was a particularly nasty homosexual," Sherrill recounts stories of Cohn's extreme promiscuity and his supposed relations with other duplicitous right-wing homosexuals, then ends his account with the following paragraph:

Typically disloyal, Cohn gave no support to homosexuals who were trying to win public acceptance. He called them "fags," did all he could to make their lives miserable, lectured against them, berated politicians for any display of tolerance toward homosexuals and urged laws to restrict their freedom. To his death he denied that he was homosexual, but the Dorian Gray scene of his dying of AIDS said it all: "Roy . . . lay in bed, unheeding, his flesh cracking open, sores on his body, his faculties waning" and with a one-inch "slit-like wound above [his] anus."

The final quotations, indicative for Sherrill not of disease but of homosexuality (or perhaps the two are not to be differentiated), are uncredited, but are taken from one of the two books under review in the article, *Citizen Cohn* by Nicholas von Hoffman.

bodied oppressions. Acknowledgment of this disproportion does not mean that the consequences of such acts as coming out can be circumscribed within predetermined *boundaries, as if between "personal" and "political" realms, nor does it require us to deny how disproportionately powerful and disruptive such acts can be. But the brute incommensurability has nonetheless to be acknowledged. In the theatrical display of an* already institutionalized *ignorance no transformative potential is to be looked for.*[13]

Signorile's initial impulse was perhaps, then, more productive: not to "out" supposedly closeted gay men and lesbians, but to "out" enforcers of the closet, not to reveal the "secret" of homosexuality, but to reveal the "secret" of homophobia. For it is only the latter that is truly a secret, and a truly *dirty* secret. As for the former, the speculation about the sexuality of celebrities, gossip is a privileged activity for queers, too.

Which brings us to Jodie Foster . . . and *The Silence of the Lambs.* Larry Kramer, who claimed in his speech that Vito Russo "was the only person who agreed with me unequivocally on everything I said and did," added, after his thank-you to Jodie Foster for starring in *Silence:* "Vito would really have screamed about that one." But Vito can speak for himself. In his introduction to *The Celluloid Closet,* entitled "On the Closet Mentality," Vito wrote,

The public should . . . be aware of the sexuality of gay actors just as it is aware of the heterosexuality of the majority. I do not believe that such a discussion is nobody's business, nor do I believe that it is one of a sexual and therefore private nature. Discussing such things in a book without the knowledge or consent of the people in question is, alas, immoral and libelous. It is immoral because unless people by their own choice come out of the closet, the announcement is valueless; it is libelous because such information has been known to destroy people's lives. Some of us will change that in time.[14]

13. Sedgwick, *Epistemology of the Closet,* p. 78.
14. Vito Russo, *The Celluloid Closet: Homosexuality in the Movies* (New York: Harper & Row, 1987), p. xi.

The last sentence is characteristic of Vito, of his fighting spirit, his optimism, and his understanding of what needed changing. Among the things we need to change is the fact that calling someone homosexual is, to this day, considered by our legal system to be libelous per se. Malicious intent does *not* have to be proved.

One thing Vito would surely have disagreed with Larry about is who to blame for his own death. Vito pointed his finger at queers only to tell us how much he loved us and to praise our courage. As for *The Silence of the Lambs*, Vito would have been the best equipped among us to show just how careless Jonathan Demme was in his characterization of serial killer Buffalo Bill, a.k.a. Jame Gumb, with his miniature poodle named Precious, his chiffon scarves, his made-up face, his nipple ring, and his murdered boyfriend. Maybe these features don't have to add up to a homophobic stereotype within the complex alignments of sexuality and pathology represented in *The Silence of the Lambs*, but they most certainly do within the history of their deployment by Hollywood, the history Vito Russo wrote.

Up to a point, Demme was careful about his portrayals in *Silence*—of both Clarice Starling and the men around her. Feminist approval of the film derives, I think, not only from the strength and intelligence of Foster's character Clarice, but also from her independence from an array of alternately annoying or sinister patriarchal figures, although just *how* independent is a matter of contention. But Clarice does reject every attempt to put the make on her; her commitment is to the captured woman. Demme ultimately failed, though, to follow through on his film's antipatriarchal logic. He let patriarchy off the hook by homosexualizing the psychopaths—Buffalo Bill, obviously, but Hannibal Lecter as well, whose disturbing appeal can hardly be divorced from his camp, effete intelligence. What straight man would get off a line like "Oh, Senator, . . . love your suit!"? Demme's homophobia is thus a matter not only of underwriting the tradition of Hollywood's stereotyping of gay men as psychopathic killers, but also of his displacement of the most horrifying consequences of patriarchy onto men who are far from straight.

In Thomas Harris's novel, Jame Gumb is not homosexual—the boyfriend he murdered was not his, but Hannibal Lecter's patient's. On the contrary, Gumb is explicitly referred to in the book as a fag basher.[15] He was refused the sex change operation he applied for at Johns Hopkins not only because he failed the requisite psychological tests, but also because he had a police record for two assaults on gay men. One has to wonder why Demme decided to leave out this information in a film that otherwise follows the novel very precisely. Would the fact that the killer was a homophobe have brought yet another murderous consequence of patriarchy too close to home?

The displacement of patriarchy's most serious consequences can also be seen in the film's illustration of another mode of feminist analysis, one that moves beyond positive-versus-negative images to the enforcement of sexual difference through psychic processes provoked in the spectator by cinematic codes. Laura Mulvey might well have written the climactic scene.[16] Deprived of agency by being the object rather than the subject of vision, Clarice Starling is stalked by the voyeuristic gaze of the spectator, who, unseen in the darkness, just like the serial killer, sees her through infrared glasses worn by Jame Gumb. There is no question where spectatorial identification ought to lie, and how it ought to be gendered: what the killer male's gaze sees is all the camera shows, and the image of the woman is trapped by the cinematic apparatus, represented in the prosthetic device the killer wears. But something unex-

15. In the novel, Dr. Danielson of Johns Hopkins reports to Jack Crawford: "The Harrisburg police were after [Gumb] for two assaults on homosexual men. The last one nearly died" (Thomas Harris, *The Silence of the Lambs* [New York: St. Martin's, 1989], p. 312). And Crawford reports to Clarice Starling about Gumb: "He's a fag-basher" (p. 322). This is not to say that Harris's portrayal of Gumb is free of homophobic stereotyping. Most of the details of Gumb's characterization in the film are taken directly from the novel. Demme added one (the nipple ring) and omitted one (Gumb's obsession with his mother). But it is important to add that stereotyping functions differently in the two mediums and that their respective histories of homophobic portrayals differ even more significantly.

16. I have in mind, of course, Mulvey's classic and often reprinted essay "Visual Pleasure and Narrative Cinema" (1975), now in her essay collection, *Visual and Other Pleasures* (Bloomington and Indianapolis: Indiana University Press, 1989), pp. 14–26.

Jame Gumb (Ted Levine) with his poodle Precious in *The Silence of the Lambs*, 1991.

Clarice Starling (Jodie Foster) cornered in *The Silence of the Lambs*, 1991.

pected happens. The tension of the scene is broken, not by Clarice's gunshots, but by an often-remarked male spectator's shout in the dark: "Shoot the fucking faggot!" Homophobia breaks the power of cinema, "proper" interpellation fails, and only then is Clarice restored to agency.

The film is thus perhaps feminist, though insufficiently, and certainly homophobic, quite sufficiently. Acknowledging these two different positions should not be impossible; although they are interdependent in the film's mapping of them, they do not have to be mutually exclusive in our reading of the film. What makes the debate about *The Silence of the Lambs* troubling, however, is its polarization along gender lines. Women, including lesbians, have tended to defend the film, while gay men usually decry it. And Jodie Foster gets caught in the middle. As B. Ruby Rich, an "out" lesbian, put it in the *Village Voice,* "Male and female desires, fears, and pleasures in the cinema have rarely coincided, so it should come as no surprise that dyke and faggot reactions to this movie are likely to diverge as well."[17] For gay men, Foster lends her prestige to the film's homophobic portrayal; for women, including lesbians, she lends her skill to a feminist one. For gay men, Foster is a closeted oppressor; for lesbians, she's a role model.

The division is a double one, for it entails, on the one hand, the identity of Foster and, on the other, the conception of identity itself. Castigating Foster as oppressor both presumes her (closeted) lesbian identity and presumes that identity precedes and determines political enactment. Praising Foster as role model, by contrast, accepts her feminism as itself constitutive of her identity. Rich insists, "I'm not willing to give up the immense satisfactions of a heroine with whom women can identify. Not willing to reduce all the intricate components of this movie down to the pass/fail score of one character. Please excuse me if my attention is fo-

17. B. Ruby Rich, contribution to "Writers on the *Lamb:* Sorting Out the Sexual Politics of a Controversial Film," *Village Voice,* March 5, 1991, p. 59. This series of short pieces on the film was partially in response to questions raised about the film's homophobic stereotyping and the threat of "outing" Jodie Foster by Michelangelo Signorile in *Outweek.*

cused not on the killer, but on the women he kills." And her defense concludes, "Guess I'm just a girl." Which is to say that in this debate, Rich's identification, her politics, emphasizes gender identity over sexual identity. As we know from her writing, in debates *within* feminism, Rich is perfectly capable of reversing the emphasis. Rich's identity is not fixed, does not determine her political identifications; rather her political identification momentarily fixes her identity: "Guess I'm just a girl." But where is the lesbian in this picture? Hasn't she again been rendered invisible? And what, if not outing, will make her visible?

Videomaker Jean Carlomusto's video *L Is for the Way You Look* provides one answer. In the central section of the tape, nine women, speaking singly or in groups, tell the story of an evening at the Lower East Side performance space PS 122 when lesbian comedian Reno was performing. What made the occasion worth talking about was that someone special was in the audience. First Zoe tells us that halfway through Reno's performance, Nancy leaned over to say, "Fran Liebowitz is over there . . . we're both, you know, we both kinda have a thing for Fran. . . ." Nancy then says she had more fun watching Fran laughing at Reno than she did laughing at Reno herself, after which Cynthia, sitting with her friend Bea, describes a commotion on the stairway as the audience was leaving. "Finally," Cynthia says, "the crowd parted a little bit and . . . ," cut back to Nancy midsentence, ". . . and all I see is this giant hair. It's almost like it could've been hair on a stick passing by, this platinum huge thing on this little black spandex." In case we haven't yet figured out what the commotion is about, Zoe adds another clue: "I turned around, and I saw her breasts, I saw this cleavage, I saw this endowment, and, oh my God, I saw the hair, and it was . . . Dolly Parton." It turns out that Hilery was there, too, and though Emily, Polly, and Gerri weren't, the news has traveled, and, after joking around about it, they decide to say they *were* there, and that Dolly had a crew cut like Nancy's, and that she was making out with Fran.

This sequence of *L Is for the Way You Look* (which was initially titled *The Invisible Woman*) is, as Carlomusto told me, not really about Dolly

Jean Carlomusto, *L Is for the Way You Look,* 1991.

Parton; it's about gossip. Dolly Parton may be the subject of the gossip, but the subjectivity represented in the video is that of the lesbians who gossip among themselves about Dolly. What matters is *their* visibility. Dolly is the absence around which a representation of lesbianism is constituted. But this is no simple structuralist lesson about representation founded on absence; rather it is meant to tell us something about the identifications we make and the communities we form through these identifications.

I don't mean to suggest that the focus of gossip on Dolly Parton doesn't matter at all. Of course it matters that Dolly's lesbianism has long been rumored and that her attendance at a lesbian performance in the company of another well-known closeted lesbian seems to confirm the rumors. But the emphasis on signifiers of Dolly's feminine masquerade—huge hair, huge cleavage, tiny spandex miniskirt—by a group of women whose masquerade differs so significantly from hers implicates their identifications and their desire in difference. None of the lesbians visible in *L Is for the Way You Look* looks femme like Dolly; compared with her absent image, they are in fact a pretty butch bunch.

Identification is, of course, identification with an other, which means that identity is never identical to itself. This alienation of identity from the self it constructs, which is a constant replay of a primary psychic

self-alienation, does not mean simply that any proclamation of identity will be only partial, that it will be exceeded by other *aspects* of identity, but rather that identity is always a relation, never simply a positivity. As Teresa de Lauretis put it so concisely in her essay on lesbian spectatorship in Sheila McLaughlin's *She Must Be Seeing Things,* "It takes two women, not one, to make a lesbian."[18] And if identity is relational, then perhaps we can begin to rethink identity politics as a politics of relational identities, of identities formed through political identifications that constantly remake those identities. As Zoe says in *L Is for the Way You Look,* "We decided to milk this for all it was worth, in terms of a female bonding experience."

Again in *Epistemology of the Closet,* Sedgwick writes:

I take the precious, devalued arts of gossip, immemorially associated in European thought with servants, with effeminate and gay men, with all women, to have to do not even so much with the transmission of necessary news as with the refinement of necessary skills for making, testing, and using unrationalized and provisional hypotheses about what kinds of people *there are to be found in one's world. . . . I don't assume that all*

18. Teresa de Lauretis, "Film and the Visible," in *How Do I Look? Queer Film and Video,* ed. Bad Object Choices (Seattle: Bay Press, 1991), p. 232.

gay men or all women are very skilled at the nonce-taxonomic work represented by gossip, but it does make sense to suppose that our distinctive needs are peculiarly disserved by its devaluation.[19]

The most fundamental need gossip has served for queers is that of the construction—and reconstruction—of our identities. Most of us can remember the first time we heard someone called a queer, or a fag or a dyke, and—that someone *not* being ourselves—nevertheless responding, within, "So that's what I am." Because the name-calling is most often a derogation, our identifications are also self-derogations. We painstakingly emerge from these self-derogations through new identifications, a process that often depends on gossip among ourselves: "Really, *he's* gay? *She's* a dyke?" "Jodie's a dyke? Then maybe I'm fabulous, too." From this, we go on to deduce the role-model defense. "If little tomboys growing up today knew about Jodie, they'd be spared the self-derogation." But the deduction misses two crucial points: first, what Sedgwick means by "an already institutionalized ignorance," and second, our conception of identity.

Little tomboys won't be told about an openly lesbian actress, whose career will in any case probably be cut short the moment she comes out. As Vito Russo famously quipped about coming out, "The truth will set you free . . . but first it will make you miserable." The eradication of the homophobia that constructs the celebrity's closet does not depend on the individual celebrity's avowal, the limitations of which we have seen again and again: Did the exemplary midshipman's confession of his homosexuality change the rules at Annapolis or the Pentagon? Did the Olympic medal winner's founding of the Gay Olympics persuade the U.S. Olympics committee or the Supreme Court to let us use that rubric? No, the eradication of homophobia—of this already institutionalized ignorance—depends on our collective political struggle, on our identity politics.

Identity politics has most often been understood, and is now denigrated, as essentialist (denigrated in certain quarters, in fact, as *essen-*

19. Sedgwick, *Epistemology of the Closet,* p. 23.

tially essentialist; this is what Diana Fuss recognizes as the essentialism of anti-essentialism).[20] We were gay, and on our gayness, we built a political movement. But is this really what happened? Wasn't it an emerging political movement that enabled the enunciation of a gay—rather than homosexual or homophile—identity? And wasn't that political movement formed through identifications with other political movements—Black Power and feminism, most particularly? Remember, the Gay Liberation Front, named in identification with Third World liberation struggles, came apart over two issues: whether to support the Black Panthers and whether women would have an equal voice. It was our inability to form alliances with those movements identifications with which secured our own identities, as well as our inability to acknowledge those very same differences of race and gender within our own ranks, that caused the gay and lesbian movements to shift, on the one hand, to an essentialist separatism and, on the other, to a liberal politics of minority rights. The AIDS crisis brought us face to face with the consequences of both our separatism and our liberalism. And it is in this new political conjuncture that the word *queer* has been reclaimed to designate new political identities.

The setbacks for the AIDS activist movement that I mentioned above avoided one of the most difficult of them: troubles within the movement itself. Our political unity has been badly shaken by our constantly increasing knowledge of both the breadth and depth of the crisis— breadth, in the sense of the many different kinds of people affected by HIV disease; depth, in the sense of the extent of social change that will be required to improve all these different people's chances of survival. It is impossible here to describe fully either the scope of the crisis or the factionalism it has caused. But consider just this: whereas at first the structure of ACT UP in New York consisted of six committees—Actions, Coordinating, Fundraising, Issues, Media, and Outreach—by 1991, when our internal difficulties emerged most damagingly, we had fourteen committees, twenty-one working groups, and ten caucuses— forty-five different subgroups in all. Apart from a few remaining com-

20. See Diana Fuss, *Essentially Speaking: Feminism, Nature, and Difference* (New York: Routledge, 1989).

mittees that are still essentially organizational and several working groups centered on actions-in-progress, these various committees, working groups, and caucuses are oriented mostly toward either specific issues—Addicts Rights, Alternative and Holistic Treatment, Insurance and Access, Healthcare Action, Medicaid Task Force, Needle Exchange, Pediatric Caucus, Police Violence, Prison Issues, PWA Housing, Treatment and Data, YELL (Youth Education Life Line)—or identities—Asian and Pacific Islanders, Black AIDS Mobilization, Foreign Nationals, Latina/o AIDS Activists, Lesbian Caucus, PISD (People with Immune System Disorders), and Women's Action.

This level of specialization does not, in and of itself, necessarily result in factionalism; it merely suggests something of the complexity of issues raised by the epidemic and of the make-up of the AIDS activist movement. But conflict does exist, and much of it concerns competing identities and contradictory identifications *across* identities. There are conflicts between men and women, between lesbians and straight women, between white people and people of color, between those who are HIV-positive or have AIDS and those who are HIV-negative. There are also conflicts between those who think we should devote all our energies to militant direct action and those who favor meeting with government officials and pharmaceutical company executives as well; between those who want to concentrate on a narrowly defined AIDS agenda and those who feel we must confront the wider systemic ills that AIDS exacerbates; between those who see ACT UP as the vanguard in the struggle against AIDS and those who see direct action as only one of many forms of AIDS activism, which also includes advocacy, fundraising, legal action, and providing services. Negotiating these conflicts is painful and perilous; it has even resulted in splits or dissolutions of ACT UP chapters in some cities.

These conflicts are not new to ACT UP, but their intensity is. Earlier in our history, they were mitigated by a queer hegemony. Most of us were gay and lesbian, and ACT UP meant for us not only fighting AIDS, but fighting AIDS as queers, fighting homophobia, and rejuvenating a moribund gay activism. In New York, we met at the Lesbian and Gay

Community Services Center; you had to confront your homophobia just to cross the threshold. Our meetings and actions, our fact sheets and chants, our T-shirts and placards, our videos and even our acronyms—everything about us was queer. We camped a lot, laughed a lot, kissed each other, partied together. ACT UP fundraisers at nightclubs were the hot ticket in queer social life.

But that hegemony didn't last. Attacks on queers escalated, both officially, with the congressional assault on government support of our culture, and unofficially, on the streets. As queers became more and more visible, more and more of us were getting bashed. Overburdened by the battles AIDS required us to take on, ACT UP couldn't fight the homophobia anymore. That, too, was a full-time struggle, a struggle taken on by the newly formed Queer Nation. I don't want to oversimplify this capsule history. Queer Nation didn't take either the queers or the queerness out of ACT UP. But it made possible, at least symbolically, a shift of our attention to the non-queer, or the more-than-queer, problems of AIDS.

It was then that new political identifications began to be made, as I said, across identities. I have already mentioned a number of identities-in-conflict in ACT UP: men and women, whites and people of color, and so forth. In spite of the linguistic necessity of specifying identities with positive terms, I want to make clear that I am not speaking of identity as nonrelational. Because of the complexities of the movement, there is no predicting what identifications will be made and which side of an argument anyone might take. A white, middle-class, HIV-negative lesbian might form an identification with a poor black mother with AIDS, and through that identification might be inclined to work on pediatric health care issues; or, outraged by attention to the needs of babies at the expense of the needs of the women who bear them, she might decide to fight against clinical trials whose sole purpose is to examine the effects of an antiviral drug on perinatal transmission and thus ignores effects on the mother's body. She might form an identification with a gay male friend with AIDS and work for faster testing of new treatments for opportunistic infections, but then, through her understanding that her friend would be able to afford such treatments while others would not, she might shift her attention to health-care access issues. An HIV-positive gay Latino might fight homophobia in the Latin community and racism in ACT UP; he might speak Spanish at Latina/o AIDS Activist meetings and English everywhere else.

Political identifications remaking identities are, of course, productive of collective political struggle, but only if they result in a broadening of alliances rather than an exacerbation of antagonisms. And the latter seems often to result when, from within a development toward a politics of alliance based on relational identities, old antagonisms based on fixed identities reemerge. Activist politics then faces the impasse of ranking oppressions, moralism, and self-righteousness. This is the current plight of AIDS activism, but it is not the whole story.

During the time that ACT UP's internal antagonisms began to tear us apart, we nevertheless won a crucial victory. Arrested for taking to the streets of New York to distribute—openly and illegally—clean IV needles to injecting drug users, a group of ACT UP queers stood trial, eloquently argued a necessity defense, and won a landmark ruling that called into question the state's laws against possession of hypodermic needles and eventually forced Mayor Dinkins to relent on his opposition to needle exchange. AIDS activists are still—I'm sorry and angry to have to say—mostly a bunch of queers. But what does *queer* mean now? Who, for example, were those queers in the court room, on trial for attempting to save the lives of drug addicts? They were perhaps queers whose sexual practices resulted in HIV infection, or placed them at high risk of infection, or made them members of gay communities devastated by the epidemic, and for any of these reasons brought them to AIDS activism. But once engaged in the struggle to end the crisis, these queers' identities were no longer the same. It's not that "queer" doesn't any longer encompass their sexual practices; it does, but it also entails a *relation* between those practices and other circumstances that make very different people vulnerable both to HIV infection and to the stigma, discrimination, and neglect that have characterized the societal and governmental response to the constituencies most affected by the AIDS epidemic.

ABSOLUTELY QUEER: that was the anonymous group OUTpost's headline claim about Jodie Foster on the poster that appeared around New York about the time *The Silence of the Lambs* was released. "Jodie Foster," the caption beneath her photograph read, "Oscar winner. Yale graduate. Ex-Disney Moppet. Dyke." Well yes, . . . but queer? Absolutely queer? Through what identification? Interviewed about queer protests at the 1992 Academy Awards ceremony, where she won her second best-actress Oscar for her performance in *The Silence of the Lambs*, Foster declared, "Protesting is constitutional. You can learn from it. Anything beyond that falls into the category of being undignified."[21] Confronted with such a statement, I'm forced to agree with Larry Kramer: "Vito would really have screamed about that one." For Vito's was a feistier kind of dignity, not Jodie's idea of dignity but Judy's, a survivor's dignity. If we really want to honor Vito's memory—as a film scholar and movie buff, as a queer, an activist, and a friend—we shouldn't forget that he loved Judy, and that his identification with her made *him* queer, not her.

21. Quoted in John Gallagher, "Protest Threats Raise Visibility at Academy Awards," *Advocate,* May 5, 1992, p. 15. In this same issue of the *Advocate,* the "etcetera" column contains a photo of Jodie Foster whose caption reads, "A first-rate actress with a third-rate consciousness we hope is straight" (p. 88).

11 THE SPECTACLE OF MOURNING

First presented at the panel discussion "The Names

Project: The Transforming Power of the Forbidden

Stitch," sponsored by the Family Planning Council of

Western Massachusetts, Springfield, October 26, 1991.

Speaking about the Names Project quilt is difficult for me, because it means speaking about ambivalence, never as easy as expressing an unconflicted attitude. But at the same time I think that it might be possible to understand this ambivalence as appropriate to the quilt, since the quilt represents the work of mourning, a process that is itself profoundly ambivalent. As Freud describes it, mourning involves the painful conflict between the wish to cling to a lost loved one at the same time that we must work through the loss and definitively give that person up.

My initial ambivalence about the quilt, which was that often voiced by AIDS activists, was partially overcome when I first visited it on the Mall in Washington during the 1987 national march for lesbian and gay rights. Walking about the quilt, I was deeply moved—by the sheer enormity of loss, by the varied sentiments about so many people's lives, and by the grief-stricken responses of fellow mourners. One thing struck me particularly about my own response. Seeing a panel bearing the name of Michel Foucault, who was an intellectual idol, whose writings I had depended on for much of my own work, and who had agreed to be a reader of my dissertation less than a year before he died—seeing that panel had less emotional impact on me than seeing, every now and then, a name I recognized as that of someone I'd only dimly known, or known about. It was those moments that most brought home to me the full extent of my own loss—not my good friends Craig, Dan, Hector, René, Robert . . . , whose loss I had directly experienced, but others who, because I didn't know them well enough, I hadn't even known had died. In other words, I had lost not just the center of my world but its periphery, too. Reflecting on these feelings, I remember at the time saying to friends that it was the symbols of the ordinariness of human lives that made the quilt such a profoundly moving experience. I hope it's obvious that I don't mean ordinary as a negative quality; I mean it in the sense that Raymond Williams did when he said that culture is ordinary. My feeling was related to the anger I've often felt about the media's reserving its attention for the deaths of famous people while at the same time the deaths of hundreds and thousands of others—those of ordinary people—go unnoticed.

Unfurling the Names Project Quilt on the Washington Mall, 1987 (photo: Jane Rosett).

Shortly after my first direct experience of the quilt, I was sent a copy of a right-wing campus newspaper containing a diatribe against safe-sex education written by President Reagan's White House AIDS advisor Gary Bauer. Accompanying his vicious text was an equally vicious illustration, a cartoon of the quilt showing two panels being sewn. The name on one was "Sodomy"; on the other it was "IV Drugs." Nothing could better corroborate what I wrote in "Mourning and Militancy": that "seldom has a society so savaged people during their hour of loss." Every AIDS joke is callous, but this is for me the most callous. It says that not only will there be no sympathy for our lives, there will be no sympathy even for our deaths. And from this my ambivalence returned. For while we know that this callousness, this savagery, has been directed at us constantly throughout the epidemic, we also know that, the cartoon notwithstanding, the Names Project quilt is one of the few efforts of our community that has been generally granted exemption from opprobrium.

To understand this ambivalence, it may be necessary to isolate two distinct functions of the quilt. The first is that it provides a ritual of mourning, and in two respects: the private mourning ritual of a person or group involved in making a panel and the collective mourning ritual of visiting the quilt to share that experience with others. The second function is what we might call the spectacle of mourning, the vast public-relations effort to humanize and dignify our losses for those who have not shared them. My ambivalence hinges on this second, spectacular aspect of the quilt: Does a visit to the quilt, or the media's approving attention to it, assuage the guilt of those who otherwise have been so callous, whether that callousness takes the form of denial or of outright disgust? Does it provide a form of catharsis, an easing of conscience, for those who have cared and done so little about this great tragedy?

Perhaps I can clarify the question with another: Will there one day be a panel on the quilt for Kimberly Bergalis? And will it memorialize those words she uttered before Congress? "I didn't do anything wrong, but I'm being made to suffer like this. My life has been taken away."[1] With those words, Kimberly Bergalis showed why she became both a darling of the media and a tool of Congressman Dannemeyer in one of his many attempts to pass wasteful, discriminatory, punitive legislation. As media activist Gregg Bordowitz said, Kimberly Bergalis is the first member of the general public with AIDS we have seen. She has never identified herself with other people with AIDS. On the contrary, she identifies herself only as the victim of others with AIDS. She represents not PWAs, but the so-called general public's fear of people with AIDS.[2]

I don't want to claim that media representations of AIDS are without contradiction, but I do want to ask what it is about the quilt that makes it so palatable to the media that paid such homage to Kimberly Bergalis

1. Quoted in the *New York Times,* September 27, 1991, p. A12.
2. See Cathy Caruth and Thomas Keenan, "'The AIDS Crisis Is Not Over': A Conversation with Gregg Bordowitz, Douglas Crimp, and Laura Pinsky," *American Imago: Studies in Psychoanalysis and Culture* 48, no. 4 (winter 1991); reprinted in Cathy Caruth, *Trauma: Explorations in Memory* (Baltimore: Johns Hopkins University Press, 1995), pp. 256–271.

as the archetypal innocent victim. For I think we must recognize that Kimberly Bergalis was a representational choice, a choice that did not extend, for example, to Belinda Mason, whose "innocence" was no doubt tarnished by the fact that she became an articulate spokesperson for all PWAs, people whose struggles she entirely took on as her own. Belinda Mason argued, in a letter written to President Bush just before her death, against the very bill that Kimberly Bergalis testified for.

Perhaps that vicious cartoon can provide an answer. When Kimberly Bergalis informed Congress that she didn't do anything wrong, we know exactly what she meant: She didn't engage in sodomy and she didn't use drugs. What the cartoon means to tell us is that the quilt is not telling the truth, that what it isn't telling us is that all these people who died of AIDS were bad people, that they were sodomites and junkies. Of course, to make its nasty point, the creators of this cartoon could hardly have included panels that said hemophilia or perinatal transmission or just plain sexual intercourse between married couples; these "innocent" modes of contracting HIV would undermine their point. But their point is what we have to attend to.

I don't think most people would espouse the belief that gay men and IV drug users deserve to die, but I nevertheless think that most people are afraid to look gay sex and drug use square in the eye as everyday facts of many, many people's lives. In everything I have written about AIDS, which has concentrated mostly on gay men, I have insisted on the determining fact of homophobia, which I believe is still the single most powerful determinant of everything everyone has suffered during this epidemic. And I've been especially critical of any response to this homophobia that makes any concessions to it. In "How to Have Promiscuity in an Epidemic," I criticized Randy Shilts for his gift of the Patient Zero narrative to the media and Larry Kramer for his condemnation of promiscuous gay sex in *The Normal Heart*. In "Portraits of People with AIDS," I asserted that Nicholas Nixon's portrayals of gay men as deathbed victims with fleshless, ethereal bodies were phobic images, images of the fear of people with AIDS as still sexual. And I contrasted these photographs with Stashu Kybartas's videotape *Danny,* a portrayal of a gay man with AIDS as both sexual and sexy. In "Mourning and Militancy," I wrote that what gay men had lost to AIDS, and what we were therefore mourning, was not only our lovers, friends, acquaintances, and community members, but also our highly developed sexual culture. And I suggested that the repudiation of that culture entailed a failure to mourn, a form of melancholia. What has been important to me is to insist on precisely what the creators of that horrible cartoon insist on: sodomy, to use their quaint, archaic word.

In seeing and being moved by the representation of what I called ordinariness in the Names Project quilt, it is partially the representation of sodomy that I saw. Not directly. There aren't a whole lot of cock rings, dildos, or Crisco labels, for example, although there are plenty of color-coded handkerchiefs. But in a myriad different details, I saw my culture, my sexual culture. I felt I knew many of these people, knew them from the bars and bath houses, from the streets and parks. But I wonder how true this is for others. I wonder what kind of ordinariness other people see. And that's one reason for my ambivalence. Does the quilt sanitize or sentimentalize gay life? Does it render invisible what makes people hate us? Does it make their continuing disavowal possible?

My ambivalence is about, on the one hand, my anger at a cartoon that would vilify our ritual of mourning by replacing the name of a person with that of a sexual act—sodomy—and, on the other hand, my desire to celebrate the sexuality of those we mourn. Because if we fail to celebrate that sexuality, then we fail to celebrate a vital part of the lives of those we mourn.

Jeff Nunokawa has written, in "All the Sad Young Men," of another difficulty that gay men have with mourning. Beginning with a reading of *The Portrait of Dorian Gray*, he analyzes the legacy of literary portrayals of gay men as always already doomed, the logical outcome of our having been pathologized from the moment homosexuality was invented as a category of nineteenth-century sexology.[3] Vito Russo saw the same

3. Jeff Nunokawa, "All the Sad Young Men: AIDS and the Work of Mourning," in *Inside/Out*, ed. Diana Fuss (New York: Routledge, 1991), pp. 311–323.

pattern in the history of Hollywood's portrayals of gay men and lesbians. At the end of *The Celluloid Closet*, he appended a necrology, in which he cataloged the causes of premature death of hundreds of gay and lesbian film characters.[4] That many in our society secretly want us dead is to me beyond question. And one expression of this may be our society's loving attention to the quilt, which is not only a ritual and representation of mourning but also stunning evidence of the mass death of gay men. It would, of course, be unseemly for society to celebrate our deaths openly, but I wonder if the quilt helps make this desire decorous.

One question I would pose about the quilt, then, is a question that I have learned to pose about any representation: Whom does it address? Who is its presumed audience? Is it for President George and First Lady Barbara Bush, who, even when implored, would not deign to walk across the street to see it?[5] Is it for the media, surveying it from helicopters? Is it for the general public, that fiction whose ugly face we saw personified by Kimberly Bergalis? Or is it for those who can read from the representation of ordinariness the sex lives of so many people whose names the panels bear? Is it for those who inhabit a culture of poverty, for whom drugs are often a way of life? Is it for those who take solace in this collective ritual of mourning, who recognize the names of friends and loved ones, of sometime acquaintances, and encounters in the dark? Of those like us and those bound to us by their struggle against both AIDS and an indifferent society?

In the film *Common Threads*, Vito Russo is shown speaking at a 1988 ACT NOW rally in front of the Health and Human Services headquarters in Washington the day before the big action at the Food and Drug Administration in Rockland, Maryland. The moment of Vito's speech used in the film was when he said, "I'm here because I don't want to have my

4. Vito Russo, *The Celluloid Closet: Homosexuality in the Movies* (New York: Harper & Row, 1981), pp. 261–262.

5. In spite of this fact, The Names Project Foundation brochure handed out on the occasion for which I gave this paper included the following anodyne and cliché-ridden blurb: "'These amazing quilts . . . prove that no one is a statistic. Every life has its own fabric, its own colors, its own soul. No two are alike.'—President George Bush, Washington, D.C."

name on that quilt over there in front of the White House." Vito died in November of 1990, and I imagine one day many panels of the quilt will bear his name. Vito must have been ambivalent about the quilt, too, because even though he was determined never to join him there, he made a panel for his lover Jeffrey. But Vito intended to survive. That was what made him such a fierce activist. Certainly some activists misinterpreted his comment about the quilt as hostility toward it. But I don't think he was hostile toward the quilt. He was hostile toward what made the quilt necessary: so many, many early deaths.

For many activists who find those deaths unacceptable, the quilt is seen as capitulation; it represents acceptance of those deaths. But this returns us to the ambivalence of mourning that I spoke of in the beginning. In an epidemic that didn't have to happen, and whose continuing to this day to spread virtually unabated is the result of political neglect or outright mendacity, every death is unacceptable. And yet death itself can never finally not be accepted. We have to accept death to continue to live. But the difference, and the resulting ambivalence, is precisely this: the difference between those of us who must learn to accept these deaths and those who still find these deaths acceptable. And who can say whether or not the Names Project quilt might cut both ways?

12 ACCOMMODATING MAGIC

First presented at "Dissident Spectators, Disruptive

Spectacles: A Conference on Watching the Media,"

Harvard University Center for Literary and Cultural

Studies, Cambridge, Massachusetts, May 15–16, 1992,

and published in Media Spectacles, *ed. Marjorie*

Garber, Jann Matlock, and Rebecca L. Walkowitz

(New York: Routledge, 1993). This is an expanded

version written in the fall of 1992.

*We think, well, only gay people can get it—it's not going to happen to
me. And here I am saying that it can happen to anyone, even me, Magic
Johnson.*
—From the press conference at the Great Western Forum

*Then came the news about Magic. In a way, that changes everything. He
is not them; Magic is us.*
—A Daily News *column of a few days later*[1]

Magic is here. Magic is now. Magic is us.
—Sports Illustrated*'s version of the same*[2]

Now everyone knows someone who's infected.
—The sportswriter's presumption

Where were you when you heard the news about Magic?
—Newsweek *suggesting the Kennedy assassination analogy*[3]

My grandfather was a basketball player, and so was my grandmother. I
have photographs of both of them proudly posing with their high school
teammates. My brother was a star basketball player and now coaches
women's college basketball, my sister married a high school basketball
coach, my nephew went to college on a basketball scholarship, and my
twelve-year-old, already five-foot-eight niece is a basketball prodigy
(since she's too young for Magic, her room is covered with Michael Jor-
dan posters). During my adolescence in the small town where I grew up,
people meeting me for the first time would note my height and the size
of my hands—big enough to palm a basketball—and say, "You must be
a basketball player." Admitting that I wasn't embarrassed me; it felt like
divulging my sexuality. In fact I *did* play basketball throughout most of

1. Earl Caldwell, "Magic: When 'Them' Becomes 'Us,'" *New York Daily News*, November 11, 1991, p. 29.
2. Leigh Montville, "Like One of the Family," *Sports Illustrated*, November 18, 1991, p. 45.
3. Charles Leerhsen et al., "Magic's Message," *Newsweek*, November 18, 1991, p. 58.

my childhood and adolescence, but being queer made me self-conscious in locker rooms, so I stayed away from organized sports. What I meant when I said I didn't play was only that I didn't turn out for the high school team. Like a lot of other queers, when I left my hometown and found out there were places where playing basketball wasn't the only measure of worth, I rarely played or watched a basketball game again. So on November 7, 1991, when I listened to Magic Johnson announcing his retirement from the Lakers because he'd tested HIV-positive, I had to ask, Who's Magic Johnson?

Of course I found out right away. By the time I watched *Nightline* that same night, I'd already learned enough about Magic to recoil at Larry Kramer's insensitivity when he declared Magic would become a pariah and die. I doubted Magic would become a pariah, and though I agreed that he'd probably die of AIDS, I knew it wasn't the right time to say it.

But I understand why Larry was so angry. Those of us who have long been coping with this crisis, who have watched lovers, friends, and acquaintances die or are ourselves infected or ill, are enraged by the constant repetitions. How many times do we have to hear "AIDS is not just a gay disease"? "The virus doesn't discriminate." "Heterosexuals get AIDS, too." "HIV is transmitted through heterosexual intercourse." "Everyone is potentially at risk." "AIDS is everybody's problem." How much longer will the us/them rhetoric remain in place? How many people have to die or become infected for it to matter? Why is attention paid only when celebrities become infected, get diagnosed, or die?

Of course, we also know the answers to our questions, but it doesn't make the repetitions any easier. One answer was broadcast the very next night, when Magic appeared on *The Arsenio Hall Show*. At his press conference Magic had said that it didn't matter how he got the virus. It was a courageous gesture, but of course it wouldn't play. So he told Arsenio, "I'm far from being homosexual. You know that. Everybody else who's close to me understands that." The crowd went berserk, cheering wildly for several minutes. What could Magic do but flash that

Magic Johnson on the *Arsenio Hall Show,* November 8, 1991 (AP/Wide World Photos).

smile?—"the most famous smile since the Mona Lisa" in *Newsweek*'s estimation.[4] The crowd evidently felt vindicated now that they were re-assured that they hadn't been duped into hero-worshiping a secret fag. Queers felt betrayed. We'd heard through the grapevine that Magic *was* a secret fag, and I guess we hoped it was true.[5] Not every queer stops playing basketball when he leaves home, and we'd like people to learn that, even if the hard way.

Writing a week later in *Sports Illustrated,* Magic repeated his denial of the rumors—"I have never had a homosexual encounter. Never"— and speculated on how he became infected. "It's a matter of numbers. Before I was married, I truly lived the bachelor's life. I'm no Wilt Chamberlain, but as I traveled around NBA cities, I was never at a loss for fe-male companionship. . . . There were just some bachelors almost every woman in L.A. wanted to be with: Eddie Murphy, Arsenio Hall, and

4. Jack Kroll, "Smile, though Our Hearts Are Breaking," *Newsweek,* November 18, 1991, p. 65.
5. Peter Vecsey, "Rumors Fly about Magic, but the Motives Are Selfish," *USA Today,* November 12, 1991, p. 6C.

Magic Johnson. I confess that after I arrived in L.A. in 1979, I did my best to accommodate as many women as I could—most of them through unprotected sex."[6]

Accommodate? "He was doing these women some kind of *favor?*" Barbara Harrison asked in *Mademoiselle.*[7] The arrogance and contempt Harrison recognized in the word choice were corroborated by Magic's friend Pamela McGee, who wrote in the *Los Angeles Times,* "Magic's closest friends always knew him as a major player and womanizer. He has had one-night stands with what he calls 'freaks' across America."[8] Like the denial of homosexuality, the misogyny does its work: promiscuity, which Johnson would come to regret and thus to condemn, was really the sin of others. Magic wasn't in active pursuit; he just acquiesced to fast women: "I know that we are pursued by women so much that it is easy to be weak. Maybe by getting the virus I'll make it easier for you guys to be strong."[9] Another repetition: women scapegoated as vectors of transmission; *their* risk—the greater risk of infection—is not the issue. And, as Martina Navratilova noted, the big-time double standard: if a woman athlete confessed to so many sex partners, she wouldn't be seen as a superstar but as "a whore and a slut."[10]

Moralizing about promiscuity has been and continues to be one of the most difficult rhetorics to combat for AIDS educators. Every queer remembers the incredulity, disdain, and disguised envy that met early accounts of gay men's numbers of sex partners. Now that the tables are

6. Magic Johnson, with Roy S. Johnson, "I'll Deal with It," *Sports Illustrated,* November 18, 1991, pp. 21–22. "Most" is something of an understatement. Johnson told the *Advocate* that he tried using condoms "just one time," but gave them up because he "didn't get the same feeling" (Roger Brigham, "The Importance of Being Earvin," *Advocate,* April 21, 1992, p. 38). For Wilt Chamberlain's account of his sexual conquests, see *A View from Above* (New York: Villard, 1991).

7. Barbara Harrison, "Do You Believe in Magic?" *Mademoiselle,* March 1992, p. 94.

8. Pamela McGee, "Friend: Magic Had Plenty of One-Night Stands," *New York Newsday,* November 10, 1991, p. 4.

9. Johnson, "I'll Deal with It," p. 22.

10. Martina Navratilova, interviewed in the *New York Times,* November 21, 1991, p. B16.

turned, the envy comes out in the open, but it poses a new crisis. When the studio audience on *The Arsenio Hall Show* cheered so wildly, their homophobia was doubly displayed, for in their gloating that Magic was no fag, they could not but demonstrate that they would rather die than entertain the idea that he could be one. Had those "freaks" that Magic accommodated been men instead of women, Arsenio's vociferously heterosexual audience *might* have wanted to heave a collective sigh of relief that they still aren't implicated in this terrible epidemic, as they've wanted to believe all along.

Playboy moved fast to accommodate Magic's news. Keeping sex safe, untroubled, unencumbered for heterosexual men is their up-front agenda, Michael Fumento's *Myth of Heterosexual AIDS* their treacherous guide.[11] More repetitions: safe anatomy—fragile anus versus rugged penis and vagina, "built," as *Playboy* put it, "to sustain the rigors of sex."[12] Safe (and racist) geography—AIDS in Africa is a different epidemic and sex in Africa is a different practice. More safe (and racist) geography—AIDS is contained in "communities"—"What will kill you in the South Bronx will make you a living legend in your home town."[13] And of course, heterosexual transmission as a deceit perpetrated by the "powerful gay lobby" to get more funding for "their" disease.

But there was still Magic. *Playboy* had some doubts: "Assuming that he did not contract the virus from his dentist (no one checked), another male (he denies the rumors), or intravenous drug use (steroids?), Magic

11. Michael Fumento's *The Myth of Heterosexual AIDS* (New York: Basic Books, 1990) argues that heterosexual transmission of HIV is enormously exaggerated by the media, by politicians, and by "the powerful gay lobby" as a means of increasing funding for a "gay disease." For Fumento, virtually every case of heterosexual transmission, and especially female-to-male transmission, is a special case.

12. James R. Patersen, "The Playboy Forum: Magic," *Playboy,* March 1992, p. 43. The fragile anus/rugged vagina hypothesis appeared as early as 1985 in John Langone, "AIDS: The Latest Scientific Facts," *Discover,* December 1985, pp. 27–52. For an analysis, see Paula Treichler, "AIDS, Homophobia, and Biomedical Discourse: An Epidemic of Signification," in *AIDS: Cultural Analysis/Cultural Activism,* ed. Douglas Crimp (Cambridge: MIT Press, 1988), pp. 31–70.

13. Patersen, "The Playboy Forum: Magic," p. 43.

is simply the newest member of a very small group of men who have contracted the AIDS virus through heterosexual contact." "Magic is an exceptional man. . . . He could accomplish more with a smile than you or I could in a year of sophisticated courtship. . . . He says he lived 'the bachelor's life,' but that is like saying he could play a little ball. Just as he redefined the guard's position on the basketball court, he redefined the number of sexual conquests that it is possible for a bachelor to achieve off the court. All his passes were caught."[14]

Playboy's Magic is a whole new "myth of heterosexual AIDS." You'd think using a condom, like being a fag, was worse than death. Paradoxically, because we queers know it's not, and because nobody will ever ask us, we have to learn to accommodate Magic.

From the moment of the November 7 press conference, Magic began urging that "safe sex is the way to go,"[15] and he's remained steadfast under intense pressure to modify his position. He is accommodating enough to tell kids that "the safest sex is no sex," but he knows, just as the kids do, that the truism is also a lie: No sex may be safe, but it's not sex. As he told *Ebony,* "That's not the reality, and I'm trying to explain that to people too. Reality is young people. . . . are going to have sex no matter what has happened to me. So if that's going to be the case, then they should practice safe sex."[16] Magic's realism about the necessity of teaching safe sex is no surprise, but the widespread acceptance of it is a significant breakthrough.

In spite of extraordinary success in slowing seroconversion rates for gay men, in spite of consensus among health educators about its efficacy, skepticism about safe sex has lingered, registered along a spectrum from "there's no such thing as safe sex" to the hedge-your-bets "r" tacked onto *safe*—not safe, but at least *safer* sex. But now, as if by magic, there

14. Ibid., p. 41.
15. Quoted in Pico Iyer, "It Can Happen to Anybody. Even Magic Johnson," *Time,* November 18, 1991, p. 26.
16. "Magic Johnson's Full-Court Press against AIDS," *Ebony,* April 1992, p. 108.

really is such a thing as safe sex. And the reason can be discerned in the same *Ebony* article, as a moment painfully reminiscent of the Arsenio episode is recalled. Magic was speaking to students at Cardozo High School in Washington. "And when he told them 'I still kiss my wife a lot,' the place went nuts—you couldn't have heard a symphony of school bells for all the screams and applause."[17] Safe sex has become truly safe, you see, because Magic has to accommodate his wife Cookie. *Ebony's* cover article was devoted to Magic and Cookie's marriage, and was meant to allay some new tabloid rumors—that Cookie had moved to the maid's room, was so afraid of contracting HIV that she wouldn't let Magic touch her. "All of those rumors are false," Cookie reassured, and "As for their marriage, 'it has only gotten stronger, it's just fine. . . .' As Magic put it, 'We are still doing our thing.'"[18]

Accommodating Magic. I want to try to make it clear how difficult this is. Behind the "there's no such thing as safe sex" line, which has been used mostly to prevent teenagers from getting safe sex education, there has always been a tacit assumption, applied equally to queers and teenagers (doubly to queer teens), that for such people sex is a luxury, an indulgence, an excess, a dissipation. We are told to give it up, desist, abstain. There has never been anything like an equivalence drawn between gay and straight sex, which is why gay men's success in stopping the spread of HIV infection with the adoption of safe sex practices has never been seen as an example to emulate. Now, though, Magic Johnson is infected with HIV, and he is blissfully married to Cookie, and so safe sex must be safe after all. Even *Playboy* will go this far: "If Magic can articulate the role of intimacy in his own life—the commitment that supersedes fear of infection—then we all stand to learn something. This is the real meaning of the marriage vow 'till death do us part.' This is the real face of love."[19]

17. Ibid.
18. Laura B. Randolf, "Magic and Cookie Johnson Speak Out for First Time on Love, Marriage, and AIDS," *Ebony,* April 1992, p. 106.
19. Patersen, "The Playboy Forum: Magic," p. 45.

Accommodating Magic—for queers—means accommodating this contradiction: Safe sex will be accepted, taught to teenagers, adopted by heterosexuals at risk, save lives—because of Magic, because it is necessary to protect the sanctity and prerogatives of his heterosexual union. Accommodating Magic—for queers—means accommodating the continued homophobic construction of AIDS discourse, apparently as unshakable today as it was when the new disease syndrome was named GRID, for Gay Related Immune Deficiency.

It is this homophobia that we endure every time we see Magic accomplish something we've worked for so tirelessly for years, to no avail. For years we tried to get the media to distinguish between HIV and AIDS; they finally found it necessary to comply in order to reassure Magic's fans that he was infected with HIV but did not have AIDS.[20] For years we asked the media for images of people with HIV disease living normal, productive lives. They gave us Magic playing the All-Star Game. For years we badgered the *New York Times* to take a critical position on George Bush's do-nothing AIDS policies. They wrote a scathing editorial headlined "Magic Johnson, as President."[21] We badgered Bush directly. He rebuked us, but admitted to Magic, "I haven't done enough about AIDS," and asked him to join his National Commission on AIDS.[22]

20. Johnson himself made it clear how badly the media had failed on this point: "Dr. Mellman quickly told me that I didn't have AIDS, that I was only infected with the virus that could someday lead to the disease. But I didn't really hear him. Like almost everyone else who has not paid attention to the growing AIDS epidemic in the U.S. and the rest of the world, I didn't know the difference between the virus and the disease. While my ears heard HIV-positive, my mind heard AIDS" (Johnson, "I'll Deal with It," p. 18).

21. "Magic Johnson, as President," *New York Times,* November 9, 1991, p. 22.

22. On January 22, 1992, prior to his first meeting with Bush, Johnson wrote the president a forceful letter asking him to become the leader he had not yet been on AIDS. The letter included three demands for increased funding: to speed research, to fund the Ryan White CARE Bill fully, and to allow Medicaid to pay for people with HIV disease, not just AIDS. On July 14, the *New York Times* reported that Johnson had told CNN that he would probably resign from the National Commission on AIDS: "We need funding," Johnson said, "and every time we ask for more funding we get turned down by the President" ("Magic Johnson Says He Is Likely to Quit Bush's AIDS Panel," p. A18). Johnson's official resignation was announced on September 25, 1992.

Wherever Magic appears—the NAACP Image Awards, the American Music Awards, on any talk show—there is adulation. His fellow players arranged a pre-All-Star Game ritual of bear hugs. The spectacle of someone who is HIV-positive being revered and physically embraced is deeply gratifying. But *our* gratification is diminished, because we know the boast to Arsenio makes it possible.

But we know something else, too. Gay men who have unequally borne the burden of AIDS in the United States know that that burden has also been unequally borne by people of color. In 1992, the *majority* of new AIDS cases in the United States was reported among people of color. African Americans account for 12 percent of the population, but more than 25 percent of total reported cases of full-blown AIDS. More than half of all women with AIDS are African American. Three out of four women with AIDS are African American or Latina. Nine out of ten children with AIDS and over half the teenagers with AIDS are African American or Latino.[23] Magic admitted that he hadn't practiced safe sex during his bachelor years because, before receiving his test results, he still thought of AIDS as a gay disease. That astonishes me, but then I recall that, before he received his test results, I didn't know who Magic was, and that would probably astonish him. Now I know very well who Magic is, and he knows very well that AIDS is devastating African American communities. His determination, from the outset, to "become a spokesman for the virus" is good news for those communities and for others affected by AIDS. For an article in *TV Guide* about the production of *Nickelodeon*'s "A Conversation with Magic" for kids, Linda Ellerbee called a friend who is HIV-positive.

I wanted to know what my friend, a gay man, thought about the enormous attention Magic Johnson's announcement had brought to AIDS. After all, so many other good people have already died without most of us seeming to notice.

23. Statistical information from the Centers for Disease Control as of April 1992.

"Yes," he said, "it's unfair. So what. . . . If it takes a Magic Johnson to see that AIDS is everybody's problem, if he can use his fame to get the government to do more, if he can raise more money to fight the disease—to find a cure—what does fair matter?"[24]

Accommodating Magic. But "fair" *does* matter. Because "fair" can also save lives, and "unfair" can be lethal.

If Magic Johnson's credibility as a "spokesman for the virus" is ensured by his defensive heterosexuality, coupled with his newfound commitment to marital monogamy, where does this leave gay men? More significantly, given Magic's express concern for African Americans, where does it leave black gay men? Responding to Magic's "far-from-being-homosexual" claim to his pal Arsenio, and to the audience response, Charles Stewart, a contributing editor of *BLK*, wrote in the *New Republic*, "One of the largest and most invisible groups affected by the AIDS epidemic, black gay and bisexual men, just became even more invisible." After detailing what he termed the double jeopardy faced by many black gay men—their alienation from gay community institutions, largely experienced as white, and black community institutions, largely experienced as straight—Stewart went on to voice his fear that Magic might "destigmatize AIDS at the cost of restigmatizing black gay men, who are still the prime risk group for this disease."[25]

Just prior to his first meeting with the National Commission on AIDS, Magic wrote to George Bush that he now knows "more about HIV and AIDS than I ever wanted to."[26] But still, like Bush himself, Magic has generally adopted an accommodating stance: He wants to save the kids. In the AIDS epidemic, however, saving kids will mean knowing more than Magic has so far let on that he does:

24. Linda Ellerbee, "Magic TV and Kids," *TV Guide,* March 21–27, 1992, p. 10.
25. Charles Stewart, "Double Jeopardy: Black, Gay (and Invisible)," *New Republic,* December 2, 1991, pp. 13, 15.
26. Letter from Earvin Johnson, Jr., to President George Bush, January 14, 1992.

—knowing, for example, that the availability of clean and free hypodermic needles for IV drug users will save not only their lives but those of their sex partners and children as well;

—knowing that the disproportionate numbers of black women with AIDS is due in part to women's greater risk than men's of infection through heterosexual sex;

—knowing that the disproportionate number of AIDS cases among African Americans includes a disproportionate number of AIDS cases among black gay men;

—knowing that black men who have sex with men often don't cop to being gay, might even say, if pressed, "I'm far from being homosexual";

—knowing that those men who have sex with men often also have sex with women;

—and knowing that kids, black kids, even the ones who play basketball, can be queer.

In 1987, when AIDSfilms produced *Changing the Rules,* the first made-for-television safe-sex education video, the stated assumption was that only straight people needed education; gay men were supposedly already informed. The assumption was wrong for a number of reasons: because the many various men who have sex with men have vastly unequal access to education materials distributed by local gay community institutions, depending on those men's self-perceived sexual identities, their geographic locations, their ethnic, racial, and class positions, and because "gay men" is not a stable, already formed, unchanging group. Children are in the process of becoming gay all the time, and they need to be educated too.

Another repetition: Magic Johnson and Arsenio Hall's video, *Time Out: The Truth About HIV, AIDS and You,* proceeds from the same assumption as *Changing the Rules,* this time, though, without directly saying so. In fact, the "gay issue" is included in several ways in this video directed at teenagers. In an early segment, a white girl tells us that one of her best friends is a lesbian and that it doesn't bother her; a boy, possibly Latino, says, "I'm openly gay. Through our knowledge and then our education, we are beginning to decrease the number of cases in the gay community, so that's been my experience"; and finally another white girl tells us she's been out as a lesbian since she was fourteen, that she knows sixteen people who have died, and that a number of those people were closeted, married, and had infected their wives. From this segment we thus learn that gay people can be tolerated by straights, that they already know about AIDS, and that they infect unknowing straights.

There is one other openly gay person in the tape. Among a number of people who talk about testing positive, a young Brazilian American explains that learning his sero-status was made easier because his lover was there for him: "I was real glad I was with my lover of that time," he says. "We both had tested together, and he tested negative and I tested positive, and he was very supportive. He didn't say, 'Well, goodbye, now, because you're positive.'"

The longest part of this segment, however, is devoted to "Jason, 22," who gets to be much more than a talking head. We first see Jason lifting weights. He's very hot. He tells us, "I don't look like the stereotypical HIV-positive person. You know, the stereotype is gay, old, sick-looking." Jason proves the stereotype wrong on each count: He's straight, young, and healthy-looking. The segment's ostensible purpose is to show that HIV-positive people can have sexual relationships. Jason has an HIV-negative girlfriend.

As a queer, it's difficult to watch the enactment of Jason's little romance and not imagine how it might have been different, perhaps because in the opening black-and-white sequence, with Jason pumping iron, the hard bodied, clean-cut, all-American boy looks so much like so many of the queers in the gyms and bars these days. What—I can't help thinking—if this guy's HIV-negative lover had been another guy instead of a girl? And what if, instead of being white, the couple had been black?

What might this video have accomplished with just these minimal changes in casting and story line?

Of course, Jason has given us ample reason to question our desire for any particular positive image to counter a stereotype, because a positive image is just what Jason is; and in being *not* gay, *not* old, *not* sick-looking, Jason only reinforces the idea that gay, old, and sick-looking are despicable things to be.

Time Out does do some important work. Its condom demonstration is no-nonsense, explicit, and accurate, except that no mention is made of the dangers of oil-based lubes. The whys and wherefores of HIV testing are helpful, except that no mention is made of the necessities for anonymity, or at least confidentiality. The abstinence issue is managed well, because being sexually active is seen as the norm among teens. This makes it possible to talk about choice and peer pressure—not to demand abstinence, but to say that it's okay to be a virgin. In "Contents under Pressure," Jaleel White raps "I'm not ready for the wild thing," and later Arsenio becomes an impromptu rapper (and in so doing seems to chide big-name rappers for not appearing in the tape) to assure his audience, "You don't have nothin' to prove."

But Arsenio evidently does have something to prove. In one of his moments with Magic, Arsenio does a gratuitous reversal riff on the difficulty women have in getting men to use condoms. "I had a girl over at my house," he tells his buddy, "and I was like suggesting that I get a condom and everything, and she copped an attitude. She was like 'Oh, I'm nasty now? I'm nasty? Why you ever bring me here if I'm nasty?' And she copped an attitude and left." Magic's lack of sympathy is no doubt meant to remind us that Arsenio is one of those L.A. bachelors that every woman wants to be with, so why fret over one that got away.

The framing conceit of *Time Out* is a basketball court-side talk between Magic and Arsenio. As the tape begins, the two of them are shown playing one-on-one; then they take a break to talk about AIDS. Their chat is casual, between friends, intended to establish the themes that will be taken up by a host of young celebrities and other talking heads. But the banter between Magic and Arsenio does more than lay out the themes; it sets the tone. Who do they assume is listening in on this talk between two straight guys at the gym?

The positive-gay-image desire sparked by *Time Out*'s portrait of Jason, or the desire for at least *one* image of a self-affirming black gay man in the video, is set in motion not merely by the tape's representational absences, but by its all-too-familiar construction of its audience. That construction returns us to the repetition with which I began: "AIDS is not just a gay disease." The statement is true, of course. But what *follows* from this truism is what really counts. What follows in *Time Out*, if we are to believe Magic's words, is that it doesn't matter how you get the virus. But if we believe what we otherwise see and hear, it does matter. As far as this video is concerned, queers need to be represented—marginally—only for the edification of a straight audience. Magic and Arsenio are entirely unable to imagine and speak to queers. No one says, "If you're gay or lesbian, you need to. . . ." Or better still, "If you're gay like me, you need to. . . ." And I think it's no accident that this absence is all the more glaring as regards African American gays and lesbians, for they appear nowhere in *Time Out*. What we really need to imagine— and to demand—is not hunky Jason as a black gay man, but Magic Johnson and Arsenio Hall looking into the camera and saying, "We want to talk to our black gay brothers and sisters, we want to talk to all you young guys who are getting it on with other guys, and all you young girls who are getting it on with other girls. We want to tell you that we respect your sexual choices, and we want to give you the information you need to protect yourselves from HIV infection. And we want to say to all our gay and lesbian brothers and sisters who are HIV-positive or have AIDS, we're fighting this fight for you, because we know you've been fighting this fight for us for a very long time." But once we imagine something like this, we begin to envision an AIDS education video very different from *Time Out*, a video that in saying "AIDS is not just a gay disease" would not be saying, implicitly, "If AIDS *were* just a gay disease, we wouldn't be making this video." *Time Out* reenacts, through its absences, its failures of imagination, and its presumption of audience,

Magic's original disavowal on Arsenio's show. In spite of all else it tries to be, *Time Out* is Magic's (and Arsenio's) way to never stop saying, "I'm far from being homosexual. You know that. Everybody else who's close to me understands that."

In his just-released autobiography, *My Life,* Johnson splits himself into two identities: Magic Johnson, superstar basketball player and super-stud bachelor; and Earvin Johnson, Jr., private person, AIDS educator, and faithful lover and husband to Cookie. In the chapter entitled "Women and Me," he writes, "Some people can't understand how I could love one woman and be with others. But there was a part of me that was always with Cookie. Maybe that was Earvin, and the other part of me was Magic."[27]

Splitting himself into these two personas, Johnson can speak in two distinct voices, claiming, for example, as Magic, that he had a lot of pleasure leading the bachelor life, and, as Earvin, that Cookie was right, he should have married her sooner. He can be both hedonist and moralist, realist promoter of safe sex and pious proselytizer for abstinence. It's also Johnson's way of explaining his broken engagements, his long delay in marrying Cookie. Finally committing to Cookie and almost immediately thereafter discovering his HIV infection, he settled on the Earvin persona . . . until the All-Star Game and the Dream Team at the Barcelona Olympics. After those new highs, the Magic guise emerged again, and so Johnson eventually returned to the Lakers. When he retired from the Lakers a second time, just a month later and almost exactly a year after the press conference at the Forum announcing that he had tested HIV-positive, he did it as Earvin, with no fanfare, simply by issuing a written statement to the press. The ostensible reason for this resignation was the fear others in the NBA had begun to express about playing full-out against Magic, a reason condensed for the television audience into the seemingly powerful image of a bleeding scratch on Magic's leg during a game. But the subtext of the second resignation sto-

27. Earvin "Magic" Johnson, with William Novak, *My Life* (New York: Random House, 1992), p. 227.

ries, buried beneath Karl Malone's and Gerald Wilkins's exaggerated—
and undoubtedly displaced—sense of their health risks,[28] was that tenacious old rumor, circulated, according to the Nets' Sam Bowie by "a lot of
male egos out there not wanting to believe they can get this from a woman
so they can go on doing what they want to do without having to worry."[29]

Johnson went over the whole thing once again with Arsenio, complaining that Karl Malone should have had the courtesy to talk to him pri-
vately about his fears before going to the press, and reassuring his pal
that he'd had things out with Isiah Thomas, who had been fingered as a
source of the rumors (ironically enough, since the whispering supposedly began in the first place because Magic and Isiah always kissed each
other before their games).

I said at the beginning of this essay that I disagreed with Larry Kramer's
Nightline prediction that Magic Johnson would become a pariah. I
thought at the time that Larry failed to understand the extent to which
AIDSphobia was dependent on homophobia. But maybe *I* failed to recognize how completely the two remain intertwined. Because he's a
straight celebrity, Magic Johnson shows a deeper, perhaps unconscious, understanding of the necessity of constantly guarding against
the taint of homosexuality now that he's infected with HIV. Just think
how he might have reacted to this astonishing statement by an Ohio
teenager in his video *Time Out:* "We think in Centerville, Ohio, it doesn't
seem like AIDS could really hurt us. It seems like it's more of, like, a Hollywood type thing—celebrities." No wonder Magic has opted for Earvin.

I also said before that I agreed with Larry that Magic Johnson will probably die of AIDS. Buried in only one story that I read about Magic was
the fact that he had a case of shingles in 1985.[30] For anyone familiar with

28. Harvey Araton, "Messages of Reality and Mortality," *New York Times,* November 1,
1992, section 8, p. 1.
29. Quoted in Harvey Araton, "The N.B.A. Discovers It Can't Outleap Reality," *New York
Times,* November 3, 1992, p. B11.
30. Leerhsen et al., "Magic's Message," p. 62.

the course of HIV disease, that is an alarming, if ambiguous, fact. We haven't been told how impaired Magic's immune system is—no T-cell counts, no markers of any kind. Magic's workout regimen and optimistic outlook are all the press reports. Magic himself wrote in *Sports Illustrated* at the time he tested positive, "I told the fellas that this is just another challenge for me. It's Maurice Cheeks in the NBA Finals in 1980 and '83 against the 76ers. It's Larry [Bird] and Dennis Johnson every time we stepped on the court against the Celtics. It's Isiah [Thomas] and Dennis Rodman in all those wars against the Pistons. It's Michael [Jordon]. It's because of all of those challenges that I'm able to face this newest challenge."[31] But Magic's determination "to fight the virus," "to beat this thing," is for us probably the most demoralizing repetition of them all. We've heard it so many times. We've wanted so much to believe it. But we can't anymore. We've had to accommodate too much. I wonder if now—with Earvin—it will be different.

31. Johnson, "I'll Deal with It," p. 21.

13 DON'T TELL

First presented as a keynote address for the

conference "AIDS Appropriations: Cultural Studies

Perspectives," Rice University Center for the Study of

Cultures, Houston, October 1, 1993.

YOU CAN'T WEAR A RED RIBBON IF YOU'RE DEAD.

You can't serve in the military if you're dead.

You can't march in the Saint Patrick's Day parade if you're dead.

You can't register as domestic partners if you're dead.

ACT UP!

Take direct action to end the AIDS crisis.
Come to our weekly meetings on Monday nights at 7:30
at the Lesbian & Gay Community Services Center,
208 West 13 Street

One person can make a difference.

Alessandro Codagnone, poster for ACT UP New York, 1993.

"Nobody talks about AIDS anymore." This observation—or accusation—was made by ACT UP on one of several different posters that appeared on hoardings around New York City in the summer of 1993. The statement is elaborated in fine print: "We've turned the lives of our missing friends and lovers into pieces of a quilt and our anger and activism into red ribbons. Now more than ever is the time to ACT UP."[1] The factious red ribbon is returned to on a second poster, whose bold type asserts: "You can't wear a red ribbon if you're dead," followed, in smaller print, by "You can't serve in the military if you're dead. You can't march in the St. Patrick's Day parade if you're dead. You can't register as domestic partners if you're dead." A third broadside demands, "If AIDS is Clinton's obsession why are so many still dying?"[2]

That question refers to a promise made by Clinton during his 1992 presidential election campaign that, if elected, AIDS would be his obsession, but the word *obsession* also recalls, to me, an article that appeared in the *Nation* in February 1989 under the headline "The Deadly Costs of an Obsession."[2] I think back to that article because *its* accusation—that AIDS had monopolized the attention of gay men and lesbians at the expense of other pressing issues—was just the reverse of what ACT UP charges—that AIDS has been displaced from our agenda by the Campaign for Military Service, domestic partnership legislation, and other gay rights concerns. In the *Nation* piece, Darrel Yates Rist assailed AIDS activists and AIDS service organizations for diverting all the energies and fundraising capabilities of gay men and lesbians away from any cause but AIDS. What about homeless gay teenagers? Rist demanded.

1. A handout with related rhetoric also appeared. Its opening paragraph reads: "People don't talk about AIDS anymore. They just die from it. AIDS is quickly becoming 'last year's news' and AIDS activism is no longer considered 'appropriate.' Instead, AIDS has become the familiar ache in the background of our days. We spend our mornings scanning obituary pages, our afternoons visiting hospital rooms and our evenings attending memorial services. Too exhausted to fight and too hurt to hope, we've turned the lives of our missing friends and lovers into pieces of a quilt and our anger and activism into red ribbons."

2. Darrell Yates Rist, "AIDS as Apocalypse: The Deadly Costs of an Obsession," *Nation*, February 13, 1989, pp. 181, 196–200. Page numbers for further citations from this article appear in parentheses in the text.

What about anti-gay violence or the rights of same-sex couples to marry? What about organizations like the Hetrick-Martin Institute (for the protection of gay and lesbian youth) or the National Gay and Lesbian Task Force? Based largely on false charges, such as one that AIDS activists deliberately exaggerate numbers of people infected with HIV to incite panic, the crux of Rist's argument was that AIDS activism is selfishly motivated by wealthy white gay men. He wrote, for example, of "an elder of the [San Francisco] gay community, a man of money and influence," who was incredulous when confronted with Rist's concern with the problems of gay youth. "When it comes to kids," Rist declared, "even the homosexual heart beats false; it beats only for men of a certain age, a certain color—in fact, a certain social class" (p. 198). And, evidently, it beats only for men. "Some angry lesbians," he wrote at another point in his discussion, "question whether bourgeois gay men ever wanted more than comfortably closeted sex anyway—and now wonder if they want more than a quick cure for AIDS in order to get back to the old days" (p. 200).

Rist seemed to think he was making an argument for gay identity politics, which in his view AIDS activists deny by inhabiting a new, peculiar sort of closet; thus: "A certain interest in AIDS has become a trendy code for suggesting one's homosexuality without declaring it, what being a bachelor and an artiste used to suggest" (p. 200).[3] But instead, by alleging the selfishness of gay white men, their inattention to race and class— and by doing so in the pages of a traditional left-liberal journal whose record on gay and AIDS issues was abysmal—Rist only thwarted his own stated cause. In the *Nation* an indictment of closetedness is hardly an indictment at all—unless, of course, it involves Roy Cohn[4]— whereas bourgeois indifference to the problems of poverty and racism

3. "In my gym, a crossroads in Manhattan, a coterie of cultish gay men plastered ACT UP's 'Silence=Death' logo everywhere in the facility and are given to working out in ACT UP or G.M.H.C. T-shirts—as though sporting such gym wear were a courageous act. But I've not seen one of that crowd so boldly advertise a more identifiably gay and therefore riskier issue" (Rist, "AIDS as Apocalypse," p. 200).

4. See Robert Sherrill, "King Cohn," *Nation,* May 21, 1988, pp. 719–725; see also "Right On, Girlfriend!" in this volume.

is damning indeed: the charge of slighting class issues has all along been the foundation of the traditional Left's resistance to the new social movements rooted in identity politics.

It is unnecessary now, as it was in 1989, to defend ACT UP's political record on questions of class, race, gender, and age or its commitment to fighting for gay and lesbian rights not directly related to AIDS. I don't wish to claim that the record is exemplary, but merely to insist that it is far more complex and far more commendable that Rist suggested.[5] What nags me now, though, on rereading the article, is Rist's equation, cravenly ventriloquized into the mouths of lesbians, of AIDS activism, the closet, and the desire for nothing but sex.

Getting laid, you might recall, is not among the things ACT UP's poster said you can't do if you're dead. Apart from wearing a red ribbon (which after all, I suppose, the dead could do), ACT UP mentioned three possibilities: serving in the military, marching in the St. Patrick's Day parade, and filing for domestic partnership benefits. None of these rights is specific to gays and lesbians, but their mention in tandem with the assertion that "nobody talks about AIDS anymore" is clearly meant to indicate both their current prominence in gay and lesbian politics and that as such they have displaced AIDS. By implicitly indicting that displacement, ACT UP could in fact be accused of too narrow an identification as a gay and lesbian group. The absurdity of ACT UP's either-or proposition regarding political causes, as well as its problematic gay-specificity, becomes obvious if we substitute an alternative formulation that doesn't allude to current gay rights issues. How about: "You can't get a job if you're dead"? "You can't benefit from affirmative action if you're dead"? or "You can't choose an abortion if you're dead"?

Though I am hardly more pleased by ACT UP's accusation than I was with Rist's, ACT UP does have a point, and it is one that has been noted by many others as well: AIDS is no longer the central issue on the gay

5. See, e.g., Douglas Crimp, with Adam Rolston, *AIDS Demo Graphics* (Seattle: Bay Press, 1990), especially pp. 84–95, and "Right On, Girlfriend!" in this volume.

and lesbian movement's agenda. This fact was starkly evident in the contrast between the 1987 and 1993 marches on Washington. Whereas people with AIDS and their lovers, friends, and supporters comprised the lead-off contingent and indelible image of the 1987 march, gay men and lesbians in military uniform were at the forefront in the spring of '93. The '93 march's stated theme, "A Simple Matter of Justice," virtually forecast the displacement. It might seem a simple matter of justice that gays and lesbians be allowed to serve as equals in the military; indeed all manner of gay and lesbian equal rights might seem a simple matter of justice. But just how could this phrase pertain to the AIDS crisis? At the very least, I think we'd have to say that AIDS raises *complex* questions of justice, and not only of justice.

The problem with ACT UP's allegation of displacement is not whether or not it's correct but its implicit moralism. ACT UP appears to attribute the displacement to apathy, bad faith, selfishness, or cowardice. Or, at best, to being led astray by President Clinton, who, in pretending to be our friend, co-opted our agenda.[6] ACT UP's poster might just as well have asked, "If AIDS is Clinton's obsession, why did he spend his limited political capital—and force us to us spend ours—on the effort to lift the military ban?" But how is it that we have been so easily duped? One reason I pose the question is that, if ACT UP and others are right about

6. It was a commonplace among media pundits that President Clinton made a fatal political blunder by announcing so early in his presidency that he would lift the ban on gays in the military. This was an issue, the media claimed, that nobody really cared about, but because it was so controversial it was destined to dominate the news, distracting us from the things that really mattered, like the economy and national health care. Who constituted this audience that didn't care about gays in the military? Thus is a "general public" constructed, a general public presumed heterosexual even as a gay constituency must be acknowledged to exist. But these sentiments were echoed in the gay press. Until recently, much of that press claimed, gays in the military was an issue most gay people didn't really care about. In *Conduct Unbecoming,* Randy Shilts is more accusatory. He insists that, since Stonewall, gay leaders simply opposed the military tout court—and thus gays in the military—as a knee-jerk leftist response, inspired as Shilts apparently thinks all gay leaders are by a 1960s counterculture mentality. In Shilts's simplistic view, gay leaders failed for two decades to recognize a crucial gay rights issue. See Randy Shilts, *Conduct Unbecoming: Gays and Lesbians in the U.S. Military* (New York: St. Martin's Press, 1993), pp. 95–97, 153, and passim. Page numbers for further citations from this book appear in parentheses in the text.

our being guilty of displacement, then I too am guilty, even as I too have at times deplored the displacement. I admit that I have been riveted by the newspaper and television coverage of the debates over lifting the military ban, just as I once followed every story or broadcast about AIDS. The spectacle of naked homophobia and victim-blaming, of threatened masculinity and reaction formation, of manipulated Senate hearings and contorted policymaking, is very hard to resist, even in its horrors and frustrations, or perhaps *because* of its horrors and frustrations. A choice tidbit from a *New York Times* story: A sailor worried, "If these people are allowed to come out of the closet, I'll be serving aboard a ship and wondering who's who and what's what."[7] For my part, I wonder why it is knowledge rather than secrecy that causes the sailor to wonder.

My interest here, however, is not to justify our displacement, or atone for it, but rather to examine it for what it might tell us about our current perspective on AIDS.

Displacement is a psychic mechanism usually of a defensive nature. The cathexis onto a particular idea—one that has perhaps become unbearable to consciousness—is withdrawn from it and displaced onto another idea. It should come as little surprise to us that we might now find AIDS an idea that has become unbearable and against which we might wish to defend. But ACT UP's broadside moralizing either fails to recognize or fails to credit the fact that AIDS has become an unbearable idea. In "Mourning and Militancy," written in 1989, I saw this moralism as related to our failure to honor the necessity of mourning; now in 1993 it reappears in a related failure to assess the depths of our despair. Perhaps, given the work of political activism, this is inevitable. Despair might be activism's undoing. But disavowal of the prevalence of despair about AIDS, or hectoring us because we feel it, will not help us overcome it.

Why do we despair? Surely because we seem no closer now than we did when ACT UP was formed in 1987 to being able to save our lives. And

7. Larry Rother, "The Gay Troop Issue: Off Base, Many Sailors Voice Anger Toward Homosexuals," *New York Times,* January 31, 1993. For an analysis of this "epistemophobia," see Kendall Thomas, "Shower/Closet," *Assemblage* 20 (April 1993), pp. 80–81.

unlike that moment, when the very fact of our growing activism afforded the hope that we could save ourselves, very few of us still truly
believe that the lives of those now infected can be saved by what we do.
Of course, we still know what is to be done. Other lives can still be saved
by preventing further transmission; the quality of lives can be improved
by preventing discrimination and by ensuring access to treatment and
services; and certainly more money and effort can be directed toward
research and education. But without hope for ourselves and our friends
many of us now turn away from these battles. Clearly though, our despair does not amount to total defeat, for as the charge of displacement
implies, we are still engaged, only in another cause. Perhaps if we can
discover in the displacement the nature of our defense, we can begin to
work it through.

The defense is easy enough to identify, at least insofar as it concerns the
redirection of our energies to lifting the military ban: It is a substitution
of the image of the healthy body for that of the sick body. We can see the
desire for the substitution already in early demands by AIDS activists
for positive images. Think, for example, of ACT UP's call, in the face of
the Museum of Modern Art's exhibition of Nicholas Nixon's close-up
photographs of disfigured, diseased, and dying people with AIDS, for
"the visibility of PWAs who are vibrant, angry, loving, sexy, beautiful,
acting up and fighting back."[8] Well, we now have the visibility of just
such people, but, of course, they are not people with AIDS, they are men
and women in uniform. What makes these bodies different from the
bodies of people with AIDS? Why do we suppose these bodies are
healthy? What constitutes these bodies as a psychic defense against our
despair about AIDS?

○

In *Conduct Unbecoming,* Randy Shilts profiles a vast number of gays
and lesbians hounded out of the military. The individual stories, poignant

8. I analyze Nixon's photographs and ACT UP's demonstration against them in "Portraits
of People with AIDS," in this volume.

and enraging, are also highly repetitious, variations on a single theme; ultimately they blur into a single narrative. It is the story of an all-American boy or girl, usually from a military family, an achiever, idealistic, politically and socially conservative, believing so strongly in his or her country as to want nothing more than to serve it, and generally doing so with excellence and honor. But the kid is haunted by a secret desire, one he or she thinks can be overcome or at least avoided by joining the military. The desire doesn't go away, it becomes more urgent, and finally the soldier accepts it. Sooner or later the investigation begins, the career ends in separation, often with dishonorable discharge, and the military has lost a great soldier, a great American. Here are portions of the beginning of one such narrative in *Conduct Unbecoming:*

Vernon E. Berg III was the eldest son of Navy Commander Vernon E. Berg, Jr., one of the most respected officers in the Navy's chaplain corps. . . . No one could believe how much his namesake resembled his father. . . . As young Vernon grew into his full five-foot-nine-inch frame and his hair turned sandy blond, he was still the carbon copy of his dad, right down to the deep blue eyes and second-tenor voice, which was why they called him Copy. . . . Copy began establishing his own track record of being a winner. . . . He was not just another track letterman at Frank W. Cox High School; he was also student-body president. At Boy's State, he was not just a delegate, he was a candidate for governor. At Boy Scout Troop 422, he was not simply another Life Scout, he was Alowat Sikima, Chief of Fire, the top position of the elite Order of the Arrow fraternity for the entire Chesapeake Bay area. Whenever local chapters of the Lion's or Rotary or Optimist's Clubs needed a good teenager to speak, they trotted out Copy Berg. . . . Only in his sexual attractions did his confidence waver. (pp. 171–172)

Copy Berg is what Shilts calls a "responsible homosexual with impeccable credentials" (249). The phrase ostensibly describes those whose cases against the military ban would stand a good chance of winning in federal courts, but it also characterizes the image repertoire marshaled in arguments for lifting the ban. The images have become familiar to all of us: from Leonard Matlovich and Miriam Ben-Shalom to Margarethe

Cammermeyer, Dusty Pruitt, Keith Meinhold, José Zuniga, and Joseph Steffan.[9]

Midshipman Joseph Steffan's autobiography *Honor Bound* fills out in detail the sort of narrative rehearsed again and again by Shilts.[10] It begins with a chapter entitled "Warren," the name of the little town in northern Minnesota where Steffan grew up. Steffan's literary conceit here is the description of his daily long-distance run, which provides the frame within which Steffan depicts Warren itself and relates his high school triumphs as a two-mile competitor in regional track meets after unpromising youthful attempts to be the athlete his father wanted him to be. Warren is one of those supposedly typical American towns where everybody knows everybody by name and you don't have to lock your doors at night. And Joseph Steffan is one of those supposedly typical products of such towns: He wins not only track meets but also science

9. Although my discussion here will focus on this image repertoire, I want at least to mention an argument for lifting the military ban that such images fail to make. It goes without saying that very few of us can live up to the image of the "responsible homosexual with impeccable credentials." This is one reason positive images—because they are idealizations—can be so disabling. More damaging still, arguments limited to standard, uncritical notions of patriotism, of noble desires to serve and even to risk one's life for one's country, sidestep the more ordinary reasons that most young people volunteer for the military: to get a job, to get an education, to get away from dead-end, deadening, or even deadly environments. This accounts, of course, for higher proportions of military personnel being drawn from the ranks of poor African-American and Latino populations. And not only are young gay men and lesbians just as likely to be poor, just as likely to be black and Latino, as are young heterosexuals, but they may have other, equally pressing reasons to find a way out of their stultifying home environments. Almost anyone who has grown up queer in rural or small-town America knows how necessary it is to survival to find a way out, eventually to find the way into those communities that will nourish and sustain our queerness. Because I grew up queer in just such a place—a small Northwestern town that has become infamous as headquarters to the Aryan Nations—I not only know this but recoil at the depiction of such places as the locus of all that is good and honorable about America.

10. Joseph Steffan, *Honor Bound: A Gay Naval Midshipman Fights to Serve His Country* (New York: Avon Books, 1992). Page numbers for further citations from this book appear in parentheses in the text. See also *Gays and the Military: Joseph Steffan versus the United States,* ed. Marc Wolinsky and Kenneth Sherrill (Princeton: Princeton University Press, 1993).

fairs; he gets elected class president, never drinks alcohol, joins a group called Teens Encounter Christ, sings in the choir, attends Boys State, graduates salutatorian, and gets accepted at the Naval Academy—typical, therefore, in the sense of exemplary. As a midshipman, Steffan is more than exemplary; in his fourth year he was named battalion commander, which made him one of the three top-ranking midshipmen in his class and put him in direct command over one-sixth of the Academy's forty-five hundred midshipmen. He also sang the national anthem at the Army-Navy football game, an honor that he performed in front of President Ronald Reagan. Again stressing the all-American flavor of his hometown, Steffan writes, "Back home in Warren my parents huddled with a dozen of their friends in front of the television. At the American Legion hall, the women's club stopped in the middle of their annual prayer breakfast and moved into the bar to watch on the big-screen television, while around town most everyone in Warren was waiting to see someone from their hometown sing on national television" (p. 101).

But for all his triumphs, Steffan is haunted by his secret, which finally brings him to personal crisis:

I was feeling very depressed, like nothing I had ever experienced in my life. At the heart of this depression were recurring thoughts about my sexuality. I was working so hard to ignore them, to shut them out, but I could not turn off a part of my own mind. These thoughts were always there, always resurfacing, reminding me that I was avoiding something. . . . I thought I could control my mind and shut off a part of my being. It was a battle I was losing. . . .

One night before midterm exams, I was trying in vain to study in my room. My ability to concentrate was at an all-time low, and I simply couldn't focus. There were so many pressures to deal with, so many things going on in my head. Finally, I just couldn't take it anymore. I slammed my books shut, threw on a pair of sweats, and walked down the stairs and out of the hall. . . .

From the beginning, I had avoided dealing with my sexuality, but it didn't feel like avoidance anymore. Now it felt like a lie—a lie whose perpetuation was beginning to sicken me, to eat away at my soul. I had crossed the line between doubt and certainty months before, but I kept lying to myself. (pp. 103–104)

A few paragraphs describe Steffan's problems reconciling his growing knowledge that he is indeed gay with his naval career aspirations. Then:

After what seemed like an hour, I finally got up and started walking back to the hall. I still didn't completely understand what it meant to be gay, or even fully accept my homosexuality. A part of me still wanted to be straight, to be "normal"—because I felt it would make my life easier. But I had taken a first crucial step toward acceptance. That step was the beginning of a long process of "coming out". . . .

For the first time in many months, I finally felt at peace with myself. I had finally stopped fighting who I knew I was and began accepting myself. . . .

Like many gay men and lesbians, I discovered that there is no hiding from yourself. Homosexuality is simply not a choice; it is an identity. (pp. 104–105)

From this moment in the narrative, Steffan always speaks with certainty about his identity, his being, what he *is*. Never once, though, does he speak of any sort of sexual activity.

The rest of the story is well known: Just six weeks before his scheduled graduation from the Academy and his assignment to the elite submarine service, Joe Steffan was forced to resign because the academy brass had discovered his homosexuality.

Steffan's court battle for reinstatement in the Navy is celebrated not only because he was such an exemplary midshipman, but also because of the grotesque bias and ignorance displayed by the presiding judge. Judge Oliver J. Gasch repeatedly referred to Steffan as "that homo" in the court room, and in a thirty-five-page ruling against Steffan, nearly one quarter was devoted to the argument that banning homosexuals from the military is necessary to prevent the spread of AIDS, an argument whose relevance to the case the government's lawyers had explicitly denied. Although Steffan and his lawyers knew they had a good case, from the beginning they were worried about Gasch: "Despite the strength of our position, we were concerned about how Judge Gasch felt about the issues surrounding homosexuality. In his research Marc [Wolinsky, one of Steffan's lawyers] discovered that Judge Gasch had recently decided in favor of the military in a military case involving homosexual conduct. Although ours was not a conduct case, we questioned whether he would appreciate the difference between homosexual status and homosexual conduct. This distinction could well determine his entire approach to the case" (p. 203). Clearly, given Judge Gasch's final opinion about protecting the military from AIDS, the distinction failed him.

The ignorance displayed in Judge Gasch's equation of homosexuals and AIDS is not his alone. I heard it voiced time and again during televised debates on lifting the ban, and time and again I waited in vain for it to be cogently disputed by opponents of the ban. Perhaps because the assertion was so often made amidst a barrage of other, more often stated irrational objections to lifting the ban, the ban's opponents let it go. But I think ignoring the equation is not merely a question of not dignifying so plainly false an argument with a reply. To me, the failure is symptomatic.

A reply might go like this: The military routinely tests for HIV infection, and its policy does not call for discharging those who test positive, but rather for monitoring their health. HIV is transmitted by unprotected anal, vaginal, and possibly oral sex and by shared hypodermic needles when injecting drugs, any of which activities may be practiced by men and women, gay and straight. Lesbians, who are five times more likely than gay men to be separated from military service for homosexuality, are proportionately at very low risk for AIDS. And gay men, though heretofore proportionately at greater risk than heterosexuals in the United States, tend to be better informed about and likely to practice risk reduction. Reinforcing the idea that only gay people get AIDS promotes the ignorance of those engaging in heterosexual sex and reduces the likelihood of their adopting risk reduction practices. Moreover, if the military turns a blind eye to the established fact that many men and women in the military engage in homosexual sex, whatever their professed "sexual orientations," there is little likelihood that homosexually explicit risk reduction education will be provided. If, however, the ban on gay men and lesbians in the military were lifted, there would be a greater likelihood of explicit AIDS education and probably of an overall reduction of HIV transmission in the military.

The failure to make this argument appears to me symptomatic because such an argument necessarily speaks about transmission, which in turn necessarily entails sex, but the ban's official opponents did not speak of sex; they spoke of identity. From the beginning, the fight to lift the military ban was an issue framed, like Joseph Steffan's court case, as one of status *versus* conduct, as identity *versus* behavior. That framing of the issue made it possible for President Clinton to believe he honored the spirit of his commitment to end the ban by accepting the policy of Don't Ask, Don't Tell. Don't Ask, Don't Tell is nearly everywhere recognized as a defeat for lesbian and gay rights and a broken Clinton promise because it legislates the closet, codifies into policy the very means of homophobic oppression. As if it were not clear enough how the closet oppresses, the military spelled it out for us. Under the new policy, it is theoretically okay to *be* gay or lesbian but it is not okay to say so. But "saying so" is not only a question of speech, it is also a question of conduct. Or, more accurately, the one automatically entails the other. Not only is homosexual sex—anywhere, anytime—grounds for separation from the military, but the announcement of one's homosexual identity leads, according to the policy, to the presumption—nominally rebuttable—of a propensity to break the rules of conduct; to say "I am gay" *means,* according to this policy, "I have engaged in or will engage in sodomy." Thus, although Clinton and the opponents of the ban argued for equal rights on the basis of status, the policy declares that homosexual status, when owned up to, is not simply status, it is also conduct, or at least the propensity to engage in illegal conduct.

Conduct is presumably what Clinton had in mind in the spring of 1993 when, during a question-and-answer session in the Rose Garden, he sought to reassure a concerned preacher that his support for lifting the ban should not be interpreted as his condoning the homosexual lifestyle.[11] The odd locution *homosexual lifestyle* may be supposed to mean many things, but I doubt that Clinton intended to allay the preacher's fear of his condoning fags listening to bel canto or dykes singing folk songs, or even dykes riding Harleys and fags wearing pumps. I think Clinton meant fags and dykes fucking, although lesbians fucking might still be unimaginable to those who employ the term *lifestyle* to encompass what they deplore. After all, how often were lesbians mentioned in the debates about the military ban when the issue was, say, close quarters or shared shower facilities? At the risk of perpetuating the invisibility, I won't have much to say about lesbians either. The reason is that the argument I intend to make is about the identities and identifications of gay men, which I think the virtual absence of lesbians from the gays-in-the-military debate only proves is not symmetrical or analogous to, is indeed entirely different from, the argument one would have to make about the identities and identifications of lesbians. Moreover, the separation of lesbians from military service is generally the result not of their perceived threat to other female military personnel, but of their refusal of the attentions of *male* personnel. Indeed, the very little that *was* said about lesbians and by women during the debates over the ban suggests that if lesbians were the issue and women were making the decisions, the ban would have been lifted with very little argument.

The new military policy's linkage, through the "presumption of a propensity," of status and conduct, even as status and conduct are conceptual-

234
—
235

11. "Most Americans believe that the gay life style should not be promoted by the military or anybody else in this country. . . . We are trying to work this out so that our country does not . . . appear to be endorsing a gay life style" ("Excerpts from Clinton's Question-and-Answer Session in the Rose Garden," *New York Times,* May 28, 1993, p. A14).

ized as two separate things, has the paradoxically salutary effect of forcing us to ask the question, Where is sex in our politics of identity? In the military's own version of our identity politics, status and conduct are in practice linked by more than this newly conceived propensity. On the one hand it is admitted that there are now and always have been homosexuals in the military. Less often discussed is the also-well-known fact that there is a great deal of same-sex sexual activity in the military, and that such activity is as condoned as heterosexual sex so long as the participants maintain a heterosexual identity. It is thus *only* the connection between homosexual conduct and homosexual identity that allows that conduct to be viewed as homosexual and therefore punishable by separation. In this manner, the military also *severs* sexual acts from sexual identities to make room for the range of sexual activities that are routinely practiced throughout the military.

In traditional lesbian and gay identity politics, we had good reason to argue that sex—sexual acts, sexual desire, sexual fantasies—does not determine lesbian and gay identity. While lesbian and gay identities were understood to be socially constructed through postulates about sexual desire and sexual acts, when claiming those identities for ourselves we sought to shift the emphasis to our shared oppression and our self-determined communities and cultures. We opposed the term *homosexual*—proposing instead *homophile,* then *gay* and *lesbian,* then *queer*—in part because the *sex* in *homosexual* was inevitably used to reduce us to our sexual desire; and with the exclusive focus on our sexuality, we were stigmatized as merely and exclusively sexual beings— and thus sexually obsessed, sexually voracious, sexually predatory. The persistence of this stereotype is obvious in arguments against lifting the ban, where the assumption is that, if allowed to come out in the open, we won't be able to keep our hands off anyone of the same sex.

By insisting on status *versus* conduct, identity *versus* behavior, opponents of the ban attempted to displace that stereotype by avoiding sex altogether. In place of the insatiable sexual predator, we were treated to the image of the gay or lesbian soldier with an exemplary service record or the young recruit with a desire only to serve his or her country. Just what it was that made the soldier or recruit gay or lesbian in the first place, what constitutes a gay or lesbian identity, was left unsaid. Unfortunately, this "unspeakableness"—"the love that dare not speak its name"— can only return us to the stereotype, which continues to do its work. And that work will be fully accomplished in the disciplinary power of the new policy, which punishes identity in the name of a propensity to conduct unbecoming.

Now, lest it seem that the formulators of the new policy have their priorities right—right, that is, in relation to more recent, antiessentialist theories of identity—I want to argue that sex for the policymakers is still *prior* to and foundational for identity. Although it is the soldier's enunciation of gay or lesbian identity that leads the military to presume conduct, the fact that the presumption of propensity *necessarily* follows the enunciation determines it as prior. With the small caveat of "rebuttable," the policy says that homosexual sex, engaged in or desired, is *essentially* what the enunciation of homosexual identity means. Nothing argued by opponents of the ban counters that essentialism. That is because, spoken or unspoken, emphasized or de-emphasized, sex *is* still the foundation of our identity politics.

It is of course Michel Foucault who has explained how we become trapped in the disciplinary apparatus through essentialist forms of identity politics. For Foucault, sex is not a material substrate existing "in itself," prior to the regulatory and normalizing regime of sexuality. Rather sex is an imaginary idea discursively produced inside the deployment of sexuality as the anchor of its operations:

The notion of "sex" made it possible to group together, in an artificial unity, anatomical elements, biological functions, conducts, sensations, and pleasures, and it enabled one to make use of this fictitious unity as a causal principle, an omnipresent meaning, a secret to be discovered everywhere. . . .

It is through sex—in fact, an imaginary point determined by the deployment of sexuality—that each individual has to pass in order to have ac-

*cess to his own intelligibility . . . , to the whole of his body . . . , to his
identity. . . .*[12]

Foucault goes on to warn that therefore

*we must not think that by saying yes to sex, one says no to power; on
the contrary, one tracks along the course laid out by the general deployment of sexuality. It is the agency of sex that we must break away from, if
we aim—through a tactical reversal of the various mechanisms of sexuality—to counter the grips of power with the claims of bodies, pleasures, and knowledges, in their multiplicity and their possibility of
resistance. The rallying point for the counterattack against the deployment of sexuality ought not to be sex-desire, but bodies and pleasures.
(p. 157)*

This strategy has left Foucault open to the charge of coy evasion. Just
what is meant by "bodies and pleasures" as opposed to "sex-desire"? To
the extent that Foucault later elaborated on what he meant, he only invited harsher criticism. In a famous instance, Leo Bersani linked Foucault with Andrea Dworkin and Catherine MacKinnon in the project of
a "pastoralizing," "redemptive reinvention of sex."[13] Bersani's criticism
emerged from his analysis of the homophobic stereotype mentioned
earlier, that is, the one that represents the homosexual as nothing but
sex. In Bersani's formulation, this stereotype becomes considerably
more specific, indeed *gender*-specific (and gender-dysphoric). The
stereotype is, in fact, a man being fucked, or to use Bersani's notorious
words, "a grown man, legs high in the air, unable to refuse the suicidal
ecstasy of being a woman" (p. 212). Significantly, Bersani's vivid description is of a representation, a representation that forms in the unconscious of "the good citizens of Arcadia, Florida," when "looking at

12. Michel Foucault, *The History of Sexuality: An Introduction* (New York: Vintage, 1990),
pp. 154–156. Page numbers for further citations from this book appear in parentheses
in the text.

13. Leo Bersani, "Is the Rectum a Grave?" in *AIDS: Cultural Analysis/Cultural Activism*,
ed. Douglas Crimp (Cambridge: MIT Press, 1988), p. 215. Page numbers for further citations from this article appear in parentheses in the text.

three hemophiliac children" with AIDS whose house they are about to burn down (p. 212). But though this representation is thus murderous in its possible effects, it is also, for Bersani, the picture of gay men's most radical achievement. For Bersani's claim is that gay men's identities are formed through what he calls variously a "loving identification" (p. 208), an "uncontrollable identification" (p. 222), indeed a "nearly mad identification" (p. 209) with our phallocentric, homophobic oppressors, but—and here is the radical achievement—we "never cease to feel the appeal of [that identity's] being violated" (p. 209). Thus it is gay men's constant *undermining* of our identities through self-debasement or self-shattering—through being fucked—that constitutes the possibility of a radically antiphallocratic gay politics. Although Bersani does not make the distinction, it seems necessary to point out that "being fucked" is *not* what Foucault means by *sex*. Indeed "being fucked" may well be more like what Foucault had in mind when he spoke of "bodies and pleasures," with breaking away from the *agency* of sex. For if getting fucked is that which undermines identity, it cannot be taken to be the foundation for identity.

At the end of his essay, Bersani noted the danger of his theory for gay men in the age of AIDS: "But if the rectum is the grave in which the masculine ideal . . . of proud subjectivity is buried, then it should be celebrated for its very potential for death. Tragically, AIDS has literalized that potential as the certainty of biological death, and has therefore reinforced the heterosexual association of anal sex with . . . self-annihilation . . ." (p. 222).

Bersani's fear had already been confirmed by Jesse Helms, who stated on the floor of the Senate in 1987, "Every AIDS case can be traced back to a homosexual act."[14] While Helms is of course entirely wrong about the facts, he may be entirely right about the representation—the one Bersani described as unconsciously formed by the citizens of Arcadia and the one that still appears as a ghostly afterimage whenever we see a

14. See *Congressional Record*, October 14, 1987, pp. S14202-S14220; see also "How to Have Promiscuity in an Epidemic" in this volume.

Bureau, *In Honor of Allen R. Schindler,* 1993.

person with AIDS. But is it possible that we also see that representation—albeit it unconsciously—when we look at, say, Joseph Steffan?

○

At about the same time in the summer of 1993 as ACT UP's posters surfaced around New York, two others, larger and more elegantly produced by the artist-design term Bureau, also appeared. Always hung as a pair, one carried the portrait of radioman Allen Schindler, the other the picture of his murderer, apprentice airman Terry Helvey. Circling above Schindler's handsome young face are the words "To die for." The story to which these posters refer was much in the news when lifting the military ban was being debated.[15] Schindler, just coming to grips with his homosexuality, was stationed in Sasebo, Japan, assigned there to the *USS Belleau Wood,* known as one of the roughest and most out of control in the navy. Schindler's journal indicated that he feared for his life after his homosexuality became known. His entry for October 2, 1992, read, "More people are finding out about me. It scares me a little. You never know who would want to injure me or cease my existence." His fears proved well founded, for shortly after he wrote the entry in his journal, he was followed into a public men's room in a park three blocks from base and brutally beaten to death by Terry Helvey with the participation of fellow airman Charles Vins. The Navy informed Schinder's mother only that he had been assaulted in a park and was dead, nothing about the perpetrators or the motive. When Schindler's mangled body arrived home, it was so disfigured that his mother was able to recognize her son only from the tattoos on his arm. Finally acknowledging Schindler's homosexuality, the navy then attempted to explain his murder as the result of a homosexual love affair gone sour, the same "unhappy gay sailor" syndrome that the Navy had concocted to explain the gun-turret explosion on the battleship *Iowa* in 1989.

The Bureau poster project creates a representation of gays in the military considerably more complex than the positive images put forward by opponents of the ban; that greater complexity obtains in the posters' registration, through a kind of doubling, of ambivalence. The pictures of the two sailors show them both perfectly conforming to descriptions of the supposedly all-American handsome guy. Think not only of Copy

15. See, e.g., "Death of Gay Sailor Is Investigated as Bias Crime," *New York Times,* January 10, 1993, sec. 1, p. 17; "Gay Sailor Tells of a 'Living Hell,'" *New York Times,* March 8, 1993, p. A15; Eric Schmitt, "Inquiry on Sailor's Killing Tests Navy on Dealing with Gay Issues," *New York Times,* May 10, 1993, p. A11.

Berg and Joe Steffan but of Scott Peck in his own father's description of him before Sam Nunn's Senate committee. Marine Colonel Fred Peck called his son "a recruiter's dream come true—6 feet 1 inch tall, blue-eyed, blond hair, and a great student."[16] The amazing ubiquity of blonds among all these good-soldier images resonates chillingly with Allen Schindler's term for the men that attracted him; he coded them in his journal as "blond things." But in the Bureau double portrait, one of the dreamboats is straight, the other gay, one a murderer, the other his victim.

"To die for"—to die for what? One's country? one's masculinity? one's sexuality? But of course "to die for" has another meaning altogether, as in "he's to die for": I think he's hot. But who? Allen? Terry? both? Can we tell them apart? Can we say who is the hotter? Whom we'd rather fuck? Whom we'd rather be fucked by? Is our identification and/or desire drawn inevitably, as Bersani's analysis might suggest, to Terry, the murderer?

The Bureau poster opens up within a simple pair of images not only the ambivalence of stereotypical representations, their pleasures and dangers, but also what is secret in them. That same summer a gay bar where I often hang out prominently displayed a series of banners and T-shirts printed with the slogans "Bomb the Ban" and "Operation Lift the Ban" along with signs that asked that patrons support the Campaign for Military Service. In the men's room—not that there's a ladies' room—of the same bar a flier advertised every first Wednesday of the month as M.I.U. night—Men In Uniform night, the night devoted to patrons who dress in military and other regalia. I don't want to overinterpret the over-the-bar versus over-the-toilet priorities of the Spike, but I do think Bureau's bringing the two together in their own statement on the ban is more true to the way we actually live our politics in relation to our desires. From Paul Cadmus and Kenneth Anger to Tom of Finland and Pierre et Gilles, the man in uniform has fueled gay men's sexual fantasies. It is these pictures of bodies and pleasures that are repressed in the positive images and rhetorics of official opponents of the military ban.

16. "A Recruiter's Dream," *New York Times,* May 13, 1993, p. A22.

"To die for"——Foucault writes that it is sex that we are willing to die for:

Hence the fact that over the centuries it has become more important than our soul, more important almost than our life; and so it is that all the world's enigmas appear frivolous to us compared to this secret, minuscule in each of us, but of a density that makes it more serious than any other. The Faustian pact, whose temptation has been instilled in us by the deployment of sexuality, is now as follows: to exchange life in its entirety for sex itself, for the truth and sovereignty of sex. Sex is worth dying for. It is in this (strictly historical) sense that sex is indeed imbued with the death instinct. (p. 156)

For Foucault, then, the death instinct emerges at the historical moment when identity becomes equated with sex. Taking Bersani's point, perhaps we may say that this seemingly inevitable association of sex and death is overcome when identity is shattered in the radical ascesis of a man being fucked. But that image——the image of the grown man, legs high in the air . . .——is now so indelibly attached to the person with AIDS that we disavow it.

Perhaps, then, displacing our attention from AIDS to gays in the military relieves us of our despair about sex and death by providing us with an image repertoire that allows us to think of death in an altogether different and largely metaphoric register——as a supposedly patriotic willingness to die for one's country. If sex is still secretly present in this displacement, as I think the Bureau poster shows it to be, that secretiveness makes possible again the coupling of sex and death that does not "literalize that potential as certain biological death." I wonder, though, if this is not also the "comfortably closeted sex" to which Darrel Yates Rist claimed AIDS activists wished to return but which in fact AIDS activists are determined to combat as a lethal displacement.

○

As a coda, I want to cite the text of still another poster. This one also showed up on the streets of New York in the summer of 1993. More discreet than the others in both proportions and tenor, it was produced by the few remaining members of the AIDS activist art collective Gran Fury after a long hiatus in their activities. The poster consisted only of four questions, printed in small black type on white paper. The questions require us to think about the despair that ACT UP's posters disavow. They ask:

Do you resent people with AIDS?

Do you trust HIV-negatives?

Have you given up hope for a cure?

When was the last time you cried?

14 ROSA'S INDULGENCE

First presented at the panel discussion "Civil Wars:

Queer Theory and the Arena of Activism," The New

School for Social Research, New York, May 17, 1994.

Recently I saw, for the first time, Rosa von Praunheim's early film *Army of Lovers*, or *Revolt of the Perverts* (1979), screened at the New Festival as part of a series called "Gay Sunshine: Documents of the Early Post-Stonewall Era."[1] The film's strident voice-over narration castigating gay men for their turn away from political struggle to indulge their sexual pleasures in bars, back rooms, and bathhouses reminded me of that self-righteous 1970s gay-lib chant "Out of the bars and into the streets." Lee Edelman has brilliantly analyzed, in his essay "The Mirror and the Tank," contemporary rhetorics of AIDS activism that return, if somewhat more subtly, to that opposition between political activism and a passive indulgence in sex, which, Edelman argues, only reaffirms the homophobic discourse of homosexual sex as always already passive—and narcissistic—indulgence.[2]

But von Praunheim's film contradicts its own rhetoric, or perhaps engages in a peculiar form of auto-critique, for there is Rosa himself, nothing if not indulgent, taking every opportunity to get it on in front of the camera. In one sequence he has sex with a porn star while the star, in voice-over interview, describes his work in the sex industry. In another, Rosa describes a film production course he taught at the San Francisco Art Institute in which the assignment consisted of having his students film him engaging in sex with another guy, the resulting very explicit film, or at least someone's resulting very explicit film, forming the sequence of *Army of Lovers* Rosa narrates.

I'm going to let this internal division in *Army of Lovers* stand for the current division between what we call queer theory and what we should probably still call lesbian and gay activism. I don't mean to polarize these positions or to draw any sort of rigid distinction between the academy and the "real world" or the "street." Rather I want to admit a certain failure of the theories we work to elaborate to change the struggles we en-

1. The New Festival is New York's lesbian and gay film festival.
2. Lee Edelman, "The Mirror and the Tank: 'AIDS,' Subjectivity, and the Rhetoric of Activism," in *Homographesis: Essays in Gay Literary and Cultural Theory* (New York: Routledge, 1994), pp. 93–117.

gage in. A single example of this division, but one that has many many ramifications, should suffice to make my point. Queer theory has worked on many fronts and with many tools to destabilize and de-essentialize sexual identity. And yet wherever lesbian and gay rights and even lives are at stake, those working for us seem still to need to insist on stable and essential sexual identities. We may scoff at Simon LeVay and his naive biological determinism, but it was LeVay, not his cogent so-cial-constructionist critic Carole Vance, who was asked to testify on our behalf against the Colorado referendum outlawing gay-affirmative leg-islation. We may deplore Richard Green and his effeminophobic sissy-boy syndrome, but it was Richard Green, not his critic Eve Kosofsky Sedgwick,[3] who was asked to submit an affidavit for Joseph Steffan's equal protection claim in his court battle to win reinstatement in the Navy.[4]

I don't mean to imply that queer theory is irrelevant to such questions. On the contrary, I think these legal arguments made on our behalf are very dangerous ones and that it is one of our tasks as queer theorists to discern the dangers and develop the means to avoid them.

Last summer I began work on a paper in which I wanted to interrogate the charge, made by ACT UP in a series of posters—but also made by many others after the April march on Washington—that AIDS had been displaced from the agenda of lesbian and gay activism by the issue of gays in the military.[5] My intent was to take the question of displace-ment seriously, to understand why that displacement would occur, and to see what it might reveal about our collective feelings about AIDS. I was interested in writing about this problem not only because I could see the dangers inherent in the Don't Ask, Don't Tell policy, but also be-

3. Eve Kosofsky Sedgwick, "How to Bring Your Kids Up Gay: The War on Effeminate Boys," in *Tendencies* (Durham: Duke University Press, 1993), pp. 154–164.
4. See *Gays and the Military: Joseph Steffan versus the United States,* ed. Marc Wolin-sky and Kenneth Sherrill (Princeton: Princeton University Press, 1993), especially "Affidavit I of Richard Green: On Homosexual Orientation as an Immutable Charac-teristic," pp. 56–83; and "Affidavit II of Richard Green: On Recent Developments in the Field of Brain Research," pp. 171–173.
5. See "Don't Tell" in this volume.

cause it involved a conflict that was also my own: On the one hand, I was absorbed by the debates about gays in the military, and, on the other, I felt guilty about turning my attention away from AIDS, a guilt I often projected by lamenting the fact that so many others seemed to be doing the same thing. The central point of my paper was that we are often unable to acknowledge our despair about AIDS and that, until we acknowledge it, we cannot begin to work through it and take the next forward step as activists. By this I don't mean returning to what we had been doing before, which I think is impossible, but determining how we can continue to struggle both against the forces opposing us and against the fear and sorrow inside us.

But writing the paper entailed its own kind of displacement. As I attempted to analyze the consequences of an image repertoire put forward by activist opponents of the military ban, I got sidetracked by the question of sex. Or perhaps I should say I routed my analysis through sex. For what I wanted to show was that our displacement involved the wish to detach gayness from the sick body of the person with AIDS and attach it instead to the healthy body of the soldier. But this, I argued, had been accomplished through a disavowal of the extent to which the soldier, too, was a sexualized image for us.

My discussion of the image repertoire of the all-American, patriotic, exemplary soldier focused on Joseph Steffan, whose celebrated reinstatement case hinged on making a distinction between status and conduct, on positing a homosexual identity distinct from sexual behavior. The new military policy, of course, allows for no such distinction, since it insists that homosexual identity necessarily entails homosexual conduct either engaged in or intended. Moreover, the courts have ruled, in several cases, that homosexual orientation is essentially determined by homosexual conduct. Nevertheless, Steffan's case and other equal protection cases argued before the courts have attempted to disentangle identity and conduct, since what must be proved to achieve suspect class status, and thus heightened Constitutional scrutiny, is a particular trait's immutability, and conduct is by definition mutable. Here is a passage from

Richard Green's argument on this point, taken from his affidavit in support of Steffan's equal protection claim:

While sexual activity among heterosexuals and homosexuals is common and diverse, significant portions of both populations engage in little or no interactive sexual conduct, both temporarily and for long periods of time, for various reasons. Indeed, there is substantial anecdotal evidence that during World War II, gays in the military simply refrained from engaging in homosexual conduct in order to avoid the harsh penalties that could be imposed. The fact that an individual is celibate for some short or long period of time does not mean that they do not have a sexual orientation, however. Celibacy, like any other sexual choice involving consenting behavior by a partner, is a healthy one when it is freely chosen.

Just what Professor Green might mean by "freely chosen" in this context is anybody's guess. But the larger question that I wanted to pose through my analysis was, Where is sex in our own theories of identity? To what extent does our antiessentialism help us through the conduct/status morass? How does it help us argue, as of course we must, for the right to our sexual pleasures as well as the right to simply be, or in this case be *in* the military?

The answer for me was to be found in the work of Michel Foucault— paradoxically, since Foucault also argues for detaching conduct from identity. But he does so not by disavowing sex, but by insisting on "bodies and pleasures" as against an identity predicated on sexual desire, the desire that Richard Green would claim is always there to determine sexual orientation even when it is held in check. Here is one of Foucault's explanations for substituting pleasure for desire:

I am advancing this term [pleasure] because it seems to me that it escapes the medical and naturalistic connotations inherent in the notion of desire. That notion has been used as a tool, as a grid of intelligibility, a calibration in terms of normality: "Tell me what your desire is and I will tell you who you are, whether you are normal or not, and then I can validate or invalidate your desire." One keeps running into this tactic, which goes from the notion of Christian concupiscence all the way through the Freudian notion of desire, passing through the notion of the sexual instinct in the 1840s. Desire is not an event but a permanent feature of the subject: it provides a basis onto which all the psychological-medical armature can attach itself.

The term "pleasure" on the other hand is virgin territory, almost devoid of meaning. There is no "pathology" of pleasure, no "abnormal" pleasure. It is an event "outside the subject," or at the limit of the subject. . . .[6]

The new policy on gays in the military proves the wisdom of Foucault's tactical move. For so long as we continue to base our claims for rights on a gay identity founded on desire, the institutions of normalization will be able to declare our desire abnormal and charge us with having broken or intending to break the rules of conduct. And even if this were not so obviously the case, any right to *be* gay that entails the requirement "freely to choose" celibacy is no right worth fighting for.

Rosa von Praunheim's exhibitions of his own sexual pleasures in *Army of Lovers* are, in this light, perhaps the most truly radical moments of his film, as opposed to the moralizing radical rhetoric on the soundtrack. But that is not really my point. I don't think the task of queer theory is to determine what is the truly radical position. Rather I think queer theory needs to take the conflict itself more seriously, including— no, especially— the conflict all of us experience about our pleasures. The gulf that I began by acknowledging is, I think, an expression of this conflict, but it should be understood not as one that we fall on one side of or the other. It is, rather, the conflict that we cannot help but experience as subjectivity itself. I realize that this is a rather un-Foucauldian statement, insofar as it accepts a premise that is central to psychoanalysis. But if Foucault himself did not experience this conflict, why would he have so insisted on the necessity of "becoming other than what one is"?

6. Quoted in David M. Halperin, *Saint Foucault: Towards a Gay Hagiography* (New York: Oxford University Press, 1995), pp. 93–94.

I want us to attend to conflict because I think it is one way that we might begin to bridge the gulf between queer theory and activist politics. That is, if we acknowledge that conflict comes not only from differences over tactics or strategy but also exists as a result of the feelings we all struggle with—feelings that are, of course, aroused in relation to the oppressions we all share—then we might be able to reach across the divide between queer theory and gay and lesbian politics.

15 DE-MORALIZING
REPRESENTATIONS OF AIDS

First presented at the conference on AIDS and

Activism organized by a coalition of activist groups

called Love+ (Visual AIDS Tokyo; Stop AIDS,

Sapporo; and Dumb Type and AIDS Poster Project,

Kyoto) in conjunction with the Tenth International

AIDS Conference, Yokohama, Japan, August 12, 1994.

Joe (Denzel Washington) listens to Andy (Tom Hanks)
explain a scene from *Andrea Chénier* in *Philadelphia,* 1993.

The most celebrated sequence of Jonathan Demme's *Philadelphia* shows its main character Andy (Tom Hanks) dancing with his IV stand to the tune of Giordano's *Andrea Chénier*. Trancelike, Andy interprets to a bored, then dumbstruck Joe (Denzel Washington), Maddelena's "La mamma morta," sung by every homo's favorite diva, Maria Callas. (Two outraged readers wrote letters to *Poz,* the monthly magazine for people with AIDS, excoriating it for misidentifying the voice as that of Montserrat Caballé—a mistake so glaring, according to one of the letters, as to "undermine the entire credibility of the magazine.")[1] As if fearing seduction, or perhaps contagion, Joe beats a hasty retreat, hesitates outside the door long enough for an ambiguous second thought, then goes home to hug his baby girl and crawl into bed with his wife. All the while—though we are rather far from Andy's stereo at this point—Callas continues singing of her reconciliation to life through heaven-sent love, and Joe experiences a silent epiphany. You can just watch him thinking, "It doesn't matter whether you're black or white, healthy or ill, straight or gay . . . love is love."

Why do I feel betrayed by this sequence? For one thing, if love is love and it doesn't matter if you're straight or gay, I want to know why Jonathan Demme didn't show Andy getting into bed with his boyfriend Miguel (Antonio Bandéras) as Callas continued to sing. After all, didn't Joe say he wasn't all that familiar with opera? So whose subjectivity is represented here, anyway? The answer, of course, is that it's the subjectivity of the spectator, constructed by Demme's film as straight and unaffected by AIDS. That spectator might not be familiar with opera either, but Andy explains this particular aria well enough for anyone to understand that opera's themes—like those of Demme's movie—are universal. To make his point, though, Demme has to forsake the subjectivity he begins by representing as so fascinating, so different, so incomprehensible, but as nevertheless supposedly also laying claim to the universal. Demme steals Callas from the dying opera queen, who reveals

---

1. "La Mamma Morta-fied," *Poz* 6 (February–March 1995), p. 16. In saying that Callas is every homo's favorite, I merely and deliberately repeat received wisdom. My own favorite singer, hands down, is Caballé, but still, my favorite *diva* is Callas.

his subjectivity through his identification with her, and gives her away—to Joe and his wife and baby, and thus implicitly to every "normal" family unit. (I didn't actually count them, but it seemed to me that there were more babies than queers in *Philadelphia.*)

The reason, I think, many of us focus on the opera scene in *Philadelphia* is that it's the only one where we can in any way recognize Andy's character as queer. If I feel betrayed by the sequence, it is because this single signifier of Andy's queerness, once displayed, is divested of its queer specificity. And what Demme seems thus to be saying is that you have to dispense with what makes a queer a queer in order to get anybody else to feel sorry that he's going to die.

There are two, conflicting propositions about AIDS, or more precisely about knowledge regarding AIDS, that I want to try to bring into relation in this essay: first, that knowledge about AIDS, gained in one time and place—often the hard way, by learning from deadly mistakes—might help others, at later times and in other places, to avoid those mistakes and thus to prevent the horrible ravages of a vast epidemic such as the one we experience in New York City, where we have, as of September 30, 1994, over 70,000 reported cases of AIDS, of whom more than 47,000 have died. And second, that knowledge about AIDS is always local, will always be bound by a particular time and place, which will often make knowledge gained in one place seem inappropriate or nontransferable to another.

There are other ways of describing this contradiction. Although AIDS is truly pandemic, and everyone everywhere will potentially be affected by AIDS, the global pandemic is really many interrelated but quite different epidemics, with different causes and different effects, affecting different kinds of people. Or still another way of characterizing this conflict is to say that while certain forms of knowledge appear to be objective and thus everywhere and always applicable, other forms of knowledge begin by admitting their subjective and local limitations.

This acknowledgment of subjectivity is something that we often see as a particular strength of art, and thus we often value art made in response to AIDS as having something unique to tell us about the personal, human side of the epidemic. It is usually to art that we turn, it is said, to see the "faces of AIDS" as opposed to the statistical abstractions of science and sociology. And because art can "give AIDS a face," we often assume that it will solicit the sympathy of those not immediately affected by the disease, thus effecting the translation of the individual situation into the shared condition. When I first wrote about AIDS, my intention was to contest this distinction between the objectivity of science and the subjectivity of art. On the one hand, I wanted to show that even the most established facts about AIDS were far from objective. All facts— social facts, scientific facts, medical facts—only in time come to be seen as true and objective, but they, no less than other things we think we know, are constructed—built on subjectively contrived ideas, hypotheses, experiments, studies, surveys, descriptions, negotiations, and so forth. On the other hand, I wanted to argue that art, or cultural work generally, had as much right to make objective truth claims as did science. Indeed, I submitted that it was the function of art not only to express the experiences of love and caring, loss and mourning, fear and despair, anger and outrage, but also to inform, to educate, and to engage in the activist struggle against the negligence of our governing institutions and the falsehoods perpetrated by our media. The simplest way to characterize the argument I was attempting to make is to say that all knowledge—whether scientific or artistic—is *interested* knowledge and thus open to contestation; knowledge of whatever sort is never free of our investments, the sense in which it is true *for us*.

In the eight years since I first made this argument, I have seen that there is a significant problem with it. For in thinking about the subjectivity of knowledge production largely in terms of competing interests and investments, I failed to account for the most crucial feature of subjectivity—that governed by the unconscious, which often works against our conscious interests. And it is this aspect of subjectivity that so often determines how any of us, including our often irresponsible governments, responds to AIDS.

Let me give an example. As everyone knows, what is now called AIDS was first reported in the United States among otherwise healthy gay men. For a short time, it was assumed by some scientists that the syndrome had something intrinsically to do with homosexuality, even though a "scientific" knowledge of sexuality would certainly understand that there can be *nothing* intrinsic to homosexuality, since intrinsically homosexuality is nothing at all. In any case, AIDS was very soon seen in people who had never engaged in homosexual sex, but the link between homosexuality and AIDS has nevertheless persisted with amazing tenacity. Lip service might be paid to such statements as "AIDS is not just a gay disease," or "AIDS is everybody's problem," but still, if you ask most Americans who gets AIDS, they'll answer, Homosexuals. There are many reasons for this, some more logical than others. To this day, the majority of people with AIDS in the United States are gay men, even if the overall percentages have steadily declined. An even greater majority of *images* of people with AIDS seen in the media are of gay men. Perhaps equally important, the people who have most visibly mobilized to fight the epidemic are gay men and lesbians. Thus the images of service providers, advocates, activists, doctors, and lawyers coping on a day-to-day basis with the epidemic are also images, for the most part, of gay men and lesbians. In addition, most of the alternative representations of AIDS are produced by gay and lesbian artists, film- and videomakers, and writers.

Still, this preponderance of images of AIDS as a gay disease has, for many years now, existed alongside the countervailing information that AIDS is transmitted by heterosexual as well as homosexual sex, that it is also transmitted by sharing needles when injecting drugs, through blood transfusions and the use of blood products, and from mother to child. But despite this information, the association of AIDS with homosexuality in the United States is still extraordinarily powerful. When the star basketball player Magic Johnson discovered that he was HIV-positive in late 1991, he said that he hadn't practiced safe sex because he thought AIDS was a gay disease. Not long after he said that, the *majority* of new cases of AIDS reported in the United States were among African Americans and Latinos, including large numbers of women and children and straight as well as gay men. How is it that Magic Johnson, who had been very engaged with the needs and concerns of African Americans, could have been unaware of the extent of devastation wrought by AIDS on African Americans?

The answer to that question is suggested by what happened to Magic himself. Shortly after he rejoined the Los Angeles Lakers in 1992, Magic was forced to retire a second time. The officially reported reason was that his fellow players in the NBA were afraid to play against him because of the possibility of a bloody accident on the basketball court, but the subtext of many of the media stories suggested that Magic quit for another reason: some of his fellow players had revived rumors that Magic was gay. Now, I doubt that those players really believe Magic is gay. I think, rather, that by claiming that Magic was gay, they were able to say, in effect, "This disease is not my problem. I don't have to worry. I don't have to use condoms when I'm out on the road having lots of sex."

"AIDS is not my problem." This simple statement (or thought) is without question the most widespread, the most tenacious, and the most dangerous formulation in this pandemic. Indeed, I think it would not be wrong to say that the statement "AIDS is not my problem" is as responsible as anything for the fact that so many people worldwide have been infected with HIV. Whether the statement is enunciated by governments in the form of refusals to acknowledge the risks to their populations, to conduct responsible education campaigns, and to fund research, or of discriminatory practices such as exclusionary immigration and travel policies; by the blood banking, blood products, and pharmaceutical industries in the form of caring more for profits than for human life; by the media in the form of failures to pursue and report accurate information and to alert their audiences to the seriousness of the threat posed by AIDS; by communities in the form of scapegoating other groups and failing to acknowledge and support their own affected constituents; or by individuals in the form of distancing themselves from those already affected by the epidemic—the result is the same: an ever growing transmission of HIV to more and more people all over the world.

Most people don't say, outright, "AIDS is not my problem." Rather they translate that statement into some version of "AIDS is the problem of others." In the United States, the statement translates as "AIDS is a gay disease" or "AIDS is a junkie's disease." In other places, it translates as "AIDS is a disease of prostitutes." In still others, "AIDS is a Western disease," "AIDS is an African disease," or "AIDS is a Southeast Asian disease."

It is by now a truism that the us/them construction of AIDS is the major obstacle to overcome, that we must all accept that AIDS is *our* problem. But what is not so commonly acknowledged is the extraordinary psychic force of the statement that AIDS is not my problem—a force so strong as to make it possible to hold fast to such a statement even when it is rationally known to be absolutely false. I know this psychic force firsthand. I remember first learning about what would later be called AIDS in the summer of 1981, when the *New York Times* first reported the discovery of a rare form of cancer in gay men. Soon after that report, news about horrible rare diseases diagnosed in otherwise healthy gay men circulated widely in New York's gay community. As it became more and more evident that an epidemic disproportionately affecting sexually active gay men was spreading, I reacted, as did many of my gay friends, with my own version of the us/them mechanism. "It's only happening to those guys who go to sex clubs." "It's only happening to those guys who take lots of drugs." "It's only happening to those guys who've had lots of sexually transmitted diseases." I reassured myself that I was not one of "those guys," the ones who get AIDS. And I did so even though I went to sex clubs, I took drugs, and I'd had my share of sexually transmitted diseases. But somehow, by some form of magical thinking—this is the force of the unconscious—I exempted myself from the category of "those guys," the others, the ones who get AIDS. I stopped exempting myself only when a close friend was diagnosed, a friend I'd had sex with, a friend who lived his life very much like I lived mine. Only then did I begin saying, "AIDS *is* my problem." Only then did I begin practicing safe sex. It could easily have been too late. And that is the terrifying moral of this story: if we wait until AIDS affects us directly, until friends or lovers or family members or we ourselves are infected, it is too late.

In the United States, it was already too late for many gay men by the time AIDS was first recognized in 1981. For that reason, gay men and our lesbian friends responded to the AIDS epidemic in a way that almost no one else responded: by saying "AIDS is our problem." With that acknowledgment, everything changes. You learn all you can and help to educate others. You begin to protect yourself and those with whom you interact. You build systems of care and support. You make demands on your social institutions and your government. You fight for the attention of the mass media, and you create your own media.

But you also run a terrible risk: In saying, "Yes, AIDS is our problem," you allow others to go on saying, "AIDS is not my problem, it's *your* problem." Even worse, some will say you *are* the problem. There is still another, even more terrible risk, one that we are only beginning to recognize: the risk entailed by the long-term effects of having to sustain changes in attitudes and behaviors in the face of so much adversity and loss. Moreover, this risk is compounded by the fact that attempts to get others to recognize the impending threat of AIDS are often predicated on the abandonment or sacrifice of those already affected.

For the most part, cultural work about AIDS has been produced by those who are directly affected by the epidemic, artists who are themselves infected with HIV or who have lost friends, lovers, family, and community members to AIDS. Art has attempted to convey what it feels like to deal with the epidemic—to be ill, to care for those who are ill, to face death, to mourn, to be outraged, to be defeated. But art about AIDS has also attempted to combat the epidemic directly—to teach safe sex practices, inform people about their risks, fight discrimination, expose the lies of governments and media, arouse affected groups to anger and activism.

When I first wrote about art and AIDS in 1987, it was the latter practices, those that directly combated the epidemic, that seemed to me most in need of recognition. I pleaded for support of art practices rooted in community activism and engaged in political struggle. Although I was not opposed to art that expressed feelings of loss and despair, I nevertheless preferred and championed politically activist cultural work. What I have come to realize, though, is that I drew too rigid a distinction between the two kinds of art about AIDS, that the feelings of loss and despair expressed in the one kind of art would become necessary in activist art as well.

In 1987, one of the works I focused on was *Testing the Limits,* one of the first of what became a significant genre of videos and films documenting the burgeoning AIDS activist movement in the United States and elsewhere. This collectively produced video featured New York City community-based organizations dedicated to fighting the epidemic in the hardest hit communities. It was highly inspirational and served as a useful organizing tool. The same collective began working immediately on a longer, second video on the same subject, which centered on ACT UP. Finally completed in 1992, the second tape, *Voices from the Front,* is similar in style and format to the first, but is feature-length, more professionally produced, and covers much more ground with much greater depth. It was far more widely seen, as it won a prize at the Berlin film festival, aired on national public television, and even had short commercial releases in movie theaters. I suppose that it might serve its uplifting objective rather well, showing as it does huge, well-organized ACT UP demonstrations that led to concrete political victories. But it can serve that objective only for those who were not members of the ACT UP it pictures; for those of us who were, the video provokes a mix of nostalgia and despair, in part because ACT UP as we knew it then no longer exists, at least in New York.

Voices from the Front ends with the famous final remarks of film scholar Vito Russo's speech at the 1988 demonstration at the U.S. Food and Drug Administration, in which he proclaims: "After we kick the shit out of this illness, we're all going to be alive to kick the shit out of this system so that this never happens again." Vito's fighting words are followed by a quick montage of images of ACT UP demonstrations, and then the words "In memoriam," whereupon we see the repetition of images of twelve of the people we just watched in the video who died before the tape's completion. The final one is Vito Russo himself. I personally find it agonizing to watch Vito's rousing "We're all going to be alive" followed by such a brutal contradiction of his words. And in the time that has passed between the tape's release and today, many more people in the video have died.

Videomaker Jean Carlomusto, who worked for a time with the Testing the Limits collective, reflects on this contradiction in the videotape *Fast Trip, Long Drop* by Gregg Bordowitz, who was also a member of the original Testing the Limits collective but left after the completion of the first tape. Sitting in her editing room at Gay Men's Health Crisis, Carlomusto says:

In the beginning, when we were shooting [video] at various protests, there was a kind of energy that was amazing. It was the energy of people really coming together, really speaking out and thinking of new and creative ways [to fight AIDS]. As time went on, it became sadder and sadder to sit in an editing room with this material, because as you would look at the material you'd start to think, "Oh, well, he's gone . . . he's gone . . . ," and it became almost your only chance to see people who you hadn't seen in a long time, or a chance to see someone who looked a lot healthier at that particular time. And it really became more and more a record of loss. In that way, the material that once had been so energizing starts to become almost a burden, difficult to watch. Because of that, it completely changed its meaning.[2]

This change of meaning has had a strong effect on the way I came to think about art and AIDS, even though it was always theoretically part of the argument I was making. I always knew that politically engaged artworks confronting the AIDS epidemic were highly contingent, that their messages would not transcend the time and place for which they were made. The AIDS activist graphics that I wrote about in *AIDS Demo Graphics*, for example, were produced for specific demonstrations, were about local issues of the moment, and thus have no meaning today except as mementos, documents, or examples of the type of work that

2. *Fast Trip, Long Drop*, Gregg Bordowitz, 1993 (distributed by Video Data Bank).

might be made for other times and places. One such graphic, produced for a 1988 demonstration at City Hall in New York, juxtaposes a photograph of then Mayor Ed Koch with the text, "10,000 New York City AIDS deaths/How'm I Doin'?" Even at the time the poster was created, it would have meant little outside New York, and now, in New York, hardly anybody remembers that Koch was always fatuously asking "How'm I Doin'?" and the number of AIDS deaths is far more than 10,000. Even a work like Gran Fury's famous bloody hand print with the headline "The government has blood on its hands" had to be revised to remain relevant. The text along the bottom of the poster that originally stated "One AIDS death every half hour" had to be changed just a few years later to "One AIDS death every twelve minutes." What makes the contingency of meaning in these two obvious examples more than just a matter of banal fact is that, whereas 10,000 AIDS deaths in New York City or one AIDS death in the United States every half hour once seemed unimaginably horrible, today we can only wish the epidemic were so limited.

But the change of meaning to which Jean Carlomusto refers in Bordowitz's video is less about this sort of contingency than about the subjective experience of the work's audience. For people who live outside New York or were not members of ACT UP in the time period documented by *Voices from the Front,* the video might very well function as intended—as a testament to the possibilities of progressive change as a result of community activism and as a stimulus to create or join an activist movement. But those of us whose own activism is represented by the video often feel violated, as once again the complexities of our lives are oversimplified—and this time not by the mass media but by our own activist artists. First we were pariahs or victims, now we are immortal heroes. But of course we are neither. We are ordinary people whose struggle against this epidemic has taken its own terrible toll. Gregg Bordowitz addresses us, only half humorously, in *Fast Trip, Long Drop,* as "the burnt out, the broken hearted, and . . . the profoundly confused."

My purpose is not to condemn *Voices from the Front* as dishonest. The failure to acknowledge the toll that death was taking on AIDS activism is not merely the failure of this video, which in many ways is an exemplary work. Instead it represents a wider failure of AIDS activism to confront the daily emotional toll that AIDS inevitably takes. The difference between the original *Testing the Limits* and *Voices from the Front* is a difference between a moment of optimism at the founding of a movement and a later moment when such optimism has become hollow and therefore false. Another way to characterize this difference is to return to what I said at the beginning of this essay—that objective information is everywhere and always also subjective.

What does this relation between subjectivity and objectivity mean for cultural work about AIDS?

To me, it means that the ways we imagine and address our audiences will be the most important thing we do, and that the rhetorics we employ must be faithful to our situation *at this moment* rather than what seemed true and useful the last time we set to work. In the introduction to *AIDS Demo Graphics,* I wanted to explain how the graphic work produced by members of ACT UP constructed its audience differently from the viewers intended by much of the art about AIDS produced within the traditional art world. Here is what I wrote:

AIDS activist art is grounded in the accumulated knowledge and political analysis of the AIDS crisis produced collectively by the entire movement. The graphics not only reflect that knowledge, but actively contribute to its articulation as well. They codify concrete, specific issues of importance to the movement as a whole or particular interests within it. They function as an organizing tool, by conveying, in compressed form, information and political positions to others affected by the epidemic, to onlookers at demonstrations, and to the dominant media. But their primary audience is the movement itself. AIDS activist graphics enunciate AIDS politics to and for all of us in the movement. . . . [Through them], our politics, and our cohesion around those politics, become visible to us.[3]

3. Douglas Crimp, with Adam Rolston, *AIDS Demo Graphics* (Seattle: Bay Press, 1990), pp. 19–20.

What I hoped to convey in this text is similar to what Gregg Bordowitz wrote about the first *Testing the Limits* video in an essay entitled "Picture a Coalition":

Imagine a screening. In a local community center a consumer VCR deck and a TV set sit on a table. Representatives from the various communities affected by AIDS sit in front of the TV. They watch a video composed of interviews with each of them. They see themselves pictured in relation to one another as they sit next to one another.

Consider this screening. It presents both means and ends for the video AIDS activist. The AIDS movement . . . creates itself as it attempts to represent itself. Video puts into play the means of recognizing one's place within the movement in relation to that of others in the movement. Video has the potential to render the concerted efforts—as yet unimagined— between groups. The most significant challenge to the movement is coalition building, because the AIDS epidemic has engendered a community of people who cannot afford not to recognize themselves as a community and to act as one.[4]

Voices from the Front works to achieve something quite different from what Bordowitz describes here, where the AIDS activist movement comes into being through the very process of self-representation. *Voices* does not presume its primary audience to be those shown in the video coalescing around their own self-representation. Rather, it presumes its audience to be on the outside looking in. The subjectivity of those represented is sacrificed to the goal of reaching others.

It must, I think, be acknowledged that the historical circumstances of people who have been coping with AIDS for over a decade have changed drastically in the past few years. Our disaffection from AIDS activism is but one indication. Another, which we are even more loath to discuss publicly, is that seroconversion rates among gay men, including those

4. Gregg Bordowitz, "Picture a Coalition," in *AIDS: Cultural Analysis/Cultural Activism,* ed. Douglas Crimp (Cambridge: MIT Press, 1988), p. 195.

De-Moralizing Representations of AIDS

gay men best informed about AIDS, have begun to rise again after a period of fairly steady decline. This means that many men who had been consistently practicing safe sex no longer are. It is difficult for us to speak openly about this because, on the one hand, we have been rightly proud of the fact that we had changed our sexual behaviors more thoroughly than anyone could have predicted. On the other hand, being open about this fact immediately draws the scorn of those who have *never* cared about our welfare. Thus the moralizing rhetoric of "relapse," "irresponsibility," "selfishness," and "compulsivity"; and sadly, the moralizing is not limited to our declared enemies. A new political group of gay men calling themselves HIV Prevention Activists has formed in New York. Their mission is to close gay sex clubs. One of their members, Gabriel Rotello, an openly gay columnist for *New York Newsday,* wrote a column sensationally entitled "Sex Clubs Are the Killing Fields of AIDS" in which he describes unprotected sex in a gay sex club as a "sex murder/suicide."[5]

But moralizing will not help any of us through this new crisis any more than will the repetition of a heroic rhetoric of our past achievements in fighting the epidemic. What is necessary now is the self-representation of our *demoralization.* We urgently need resources to help us cope with the consequences of losing hope for a cure for AIDS, of dealing with loss upon loss, with so much hatred directed at us, and with the simple and horrible fact, very rarely given voice, that all of us will almost certainly live with AIDS for the remainder of our lives, however long that may be. When most of us began practicing safe sex, we made a kind of bargain—saying, in effect, I'll make this sacrifice for now, until AIDS is over with. But who among us foresaw that the sacrifice would be forever? Who is psychically able to accept the consequences of "forever"?

The singular achievement of Gregg Bordowitz's film *Fast Trip, Long Drop* is that it dares to represent this demoralization, embodied in the film in the person with AIDS, Bordowitz himself. But though the film is

5. Gabriel Rotello, "Sex Clubs Are the Killing Fields of AIDS," *New York Newsday,* April 28, 1994, p. A42.

autobiographical, the subjectivity represented is not individualized as Bordowitz's own. There are two central characters in the film, both played by Bordowitz: Gregg Bordowitz and Alter Allesman (Yiddish for "ole everybody"). The first is funny, sad, lonely, searching, fatalistic. The second is cynical, defiant, furious, dangerous. We can rarely be sure, though, which is which, except when Allesman appears on the television show "Thriving with AIDS," produced by Bordowitz (a parody of "Living with AIDS," which Bordowitz actually produced for Gay Men's Health Crisis).

The central metaphorical tale in *Fast Trip, Long Drop*, the trope for which the film is named, is the story of the death of Bordowitz's father, Leslie Harsten, whom Bordowitz never really knew. When Harsten was thirty, Bordowitz's age when he made *Fast Trip*, he went to Idaho to watch Evel Knieval's daredevil jump over the Snake River Canyon in a homemade missile. About midway over the canyon, the contraption abruptly descended into the gorge (A newspaper story reporting the event was headlined "Fast Trip, Long Drop"). Evel Knieval survived, but Leslie Harsten did not. Crossing a highway intersection after leaving the spectacle, Bordowitz's father was killed when he was hit by a pick-up truck and then a camper. Reiterated throughout the film with stock footage of crazy daredevil stunts, this is a true story about the indeterminate relations of risk and chance. Evel Knieval dared fate and survived; Harsten was killed by sheer happenstance. When Bordowitz recounts a drunken episode in which he begged a man to fuck him, remembering that they should have used a condom only after the guy came, he is telling another story of risk and chance, one that may or may not prove fatal, and one that many of us could tell about ourselves.

These funny/harrowing tales of risk and chance open out within the film to encompass more complex reflections on the history of human misery, how it is that we find agency and meaning within historical circumstances not of our own making. Taking his Jewish heritage as one context for his reflections (the film uses Klezmer music throughout), Bordowitz narrates over archival footage from pre-World-War-II shtetls and Eastern European Jewish cemeteries. He begins by remembering

Gregg Bordowitz, *Fast Trip, Long Drop,* 1993.

that his grandfather once told him that in the shtetl, epidemics of cholera and typhus came and went and that survival was a matter of luck. He goes on:

People have been dying and suffering of all kinds of things for some time. I guess I'm just a part of history. Until now, youth and ignorance have afforded me a kind of arrogance. I thought I was unique, my suffering was different, my misery was a new kind of misery. What's new about it is the way we speak about it, the meanings we make about it. What's not so new is the misery. Can one become resigned to the fact of misery without losing one's hope? I guess what's unique about my pain is that it's mine, mine to feel and mine to represent, mine to overcome, mine to resign to, mine. At first, owning it, acknowledging it, seemed like a revolutionary act. Now, accepting the fact of my own mortality has become the hardest thing I'm facing, and I have to do it. The task has appeared to me with great force, with urgency. It grabbed me and shook me. It won't let go.

Bordowitz's attempts to assert agency have already appeared in *Fast Trip* as the record of his work with ACT UP as an organizer and documentary videomaker. But after this reflection on his own fate, and immediately following the statement, "Before I die I want to be the protagonist of my own story, the agent of my own history," what we see is Bordowitz's belated attempt to learn to drive. Bordowitz approaches his new task warily; car crashes, after all, have been a leitmotiv of *Fast Trip*. But warily, too, because the date of the driving lesson is given in the film as June 1995 (the film was completed in the fall of 1993). It represents, as Bill Horrigan wrote, "a modestly hopeful projection, a vision of perfect ordinariness poignant for that very reason."[6]

Poignant, too, because—hedged, held amidst day-to-day contingencies, historically pondered—it is hope that neither rings false nor promises transcendence. It is not the rousing hope of *Voices from the Front*, which, in reminding us how blindly we once kept the faith, speaks to us now only of loss; nor is it the humanist hope of *Philadelphia*, which trusts far too much in the homophobe's progress and leaves the queer with his slightly mad vision of heaven-sent love. In this respect, the function of the opera scene in *Philadelphia* is not unlike the magical happy ending of the film *Longtime Companion*, where all those who have died in the epidemic suddenly come back to life, run down the boardwalks of Fire Island Pines and onto the beach. It is therefore not surprising that Maddelena's aria of love and transcendence is reprised one more time at the end of *Philadelphia*, just as Andy, on his deathbed, says to Miguel, "I'm ready."

Fast Trip, Long Drop has a coda following the credits that speaks very differently of death. Lying in his bed, smoking a cigarette, Bordowitz looks at the camera and says, "Death is the death of consciousness, and I hope that there's nothing after this." Then he begins to giggle, then to laugh openly, then to cough, whereupon he drops his cigarette on his chest. "Shit," he says, then, "Cut." No transcendence, no catharsis, the end.

6. Bill Horrigan, "One-Way Street," *GLQ: A Journal of Lesbian and Gay Studies* 1, no. 3 (1994), p. 368.

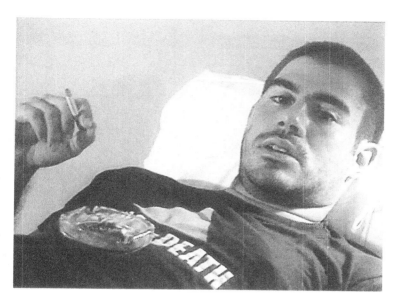

Gregg Bordowitz, *Fast Trip, Long Drop*, 1993.

16 PAINFUL PICTURES

First presented at the discussion "Have You Always

Been Artistic? A Seminar on Artistic Practice and

Queer Cultural Politics," held at the Museum of

Contemporary Art, Sydney, in association with the

Sydney Gay and Lesbian Mardi Gras Festival,

February 25, 1995.

A few years ago I gave a lecture in which I criticized the ways in which museum officials sought to defend Robert Mapplethorpe's photographs against the criminal charges brought against the Cincinnati Art Museum and its director for exhibiting them in *The Perfect Moment*.[1] I was concerned about the evacuation of the photographs' sexual contents through an insistence on their purely formal aesthetic qualities. To score my critical points, I played my audience for laughs, first showing them Mapplethorpe's self-portrait with a bullwhip shoved up his rectum while reading Janet Kardon's description of the work, which she called "a figure study": "The human figure is centered," she testified. "The horizon line is two-thirds of the way up, almost the classical two-thirds to one-third proportions. The way the light is cast, so there's light all around the figure, it's very symmetrical, which is very characteristic of his flowers. . . ."[2] I followed this excerpt from Kardon's defense with a statement by Robert Sobieszak, who sought to redeem Mapplethorpe's S&M photographs by suggesting that they portray a difficult psychological quest. Sobieszak claimed, "[The *X Portfolio* photographs] reveal in very strong, forceful ways a major concern of the artist . . . a troubled portion of his life that he was trying to come to grips with. . . ."[3] At this moment I switched to a slide of the *X Portfolio* picture titled *Helmut and Brooks*, a photograph of fist fucking. I thought it would be funny to accompany the phrase "trying to come to grips" with the image of a fist thrust up a rectum. Except for when I gave the lecture to predominantly gay audiences, though, I didn't get a lot of laughs at this point. Indeed, after I first presented the lecture, one of my university colleagues told me that she had found it almost unbearable to look at that photograph, in which she could see only excruciating pain. At the time, I didn't know how to respond, perhaps because I hadn't really thought enough about the photograph. It had served my purposes merely as the punch line of

1. The lecture derived from "Photographs at the End of Modernism," the introduction to my book *On the Museum's Ruins* (Cambridge: MIT Press, 1993); see also Janet Kardon, *Robert Mapplethorpe: The Perfect Moment* (Philadelphia: Institute of Contemporary Art, 1988); and Richard Bolton, *The Culture Wars: Documents form the Recent Controversies in the Arts* (New York: New Press, 1988).

2. Quoted in Jane Merkel, "Art on Trial," *Art in America* 78, no. 12 (December 1990), p. 47.

3. Quoted in Merkel, "Art on Trial," p. 47.

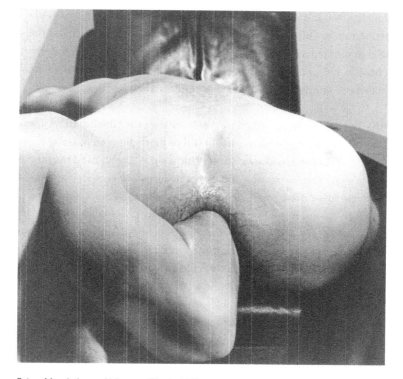

Robert Mapplethorpe, *Helmut and Brooks*, 1978
(© The Estate of Robert Mapplethorpe. Used with permission).

a joke and, I thought, to show both how inoffensive and how beautiful the photographs on trial really were. The pleasures of fist fucking are not something I necessarily take for granted, but neither are they entirely foreign to me (indeed, I used to be regularly approached in gay bars because my hands are so visibly larger than most—some people just can't resist a challenge).

Looking again at *Helmut and Brooks,* I feel a bit more charitable toward Janet Kardon and Robert Sobieszak. One cannot begin to describe the photograph adequately without mentioning its compositional symmetries, its tonal subtleties, its sheer formal beauty, and, at the same time, the photograph's impact surely resides in the contrast between those qualities and the challenge of its subject matter. Whether we see fist fucking as painful or pleasurable—or pleasurable because painful—we cannot but be impressed by the photographic staging of this extreme sexual moment in a spare, well-lighted studio, a set-up where we have come to accept a bell pepper or a nude body, perhaps, but not a sexual act whose intensity cannot be faked for the camera.

Another argument proffered by the defense at the Cincinnati trial was that the offending photographs should properly be seen in the context of Mapplethorpe's work as a whole. This would have allowed the jury to see the same studio setting and the same formal beauty as it appeared in classically posed nudes, exquisite flower arrangements, and glamorous portraits. In one of a number of highly prejudicial rulings, the judge in the case disallowed that contextualization. But there is another contextualization, more interesting to me, that no one thought worth arguing for—that of the sexual subculture in which Mapplethorpe participated at the time he made the *X Portfolio* pictures. Clearly no one thought any advantage could be gained by describing the sexual pursuits of the gay leather scene and analyzing Mapplethorpe's restaging of those pursuits for studio pictures of striking beauty and originality. That task was left to queer theorists such as Richard Meyer, Paul Morrison, and Gayle Rubin.[4]

I am, of course, aware that arguments are made in courts of law in order to win cases and that arguments are made in academic arenas for other purposes entirely, but I think the discrepancy in this instance can be instructive. If we begin by admitting that many of the pictures in Mapplethorpe's *X Portfolio* depict gay male sexual practices that we cannot hope to defend in front of a jury, then we might understand that there is something about these practices that is inimical to American democ-

4. See Richard Meyer, "Robert Mapplethorpe and the Discipline of Photography," in *The Lesbian and Gay Studies Reader,* ed. Henry Abelove, Michèle Aina Barale, and David Halperin (New York: Routledge, 1993), pp. 360–380; and Paul Morrison, "Coffee Table Sex: Robert Mapplethorpe and the Sadomasochism of Everyday Life," *Genders* 11 (fall 1991), pp. 17–36. Gayle Rubin's argument was presented at a conference in conjunction with the showing of *The Perfect Moment* at the Institute of Contemporary Art, Boston, in 1990.

racy as presently constituted, something whose defense would therefore be, at the same time, a contestation of the limits of our democracy.

I don't want to claim that fist fucking is something every gay man does,
or wants to do, or even approves of. But I do want to claim that what we
do *sexually* is the root cause of the hatred directed at us and, moreover,
that many arguments for tolerance of gay men and lesbians attempt to
obfuscate that sexuality. Here is an example of what I mean, drawn from
a very different context: In the made-for-network-TV movie *Serving in
Silence*, produced by Barbra Streisand and starring Glen Close and Judy
Davis, Close, playing Colonel Margarethe Cammermeyer, is asked by her
military interrogator to clarify her statement that she is a lesbian. "You
are currently active as a lesbian?" he asks. "I am in a relationship with a
woman," she responds. "A sexual relationship?" he inquires. "It's not
about that," Cammermeyer replies. "It's about who I am. I am a lesbian."

This film is unlike most social-issue films made for American television
in that it makes no attempt to give a so-called balanced view. No one is
allowed to defend the military's anti-gay policy; it is presented as the result of blatant prejudice. Cammermeyer is shown to be a great soldier, a
perfect mother and daughter, a model citizen, a true American hero.
But I would submit that her perfection is entirely dependent on the idea
that her lesbianism is a matter of identity, not sexuality, of identity not
in any way even based on sexuality. Indeed her lesbian identity is something that, according to the movie's narrative, can be known to her husband and children even before Colonel Cammermeyer acknowledges it
to herself, much less acts on it.

The absurdity of this nonsexual lesbianism could perhaps be accounted
for by the strictures of American TV, or for that matter by the simple repetition of a prejudice whose most famous proponent was Queen Victoria, except for the fact that it so exactly reproduces the arguments made
by various gay and lesbian activists during the struggle, in 1993, to
rescind the ban against gays and lesbians in the U.S. military. The distinction between status and conduct, identity and behavior, was the
linchpin of those arguments. And the predictable result was that homo-

sexual conduct is still punishable with separation from the military. But the military further outsmarted its lesbian and gay antagonists by insisting on the basis for identity that we ourselves felt better left unspoken. In the military's new policy, a gay identity freely admitted to automatically presumes that the soldier has either committed homosexual acts or intends to do so and is therefore subject to separation in any case.

The TV movie *Serving in Silence* also illustrates rather well the political conditions in which queer cultural politics now operate in the United States. President Clinton's feeble attempt at lifting the military ban against gays and lesbians met with fierce resistance articulated in the most clichéd and vicious homophobic terms and resulted in virtually total defeat. At the same time, gay and lesbian military personnel became so visible during the debates and were so generally admired for their patriotic service that a film entirely sympathetic to their cause has now aired on national television. This political paradox derives, I think, from the fact that the visible image so readily admired always ultimately gives way to another that is just as readily vilified.

The dramatic increase in queer visibility did not begin with the gays-in-the-military issue, of course, but with AIDS. For all our attempts to become visible in the years after Stonewall, nothing we were able to do for ourselves ensured our visibility so much as the horrible crisis that beset our communities in the early 1980s. It goes without saying that that visibility came at a terrible cost, the cost of hundreds of thousands ill, dying, and dead. But the cost is not only in lives but in the sort of visibility we achieved. On the floor of the Senate in 1987, arch-homophobe Jesse Helms stated that "every AIDS case can be traced back to a homosexual act."[5] Some four years later, on the tenth anniversary of the first official reports of what is now called AIDS, an editorial in New Hampshire's right-wing *Manchester Union Leader* repeated Helms's opinion: "Homosexual intercourse is the genesis of every single case of AIDS in that every case is traceable—either directly or indirectly—to that practice. However the disease is transmitted, the sexual perversion that is anal

5. *Congressional Record,* October 14, 1987.

intercourse by sodomites is the fundamental point of origin."[6] In other words, what has really become visible is not queer subjects but a fantasized, phobic image of anal sodomy. Even if the quoted statements are those of extremists and completely false, I think we must take seriously the idea that this image haunts every image of a gay man that comes into public view.[7] And the fact that lesbian sex cannot even be spoken might well also be a function of the force of this phobia about gay male sex. It is instructive in this regard that opponents of lifting the military ban almost entirely ignored lesbians in the military, even though lesbians are five times as likely as gay men to be drummed out of the service because of their homosexuality. Their arguments focused instead on male soldiers worried about their backsides in combat situations or being afraid to enter the shower in the barracks.

My sense is that gay men and lesbians rushed into the battle to lift the military ban, and away from the battle against AIDS, because they thought that, by separating identity from behavior and focusing on images of model citizen-soldiers, they could for once leave sex out of the equation. And I think we lost that battle precisely because we underestimated the degree to which, reinforced by AIDS, the phobic image of anal penetration haunts every image of homosexuality: Even the picture of a healthy homosexual or a patriotic lesbian is always already contaminated with that image.

What I am arguing is that images have a psychic component that cannot be negated by simply making that component invisible. In his own way perhaps even Jesse Helms realized this. It has always been curious to me that, in attacking Mapplethorpe, Helms did not much concentrate on the S&M images of the *X Portfolio*. He was far more intent on stirring up fears about two rather innocent portraits of children. But a single

6. Quoted in Andrew Merton, "AIDS and Gay-Bashing in New Hampshire," *Boston Sunday Globe,* June 9, 1991, p. 2NH.

7. Leo Bersani made this point in "Is the Rectum a Grave?" in *AIDS: Cultural Analysis/ Cultural Activism,* ed. Douglas Crimp (Cambridge: MIT Press, 1988), pp. 197–222, esp. 211–212.

statement might suffice to explain his tactics: "This Mapplethorpe fellow . . . was an acknowledged homosexual. He's dead now, but the homosexual theme goes throughout his work."[8] Helms absolved himself of the necessity of having to speak about fist fucking or any other of the terrifying acts of sexual perversion depicted in Mapplethorpe's *X Portfolio*. Mapplethorpe was a homosexual and he died of AIDS. Enough said—enough said, because that picture of anal penetration is already firmly in place.

I wonder now if my university colleague's sense of excruciating pain on seeing a slide of Mapplethorpe's *Helmut and Brooks* was not in fact the pain of recognizing—at least unconsciously—that struggles for gay visibility and rights will always be stopped short by such an image. For the torment registered in that image is not, after all, that of the body of the receptive participant, who we might well suppose is loving his submission, but of every gay man—and every lesbian—who will suffer because of the image's force in the homophobe's unconscious.

I will conclude by saying that, in my view, two things are now inescapable for queers in the United States: the AIDS epidemic, which appears to be something all of us will live with, in one way or another, for the rest of our lives; and a fear and loathing of homosexuality based on straight men's phobic fantasies of anal penetration. And if these things are inescapable—and inescapably related to each other—we cannot afford to engage in a politics that denies them, obfuscates them, or downplays them in any way. Rather we must make them the very grounds of our political struggle. Sometimes even a formally beautiful photograph can make that clear to us.

8. Quoted in Maureen Dowd, "Jesse Helms Takes No-Lose Position on Art," *New York Times,* July 28, 1989, p. B6.

17 SEX AND SENSIBILITY, OR SENSE AND SEXUALITY

First presented as a keynote address for the

conference "QueerZone: Mediating Community,"

sponsored by the University of Western Sydney,

Napean, in conjunction with the Sydney Gay and

Lesbian Mardi Gras Festival, February 19, 1998, and

published under the title "Melancholia and

Moralism" in Loss, *ed. David L. Eng and David*

Kazanjian (Berkeley: University of California

Press, 2002).

In the national gay-bashing media frenzy over so-called gay serial killer Andrew Cunanan, the man who shot Gianni Versace in the summer of 1997, the compelling question was, Why did he do it? What happened to this "excessively charming" guy that set him on a murder spree? There was a lot of wild speculation—about the fear of aging (at 27!), the inevitable result of dabbling in S&M,[1] or just running out of luck—but what finally made sense as an explanation was the conjecture that Cunanan had tested HIV-positive back in San Diego and so sought his revenge on other gay men.[2] Insistently clear in the tenor of this conjecture—and in the obvious disappointment when it was later reported that Cunanan posthumously tested HIV-negative—was that it would have simply and definitively solved the whole bizarre mystery. If he had indeed tested positive, no more explanation for his killing spree would need to be sought.

This conclusion was presented by the media as so foregone, as having such utterly compelling logic, that no one seemed able to reply, with much *more* compelling *evidence:* Hundreds of thousands of gay men have tested HIV-positive over the course of the AIDS epidemic, yet, so far as we know, not one of them has turned into a killer as a result. Why then does the "logic" so magically trump the evidence? What exactly is this logic?

Remember Patient Zero? As portrayed by Randy Shilts in *And the Band Played On,* he was the Canadian flight attendant who brought AIDS to the North America, the vengeful guy who would switch on the lights after a bathhouse encounter, point to his KS lesions, and say to his sex partner, "I'm going to die and so are you."[3] Skepticism about this story was, to Shilts, "the typical crap I get from certain segments of the gay

1. The S&M-serial-murder connection was most belabored by Maureen Orth, "The Killer's Trail," *Vanity Fair,* September 1997, pp. 268–275, 329–336.
2. See Joel Achenbach, "The Killer Virus Motive: Unfounded Rumor Casts HIV as a Villain in Slaying," *Washington Post,* July 19, 1997, p. F1.
3. Randy Shilts, *And the Band Played On: Politics, People, and the AIDS Epidemic* (New York: St. Martin's Press, 1987), p. 165.

press. . . . The fact is, Patient Zero did exist. . . . The mainstream press loved my book."[4]

Indeed, they did. Patient Zero was just the scapegoat they were looking for. Not only did his story "explain" how AIDS spread throughout America, but the explanation had all the attraction of a story everybody already knew—the story of gay men's sexual compulsion coupled with murderous irresponsibility. In the meantime Shilts himself became a minor media celebrity and *the* media spokesperson on gay and AIDS issues in the United States, until he himself succumbed to the disease in 1994.

Shilts's popular success and the tactics that won him that success have not been lost on the current generation of gay journalists. And so, sadly, the homophobia and scapegoating of HIV-positive gay men that was fueled by Shilts's Patient Zero story have been revived. The turning point was Michelangelo Signorile's *New York Times* op-ed piece "H.I.V.-Positive, and Careless," published in February 1995.[5] In the piece, Signorile misrepresents prevention theorist Walt Odets's plea for safe-sex information targeted specifically at HIV-negative men to be a condemnation of sensitivity toward HIV-positive men, and in the process he pits the two groups against each other.[6] Signorile acknowledges having had unsafe sex and being afraid to be tested. His solution to the emotional conflict brought about by these circumstances is to look for someone to blame. He doesn't condemn positive men outright. Instead he indicts "Byzantine AIDS organizations" for their refusal "to emphasize the particular responsibilities of HIV-positive men." He then goes on to blame positive men by inference. After suggesting that his own unsafe activity might result from misplaced confidence after testing negative, he writes, "On the other hand, I'm frightened that finding out

4. Quoted in "Randy Shilts's Miserable Failure," in this volume.
5. Michelangelo Signorile, "H.I.V.-Positive, and Careless," *New York Times,* February 26, 1995, p. E15.
6. See Walt Odets, *In the Shadow of the Epidemic: Being HIV-Negative in the Age of AIDS* (Durham: Duke University Press, 1995).

I was *positive* might also play into my carefree nature, that I might in my darkest moments care little about the concerns of an HIV-negative man."

To understand just what Signorile is saying here, it helps to read his elaboration of this statement as it appeared in his *Out* magazine column on the same subject: "Not knowing my status seems to keep me concerned about putting *others* at risk, perhaps because I understand personally their struggle to remain HIV negative. But if I knew I were positive, I'm afraid that in my darkest moments I might have less concern for my partners, that I might be less inclined to sympathize with the difficulties of HIV-negative guys."[7] In the psychic mechanism known as projection, Signorile defends against his internal conflicts about having unsafe sex by expelling his fears outward. He takes his imagined positive self as the reality of men who are actually positive and thus assumes positive men are unable to sympathize with those who are negative and perfectly willing to infect them. Signorile magically converts his worries about his own risky behavior into fear of the irresponsibility of HIV-positive men.

The temporality of the shift to a renewed climate of moralism signaled by Signorile's "H.I.V.-Positive, and Careless" is clearly captured in the following: "Ten years ago the gay community was fighting off hate-mongers who were intent on locking up H.I.V.-positive people; as a community we needed to foster self-esteem among H.I.V.-positive gay men and to guard against attempts to stigmatize them. Now it seems that some of what we did for those who are positive was at the expense of those who are desperately trying to stay negative."[8] "Ten years ago," attempts to stigmatize HIV-positive people seemed a legitimate concern, while "now". . . what? Stigma is no longer a problem? Sensitivity to stigma has become too burdensome? Has hurt those who are negative? Has prevented us from demanding "responsibility" from those who are positive? Several assumptions appear to be operating here. First—and this is a distortion of recent history that appears throughout Signorile's

7. Michelangelo Signorile, "Negative Pride," *Out* 20 (March 1995), p. 24.
8. Signorile, "H.I.V.-Positive, and Careless," p. E15.

writings and those of his fellow mainstream gay journalists—is the dangerous and counterfactual view that homophobia and AIDS phobia are no longer the threats they were "ten years ago." Second is the implication that fighting the stigma attaching to HIV-positive people amounts to granting them license to be "irresponsible"—*from which follows the highly stigmatizing implication that HIV-positive people are naturally inclined to be irresponsible.* We need only to look at the "logic" of the speculation about Cunanan's murderous motive to see this stigma in full force.

A particularly alarming consequence of this narrative about "ten years ago" as opposed to "now" is the fact that de-sensitizing ourselves to the stigma of homosexuality and AIDS has led to the tendency of gay journalists themselves to stigmatize HIV-positive gay men, something that, with the notable exception of Randy Shilts, had not heretofore occurred. Take, for example, the *Advocate* of July 8, 1997, whose cover carries a picture of Brad Davis and the following text: "Sex, drugs, & bathhouses are back . . . A new bio of gay icon Brad Davis reminds us of the dead end we face," followed in large type by "Bad Brad." Inside, under the rubric "The Return of Our Bad Habits," are three stories: "Men Behaving Badly," a distillation of Signorile's screed against the gay party circuit in his book *Life Outside*; "Slipping Up," an article about the return of unsafe sex; and "Our Man Brad," an indictment of Davis's "lifestyle" and gay men's supposed emulation of it.[9] Ostensibly a preview of Susan Bluestein Davis's biography of her late husband, this story is in fact a malicious portrait of Davis as a drug-taking promiscuous hustler. A pull-out quote on the first page reads, "Since his excesses killed him, why are we still hooked on his tragic glamour?" And the story turns to the reigning authority for the cautionary note it is hammering home: "If Davis represents anything for gay men today, Signorile says, it should be a warning about the perils of excess." There is no attempt to understand and sympathize with Davis's life or to mourn his tragic death from AIDS. As the religious Right would say, he got what he deserved.

9. David Heitz, "Men Behaving Badly"; John Gallagher, "Slipping Up"; Robert L. Pela, "Our Man Brad," *Advocate* 737 (July 8, 1997), pp. 26–38.

Signorile was at it again in his July '97 column for *Out* magazine, "Bareback and Reckless."[10] Puffed up with moral indignation, Signorile seems to have entirely forgotten his own "carefree nature," as he now feigns utter incomprehension that there could be "a significant number" of gay men "willfully and sometimes angrily defying safer sex efforts, rebelling against the rest of us, and thereby keeping HIV transmission thriving, affecting adversely the entire gay world." Signorile does not target positive men specifically here, although he singles out *Poz* magazine, "which," he writes, "sometimes seems to eerily glamorize AIDS." Rather, the divide Signorile now enforces is that between the "responsible" and the "irresponsible."

This divide is everywhere present in moralistic attacks by the new gay journalists on gay men's sexual desires, behaviors, and public sexual spaces. Larry Kramer has a long and ignominious history of these attacks, and in 1997 he outdid even himself. In a barely coherent article billed on the cover of the *Advocate* as "AIDS: We Asked for It" and retitled inside "Sex and Sensibility," Kramer lambasts Edmond White for writing so much and so explicitly about sex in his novel *The Farewell Symphony,* excoriates any gay person who has the temerity to question the desirability of gay marriage, and ultimately concurs with Patrick Buchanan from the early days of AIDS: "We brought AIDS upon ourselves by a way of living that welcomed it. You cannot fuck indiscriminately with multiple partners, who are also doing the same, without spreading disease, a disease that has for many years also carried death. Nature always extracts a price for promiscuity."[11]

Andrew Sullivan, who wrote a November 1996 cover story for the *New York Times Magazine* declaring the AIDS epidemic over, has one nagging fear about the new combination therapies that have so miraculously spelled the "plague's end": not that they might fail—indeed are failing for many people with AIDS who are not drug-naive—or that the vast majority of people with HIV infection throughout the world won't

10. Michelangelo Signorile, "Bareback and Reckless," *Out* 45 (July 1997), pp. 36–39.
11. Larry Kramer, "Sex and Sensibility," *Advocate* 734 (May 27, 1997), p. 59.

have access to them. Sullivan's fear is that these new drugs will give gay men the freedom to go back to their bad old promiscuous habits.[12] And Gabriel Rotello is especially insistent about the difference between the good gays and the bad. "Indeed," he writes in his book *Sexual Ecology*, "the gay world may experience a general cleavage between those who adopt a lifestyle of sexual restraint and those who drift further into acceptance of a homosexuality that is inevitably diseased and death-ridden."[13]

These journalists virtually *invite* a restigmatization of AIDS. "What remains to be seen . . . ," Rotello writes, "is how sympathetic the great moderate to conservative center of society will be to a social movement many of whose most articulate members seem complacent about risking death on a massive scale, and whose very source of difference—sexuality—is seen as the behavior leading to the problem."[14] An earlier phrasing of this statement in Rotello's book is more revealing still: "It remains to be seen whether the liberal and moderate allies of gay people will feel compelled to fight the AIDS battles of the future, or fight them very hard, when the vast majority of sufferers are perceived, even by themselves, to have 'no excuse.'"[15]

Here is the most chilling divide, and the new justification for stigma: men who become positive *now*—Signorile's "now" again. The problem "now" as opposed to "ten years ago" is revealed to be the difference between those who have an excuse—they didn't know—and those who have no excuse—they knew. If you slip up *now*, if you get infected *now*, it's your own fault, and what's more *you know it's your own fault*. The ACT UP slogan "All people with AIDS are innocent" no longer holds for you.

12. Andrew Sullivan, "When Plagues End: Notes on the Twilight of an Epidemic," *New York Times Magazine,* November 10, 1996, pp. 52–62, 76–77, 84.
13. Gabriel Rotello, *Sexual Ecology: AIDS and the Destiny of Gay Men* (New York: Dutton, 1997), p. 287.
14. Ibid., p. 284.
15. Ibid., p. 280.

The recent emergence of this small coterie of conservative, openly gay media spokesmen, who virtually monopolize discussion of lesbian and gay issues in the American mainstream media, is one of the contradictory effects of the relative success of struggles for lesbian and gay visibility and rights in the United States. These journalists have achieved and maintained their power—whether naively or cynically—by adopting positions on lesbian and gay issues that are commonsensical, simplistic, reductive, and often classically homophobic. Nevertheless, thanks no doubt to the novelty of openly gay men occupying positions of national prominence, they have become minor celebrities even among many lesbians and gay men, winning community service awards, speaking engagements, and lucrative publishing contracts with trade publishers for books aimed at a gay market. They dominate discussion in the lesbian and gay press as well, which has, during this same conjuncture, mainstreamed itself as just one more variant of consumer lifestyle journalism. Whereas formerly the lesbian and gay press—usually local, financially insecure, and politically engaged—played a central role in constructing community and solidarity through fostering open discussion among a wide range of voices, the current gay media seek to deliver a privileged segment of self-identified gay people to product advertisers. Their means are no different from those of the American media more generally: They focus on celebrity, fashion, and entertainment. Anything truly vital about queer life and subcultural expression is considered too marginal for the magazines' imagined readers. Politics is equally off-limits, except a narrowly defined politics of assimilation, on the one hand, and, on the other, a politics of manufactured controversy, highly sensationalized to bolster circulation.

Meanwhile, another, also contradictory, result of our struggle for rights has been the recent flourishing within the academy and academic publishing of radical queer theory—contradictory in this case because queer theory generally calls into question the idea of stable, coherent lesbian and gay identities that formed the basis of our earlier politics. Although queer theory thus represents a break with earlier lesbian and gay studies, and although it is far from homogeneous in its complex arguments about identity and difference, one aspect of this work is quite univocal and continuous with earlier scholarship: It can be defined, fundamentally, as antihomophobic. Indeed, queer theory is if anything more concerned with and more sophisticated about the operations of homophobia, or what is sometimes called hetero-normativity, than were lesbian and gay studies or gay liberation politics.

The vitality of queer theory cannot, however, be counted an unqualified success. Its place in the academy is still hotly contested and structurally weak, and all academic intellectual work in the United States is relegated to the margins of mainstream discussion, and is still further marginalized today after more than a decade of relentless right-wing attacks on the academy, which the liberal media has been all too happy to participate in.[16] The gay lifestyle media has contributed to the marginalization, too, scoffing at queer theory whenever it bothers to notice it at all. The now canonical texts of queer theory within the U.S. academy— among them Judith Butler's *Gender Trouble* and *Bodies that Matter,* Lee Edelman's *Homographesis,* Diana Fuss's *Inside/Out,* David Halperin's *One Hundred Years of Homosexuality* and *Saint Foucault,* Eve Kosofsky Sedgwick's *Epistemology of the Closet* and *Tendencies,* and Michael Warner's *Fear of a Queer Planet*—these books have rarely been reviewed by, nor have they influenced the arguments and positions articulated in, the gay lifestyle media. What is given generous attention instead are books by gay celebrity journalists: Bruce Bower's *A Place at the Table* and *Beyond Queer,* Gabriel Rotello's *Sexual Ecology,* Michelangelo Signorile's *Life Outside: The Signorile Report on Gay Men: Sex, Drugs, Muscles, and the Passages of Life,* and Andrew Sullivan's *Virtually Normal* and *Gay Marriage: Pro and Con.*

If, following Michel Foucault, a central tenet of queer theory has been an analysis of, and resistance to, normalizing technologies of power, the central precept of these journalists has been acceptance of normalization and vilification of anyone whose way of life might challenge an uncriti-

16. For two particularly scurrilous examples, see Lee Siegel, "The Gay Science," *New Republic,* November 9, 1998, pp. 30–42; and Martha C. Nussbaum, "The Professor of Parody," *New Republic,* February 22, 1999, pp. 37–45.

cal compliance with institutionalized norms. The journalists repudiate the legacies of gay liberation, whether militant, democratic activism, resistance to state regulation of sex, or the creation of a vibrant alternative culture; they portray women, including lesbians, as existing to moderate male sexual behavior as a function of their biology; they argue that gay marriage will be a panacea for everything from AIDS to access to any other rights we could reasonably expect (Andrew Sullivan has famously written, "Following legalization of same-sex marriage and a couple of other things, I think we should have a party and close down the gay rights movement for good");[17] they even extoll what Signorile calls, with no qualms whatever, "small-town American values."[18] As Michael Warner wrote, "For them, the legitimate outcome of a politics of sexuality is a happy lesbian or gay identity in a 'normal,' private home: mature, secure, and demure."[19]

This is *not* a productive intellectual debate; in fact, it is no debate at all. Queer theorists rarely address the mainstream writers or attempt to write for mainstream publications, and the journalists only sneer at queer theory, without having understood—or probably even read—a word of it. The dangerous consequences of this failure of engagement extend well beyond intellectual discussion.

In the summer of 1997—the summer of Andrew Cunanan's murder spree—a group of us in New York City attempted to intervene in this situation. We came together over a number of interrelated concerns: the threat to HIV prevention posed by Gabriel Rotello's claim that safe sex has been a failure and his contention, agreed on by his fellow journalists, that monogamy and marriage are the only way to end the AIDS epi-

17. Quoted in *Out Facts: Just about Everything You Need to Know about Gay and Lesbian Life,* ed. David Groff (New York: Universe, 1997).
18. Michelangelo Signorile, *Life Outside: The Signorile Report on Gay Men: Sex, Drugs, Muscles, and the Passages of Life* (New York: HarperCollins, 1997); see especially chapter 5, "The Deurbanization of Homosexuality," pp. 181–207.
19. Michael Warner, "Media Gays: A New Stone Wall," *Nation,* July 14, 1997, p. 15.

demic; the harassment and shutting down of public sexual culture as a result of Mayor Rudolph Giuliani's so-called quality of life campaign; the exclusion of lesbians from media discussion and the portrayal of lesbian sexuality as properly private, domestic, and monogamous; and, finally, the exclusion from mainstream and gay media discussion of anyone but this select group of conservative gay writers. We called ourselves Sex Panic! ironically, to call attention to the fact that we felt we were in the middle of one. Within a few months of our first meeting, we held two successful community teach-ins, got a number of pieces published in the media, and sparked an outcry throughout the gay press. Attention to Sex Panic! culminated the following November in a front-page Sunday Week-in-Review article in the *New York Times*, revealingly titled "Gay Culture Weighs Sense and Sexuality" and illustrated with a pair of photographs, one showing two smiling, confetti-covered men at their gay wedding ceremony, the other, two faceless male bodies in the dark corridor of a sex club.[20]

Perhaps the most painful lesson we learned in our brief existence was just how difficult it is to get the media to hear our side of the story. The media construction of the issues is spelled out in the *New York Times* title: on the one side is "sense"—a group of gay journalists trying to stop the continuing spread of HIV by getting gay men to adopt normal, responsible behaviors, while on the other side is "sexuality"— Sex Panic! fighting for gay men to be as promiscuous as they want to be. One journalistic account, albeit written by a young academic who claimed to be a queer theory groupie, encapsulated the media's reductive version of the debate: "These disagreements pit the value of gay male promiscuity against the dangers of HIV transmission."[21] Sex Panic!'s positions were allowed a quoted sentence here and there, lifted out of context and made to conform to the predetermined framing of the issues. And frankly, none of us in Sex Panic! was particularly

20. Sheryl Gay Stolberg, "Gay Culture Weighs Sense and Sexuality," *New York Times*, November 23, 1997, section 4, pp. 1, 6.

21. Caleb Crain, "Pleasure Principles: Queer Theorists and Gay Journalists Wrestle over the Politics of Sex," *Lingua Franca*, October 1997, p. 28.

adept, when speaking to the media, at sticking to basic points, hammering them home, and guarding against saying something that might easily be misconstrued when reduced to a sound-bite. Our insistence that the issues were complex was taken as dangerous relativism or prevarication—failure to take an ethical position in life-and-death circumstances. The celebrity gay journalists, by contrast, are very practiced at speaking the media's language and readily resort to demagoguery; moreover their insider status gives them easy access. As the novelist Christopher Bram said of Larry Kramer, "He likes to call himself a voice crying in the wilderness, but his wilderness is the op-ed page of the *New York Times.*" And indeed Larry Kramer went right to the *Times* op-ed page with a piece attacking Sex Panic! Here is part of what he wrote:

The facts: a small and vocal gay group that calls itself Sex Panic has taken it upon itself to demand "sexual freedom," which its members define as allowing gay men to have sex when and where and how they want to. In other words, this group is an advocate of unsafe sex, if this is what is wanted, and of public sex, if this is what is wanted. It advocates unconditional, unlimited promiscuity.

The facts: public sex means sex in parks, in public restrooms, in bathhouses, in the back rooms of bars and discos, at weekend parties, on beaches—anywhere men can gather. . . .

(A question: why is public sex a civil right? I do not want to see straight people copulating in the park or in public restrooms. And I do not believe that heterosexuals view such acts as theirs by right.)

The truth is, most gay men live calm, orderly lives, often as couples, and they are embarrassed by what Sex Panic espouses. They are ashamed this issue has surfaced again. . . .

Without a strong, vocal opposition, Sex Panic is on the way to convincing much of America that all gay men are back to pre-AIDS self-destructive behavior that will wind up costing the taxpayer a lot of extra money. In-

deed, what Sex Panic is demanding could easily allow our enemies, as well as many of our straight friends, to deny all gay people what rights we've won or are still fighting for.[22]

The day this column appeared, an e-mail went out to members of Sex Panic! asking for letters to be written to set the record straight, and many did so. The following day, five letters were printed under the headline "Defenders of Promiscuity Set Back AIDS Fight." Not one was by a member of Sex Panic! and not one disagreed with Kramer's position. Three days later, three more letters appeared, this time opposing Kramer. Published under the rubric "In Debate, Gay Men Aim to Find Middle Path," one letter came from Berkeley professor and queer theorist Leo Bersani. Bersani confidently refuted the most damaging of Kramer's assertions—that "gay men created a culture that in effect murdered us"—but ended his letter with the following question: "Is it possible for gay men to have a debate that is not defined by self-destructiveness on the one side and, on the other, a hysterical aversion to sexual pleasure?"[23] This sounds like a commonsense question—and that is precisely the problem. What is this self-destructiveness? Bersani refers to "a small number of gay men" who "suggest that unsafe sex is fine." It is not clear that Bersani attributes this opinion to Sex Panic! but he makes no attempt to distinguish it from Sex Panic!'s position. This is, I think, a telling example of the perils of speaking about such complex issues to the mainstream media. Although it is true that a few gay writers have provocatively celebrated the pleasures of unsafe sex, sometimes without providing the necessary context to make their celebrations comprehensible,[24] the current debate can only be seen as defined by such provocations if they are conflated with attempts to understand why gay men have unsafe sex and to explain why simple condemnation of unsafe behavior will not help.

22. Larry Kramer, "Gay Culture, Redefined," *New York Times,* December 12, 1997, p. A23.
23. Leo Bersani, "Homophobia Redux," *New York Times,* December 16, 1997, p. A30.
24. Most famous among the provocateurs is porn star and writer Scott O'Hara, who founded the queer sex zine *Steam* in 1993. See Scott O'Hara, *Autopornography: A Memoir of Life in the Lust Lane* (New York: Harrington Park, 1997).

In a number of important theoretical texts—primarily *The Freudian Body* and "Is the Rectum a Grave?"—Bersani, following the psychoanalyst Jean Laplanche, has made the argument that sex is constitutively masochistic because it brings about a shattering of the self.[25] Sex provides "pleasure in giving up what our civilization insists that we retain—our ego boundaries."[26] But where the masculine (heterosexual) psychic position is characterized by a "paranoid defensiveness" against this fundamental, self-shattering masochism, the result is a "hyperbolically defended and armored" ego, "willing to kill in order to protect the seriousness of [its] statements."[27] Gay male sex represents, by contrast, the radical potential of the ego's continual deflation leading to self-extensibility. The final sentence of Bersani's famous essay "Is the Rectum a Grave?" reads: "Male homosexuality advertises the risk of the sexual itself as the risk of self-dismissal, of *losing sight* of the self, and in so doing it proposes and dangerously represents *jouissance* as a mode of ascesis."[28] (It should be emphasized that Bersani privileges gay male sex only insofar as it is understood as a heuristic category for rethinking the relations of psychic and social life.)

Now, whether or not we agree with Bersani's sexual theories, I think we can certainly agree that Bersani's resorting to a pop-psychology notion of "self-destructiveness" to describe one side of the current debates about gay male sexuality thoroughly contradicts his own theoretical propositions—propositions that hinge precisely on the *self*-destroying potential of sex. To adopt a seemingly reasonable position, to "find a middle path" in the words of the *Times*, may be a strong temptation

25. Leo Bersani, *The Freudian Body: Psychoanalysis and Art* (New York: Columbia University Press, 1986); "Is the Rectum a Grave?" in *AIDS: Cultural Analysis, Cultural Activism,* ed. Douglas Crimp (Cambridge: MIT Press, 1988), pp. 197–222. See also Tim Dean, Hal Foster, and Kaja Silverman, "A Conversation with Leo Bersani," *October* 82 (fall 1997), pp. 3–16.

26. Quoted in Dean et al., "A Conversation with Leo Bersani," p. 7.

27. Bersani, quoted in Dean et al., "A Conversation with Leo Bersani," p. 8; and "Is the Rectum a Grave?" p. 222.

28. Bersani, "Is the Rectum a Grave?" p. 222 (emphasis in original).

when writing for the mainstream media, but when your entire intellectual project is devoted to celebrating sex as a radical force opposed to self-contained mastery, a *jouissance* beyond sense, it is an act of extraordinary intellectual self-betrayal.

Bersani's self-betrayal points to what is missing from media debates about gay sex, that is, any genuinely theoretical understanding of what sex is, of the deeply disruptive, anticivilizing psychic force of sex. The mainstream media and conservative gay journalists alike treat sex as a simple behavior, obedient to will and reason, as if it were no different from, say, driving a car. When driving, there are rules and regulations and courtesies that any responsible person will follow in order to remain safe and help ensure the safety of others on the road. Although there are many uncivilized drivers, to be a civilized driver does not require overcoming insurmountable psychic conflict. Sex, however, represents nothing but conflict in relation to civilizing impulses.

Why, then, do gay men have unsafe sex, and how do we talk to the media about it? Certainly the vast majority of gay men who have unsafe sex are still those who have not been given the information and support that would help them protect themselves. Federally funded, sexually explicit HIV education targeted directly at gay men is still effectively curtailed in the United States by so-called community-standards regulations.[29] Young men in particular, and especially young men of color, very rarely have access to homosexually specific HIV education at the time they begin sexual experimentation. They are, not surprisingly, statistically the most vulnerable to HIV transmission. Because this is not what the current debates focus on, these young men are rendered all the more invisible and vulnerable. At issue instead, in the current furor over unsafe sex, are those of us who have been well exposed to HIV prevention education, who know the risks of unsafe sex, and who still, at least occasionally, have unsafe sex. Why do we do it?

29. On this subject, see Cindy Patton, *Fatal Advice: How Safe-Sex Education Went Wrong* (Durham: Duke University Press, 1996).

I have a simple answer: We are human. When I say this—that we have unsafe sex because we are human—what I mean is something like what Bersani intends when he theorizes sex as constitutively masochistic, potentially ego-shattering, opposed to self-mastery. But how to put this to, say, the *New York Times*? As an exercise—an exercise, it turned out, in futility—I decided to see how I might write about this issue for the *Times*. So here is a piece I submitted to the op-ed editor shortly after Larry Kramer's piece on Sex Panic! appeared.

○

Why do gay men continue to have unsafe sex, knowing how dangerous the consequences can be? Many voices in the media, prominent gay journalists among them, tell us it's because we are self-destructive, or just plain fools. But hectoring won't help anyone practice safe sex. HIV prevention is, unfortunately, not a simple matter; if we pretend it is, the result could be more, not fewer infections. Exhorting gay men to just grow up and be responsible ignores how powerful and charged with conflict sex is for everyone. Imagine then how much more conflicted it must be for gay men living in the midst of the AIDS epidemic. In a society that shows its disapproval of gay sex in countless ways—messages we all receive from infancy to adulthood—gay men's most basic, life-sustaining desires and pleasures become especially fraught. Add to this the fact that each of our sexual encounters might lead to the transmission of a deadly virus, and you might begin to understand the distress that so many of us have endured for the better part of two decades.

During this time, the majority of gay men have practiced safe sex most of the time, and untold numbers of lives have been saved. Anyone who thinks this has been easy should think again. The assumption that using a condom every time you have intercourse—every time, no exceptions—is just plain good sense disregards all the powerful drives and emotions that can get in the way of "good sense" during sex: the need to express feelings of trust and intimacy, the desire to live in the moment, to overcome shame, to break the rules. Every one of us feels these emotions, simply because we are human. To suggest that gay men should not feel them, or should put them aside for the rest of our lives, is to deny us our humanity.

If discussions of gay sexual behavior began by acknowledging the extraordinary difficulties gay men have lived with, both before and during the epidemic, and how bravely and ethically most of us have lived with these difficulties, I doubt anyone would be so quick to label our behavior self-destructive. Indeed, the opposite is the case. Gay men's behavior throughout the AIDS epidemic has been profoundly self-protective. In our struggle to protect our lives, many of us have also fought to preserve the publicly accessible sexual culture that has nurtured us, provided a sense of community, solidarity, and well being—given us, in fact, the courage and will to save ourselves. Where did we learn about safe sex? From the government? In school? Of course not. We learned about safe sex in our own community, from each other, in bars, bathhouses, and sex clubs. But first, of course, we had to invent safe sex.

When others characterize gay sexual culture as destructive, as having caused AIDS in the first place, is it any wonder that we protest? As a member of the activist group Sex Panic! which came together over concerns about continuing high rates of HIV infection, I don't demand unconditional sexual freedom. Rather I ask that the rich, distinctive social world gay people have worked so painstakingly to build be honored and supported—not because it is perfect, but because without it we have only the isolation, alienation, and abjection that so many in this society would impose on us. If always practicing safe sex is difficult for us to sustain now, how much more difficult would it become if we had no public community support?

The current push for economic privatization and the ceding of urban space to private entities shielded from public accountability find a counterpart in the vilification of public gay culture, whether what is opposed are bars and nightclubs, political activism, or just "flaunting it in public." But those who call for a complete reconstruction of gay culture seem to forget that the social norms they consider responsible and civilized are the very norms that have always stigmatized and shunned us, and against which we had to find an alternative. Why should we adopt them now? Why should we abandon the life-affirming and plea-sure-filled world that we have created, where we have learned genuine responsibility to one another, for a world that only grudgingly tolerates us? Whether or not it is important for gay people to gain the right to marry—and this is far from agreed on among gay people— it is dangerous to assume that marriage would make us safe from AIDS. Studies showing that fewer than half of heterosexual couples with one HIV-positive partner consistently practice safe sex suggest otherwise.

This is not a debate between so-called ordinary homosexuals and a marginal group of sex radicals. Nor is it a debate about monogamy ver-sus promiscuity. These false oppositions denigrate the culture all gay people have made. Unlike other oppressed groups, we gay people do not acquire our culture as a birthright. We have to create it after we find our way out of the hostile environments we grow up in, often including our own families. Among our greatest achievements are the diverse possibilities we have invented for the expression and fulfillment of af-fectional and sexual relations. These possibilities are a function of our public world, overlapping communities of interest and desire, where we find each other and learn to care about each other. When that public realm shrinks—when the city closes down our bars and clubs for cabaret license violations and other trumped up charges—we lose much more than places for sex. We lose the places where our lives have taken on social meaning and made it possible for us to overcome the at-omized, private, and often secret identities that most of us lived with before finding others like ourselves.

Anyone who truly cares about slowing the HIV infection rate in gay men might begin by learning more about how we've survived thus far— against overwhelming odds. Maybe then we'll get some of the genuine support we need in our efforts to maintain the safe sexual behavior we have worked so hard to practice all along. And it might help to remember, when some of us fail: We too are human.[30]

○

An HIV prevention leader and personal friend of mine asked, in a news story about AIDS, "Am I the only one tormented with nagging curiosity, anxiety, and doubts when I learn that another friend has seroconverted?" I knew who he was tormented about. He was tormented about me. He never said this directly to me, but his indirection has been easy to read. Here is what I think his curiosity, anxiety, and doubt are about: He knows me from the time we were fellow members of ACT UP in the late 1980s. He knows that I am one of the lucky ones, someone who was sexually very active in New York City during the 1970s and early 1980s who nevertheless remained HIV-negative. He knows that I have written, taught, and lectured extensively about AIDS. He knows that I began practicing safe sex in the mid-1980s, and that I understand the risks of unsafe sex. He and I have had many discussions about prevention, and particularly about how new prevention strategies can be developed that take account of the difficulties of maintaining safe sex practices over the long term, in the face of powerful fantasies of unsafe sex and transgression, of growing despair and survivor's guilt, of the fact that sex is not amenable to rational will. Knowing all this, what he is really curious to ask is, How can you—you of all people—have seroconverted? His anxiety and his doubt follow that question with another: If you can seroconvert, is it possible that I too could seroconvert? Or my boyfriend? My other negative friends? Is *anyone* safe?

My answer again is simple, and it is the same answer. I seroconverted because I am human. And no, no one is safe, not you, your boyfriend, or any of your negative friends. Because you and they are human too. My only disappointment in all this is that I should have to protest my hu-

30. This opinion piece was submitted to Katherine Roberts, op-ed page editor of the *New York Times,* on January 26, 1998; the newspaper indicated no interest in publishing it.

manity to a friend. Still, I understand it, for to accept my humanity is to accept my frailty. Or to put it differently, it is to accept that I have an unconscious. It is to accept that everything I experienced, everything I knew, everything I understood could not guarantee my safety.

Perhaps my motive for writing an op-ed piece to the *Times* now appears in a different light. But I want to protest that it is not written only in self-defense. It is written against the fantasy of absolute safety. For this is, I think, the most dangerous thing of all about the renewed moralizing about having unsafe sex and becoming infected now. The moralizing is, in fact, a psychic defense. If we tell ourselves that only irresponsible fools still expose themselves to HIV, we allow ourselves to imagine that we are safe, since few of us would say of ourselves that we are irresponsible fools. Even if we did, we would very likely still think it possible to stop being an irresponsible fool—and then we'd be safe. But if even the educated, rational, and responsible among us can become infected with HIV; if AIDS activists and prevention educators can seroconvert *now,* then we have to think differently, with still greater complexity and self-understanding, about protection. We have to think about the force of our own unconscious, of our terrible vulnerability, of the fact that we, too, are human. And we have to accept the possibility, even the inevitability, that some of us will fail.

How might queer theory help us do this? How does saying that we are human differ from the conservative journalists' traditional humanist view that we are no different from anyone else save for whom we choose to love? The answer to this question is as complicated and disputed as all the work of queer theory occupying the shelves of our university libraries. But I will attempt to shorten the answer to a few sentences. Queer theory, like much recent postmodern theory, tells us that humanity is not a universal and natural condition of being but a contingent and cultural construction of historical, social, linguistic, and psychic forces. Knowing this, queer theory also knows the political urgency of understanding how and why we are denied our humanity within and through those very forces. The abjection of homosexuality is not a simple matter of ignorance to be overcome with time, education, and "progress," but a deep-seated psychic mechanism central to the construction of normative subjectivity and thus of social cohesion. Armored with this understanding, we can protect against sacrificing our humanity in the very act of struggling to get it recognized, or purchasing it at the cost of another's humanity, which is the perilous ethical cost of accepting the regimes of the normal. What queer theory has yet to learn is no less urgent: How do we make what we know knowable to legions?

INDEX

Figures are indicated by bold page numbers.

Living with HIV and AIDS, 87, 100, 175, 219–220, 228. *See also* People with AIDS (PWAs)
self-representations important in, 258, 267, 268, 270
Longtime Companion, 270
Los Angeles, 113–114
Los Angeles Contemporary Exhibitions (LACE), 110

MacKinnon, Catherine, 238
Malone, Karl, 219
Manchester Union Leader, 278–279
Mandatory HIV antibody testing, 148–149
Mapplethorpe, Robert
appropriating classical styles, 152, 154, 155, 162, 162–163
Helmut and Brooks, 23, 274, 275, 280, 281
X Portfolio series, 274–277, 281
Marshall, Stuart, *Bright Eyes,* 40, 103, 112
Mars-Jones, Adam, 120
Marta (Ebert and Landry), 21–22
Mason, Belinda, 199
Matlovich, Leonard, 229
Maturity narrative (AIDS=maturity), 4–5, 6–8, 7n.10, 13–14, 16, 103, 106–107. *See also* Moralistic discourse
McGee, Pamela, 207
McNeil/Lehrer Report, "AIDS in the Arts," 29n.4, 29–30
Media representations of AIDS and PWAs, 86, 95n.2, 101. *See also* "Faces of AIDS"; Hollywood and mainstream films; Press coverage of the AIDS epidemic; Television coverage of AIDS and PWAs
hyping of Magic Johnson's heterosexuality, 205–210, 206, 212, 213, 218
"Patient Zero" hype, 51, 54, 124
phobic fantasies and, 106, 124
response to Rock Hudson's death, 49–51, 55
reversals of, 102 (*see also* Alternative AIDS media)

stereotypical, 91–92, 97, 99–100, 146, 215–216, 257, 258
Medical treatments for AIDS. *See also* Research and AIDS
drug trials and FDA approval process, 2, 8, 36, 174
lack of access or unequal access to, 2, 59, 286–287
new and combination treatments, 2, 9n.4, 90n.8, 103
Meinhold, Keith, 230
Melancholia, 8n.13, 9, 141–142, 143, 144. *See also* Freud, Sigmund; Mourning
Memorial services, 135–136
Vito Russo memorial, 170–175
Metropolitan Health Association, 38–39, 78
Metropolitan Museum of Art (NY), 167–168
Meyer, Richard, 276
Meyers, Woodrow, 170
Military ban on gays and lesbians, 226n.6, 226–227, 228–230, 230n.9, 232–235
Campaign for Military Service, 19, 23, 223
"Don't Ask, Don't Tell" policy, 234–236, 242, 247, 250
opposition to displacing AIDS activism, 223–224, 248, 279
Miller v. California, 157n.5, 157
Modernism, 152, 163
Moffett, Donald, 17, 18
MOMA. *See* Museum of Modern Art (New York)
Monogamy, 56, 64, 213, 290. *See also* Gay marriage
AIDS education promoting, 65–66
Moon, Michael, 134–135
Moralistic discourse, 8, 11–13, 16, 218, 284
AIDS activism and, 8–9, 227
AIDS as a morality tale, 4–5, 6–8, 7n.10, 13–14, 16, 103, 106–107
as community values, 76–77
critique of, 19–20 (*see also* Psychological processes)

Made in the USA
Coppell, TX
13 January 2024

27644441R00184